WITHDRAWN FROM
CANISIUS COLLEGE LIBRARY

Letters from Baltimore

Henry Louis Mencken, 1880–1956

H.L. Mencken

Letters from Baltimore.

The Mencken-Cleator Correspondence

Edited by P. E. Cleator

Rutherford • Madison • Teaneck
Fairleigh Dickinson University Press
London and Toronto: Associated University Presses

Also by P. E. Cleator:

The Past in Pieces
Lost Languages
Archaeology
Treasure for the Taking
Ancient Rome
Castles and Kings
Let's Look at Archaeology
Exploring the World of Archaeology

Underwater Archaeology
Archaeology in the Making
Weapons of War
Rockets through Space
Into Space
An Introduction to Space Travel
The Robot Era
Metals

© 1982 by Associated University Presses, Inc.

Associated University Presses, Inc.
4 Cornwall Drive
East Brunswick, N.J. 08816

Associated University Presses Ltd
27 Chancery Lane
London WC2A 1NS, England

Associated University Presses
Toronto M5E 1A7, Canada

Library of Congress Cataloging in Publication Data

Mencken, H. L. (Henry Louis), 1880–1956.
   Letters from Baltimore.

   Bibliography: p.
   Includes index.
   1. Mencken, H. L. (Henry Louis), 1880–1956—
Correspondence. 2. Cleator, P. E. (Philip Ellaby),
1908–   . 3. Authors, American—20th century—
Correspondence. I. Cleator, P. E. (Philip Ellaby),
1908–   . II. Title.
PS3525.E43Z49   1982   818'.5209   78-75176
ISBN 0-8386-3075-8   AACR2

Printed in the United States of America

To the memory of Rosalind C. Lohrfinck,
"Mr. Mencken's secretary for twenty-seven years"

CONTENTS

List of Illustrations   9
Foreword   11
Acknowledgments   17
Abbreviations for Sources   19
Editorial Note   21
Personal Preamble   25
1   A Meeting of Minds   37
2   My Kingdom for a Hearse   97
3   Dear Cleator, Dear Mencken   181
4   Last Days   241
Aftermath   256
References   266
Index   267

LIST OF ILLUSTRATIONS

Frontispiece. Henry Louis Mencken, 1880–1956
1. Baltimorean Buffooneries—1   41
2. Mencken and Nathan   53
3. Cleatorian Landscape   71
4. Cleator and Companion   72
5. The Mencken Epigraphs—1   93
6. Intimation of Disaster   110
7. Mencken and Nathan   121
8. The Architecture of War   134
9. The Mencken Epigraphs—2   141
10. Cleator and Friends   153
11. The Mencken Epigraphs—3   176
12. Baltimorean Buffooneries—2   185
13. The Mencken Notepaper   186
14. The Mencken Epigraphs—4   190
15. The Mencken Epigraphs—5   199
16. The Mencken Epigraphs—6   208
17. The Mencken Epigraphs—7   218
18. The Mencken Epigraphs—8   225
19. Baltimorean Buffooneries—3   228

FOREWORD
By Carl Bode

Mencken's most faithful English correspondent was also the most farsighted. For P. E. Cleator founded the British Interplanetary Society in 1933 and published as his first book *Rockets through Space*. At twenty-two, in 1930, he happened on Mencken's writing in the form of *Treatise on the Gods,* read it avidly, and then devoured every other book by Mencken he could find. Only when he had a book of his own to send Mencken did he initiate their correspondence. It continued for a dozen years, flourishing despite the impact of World War II, and then shrank into occasional notes after Mencken's disastrous stroke of fall 1948.

The two men had a good deal in common. The ideas Cleator encountered in *Treatise on the Gods* were close to his own; both men were confirmed agnostics with a slightly sardonic view of the God business. Both men were attracted by science though neither had much scientific training. Cleator, however, trained himself and eventually produced half a dozen scientific books. Both men made a living as professional writers, with Mencken reaching a wide public. Both men viewed big government and its hydra-headed regulations with implacable hostility. When World War II arrived they exchanged horror stories about the rank abundance of government red tape. Both men stood opposed to the vast suffering any war brought, and both were determined to have nothing to do with it if at all possible. Cleator had conscientious scruples against military service, barely escaping jail because of them. As a young man Mencken found war interesting to observe but even then wanted no particle of it for himself.

Finally, despite the fact that both men were immersed in the present, they kept in their letters a touch of old-style decorum. For ten years, in point, their salutations were formal. It wasn't till the summer of 1946 that Mencken burst out with "In the name of God the Father, the Son and the Holy Ghost, why should you and I go on mistering each other?" At that, it simply became "Dear Cleator," never "Dear Phil." And never of course "Dear Henry"—"Dear H.L.M." was more businesslike.

The correspondence carried with it Mencken's customary verve and wit. From his seat in the tent he described the American political circus for Cleator. He set down a number of domestic and foreign political predictions, most of which proved to be wrong. For instance, in 1939 he assured Cleator that President Roosevelt couldn't win a third term in office and in 1943 he stated that the end of World War II was imminent. He mentioned some of the prevailing oddities of American life. He wrote about his own writing, telling Cleator about its current—and always burdensome—condition. During the final years of their correspondence he often groaned to Cleator about the trials of producing supplement II of his already classic *American Language*. Cleator sympathized. In turn Mencken sympathized with Cleator when he failed to find a publisher for a book of his or the publisher couldn't find the paper, because of wartime shortages, to print it. Also, as a confirmed hypochondriac and connoisseur of man's ills, Mencken reported on his medical misadventures and commiserated with Cleator on his. By now a self-made authority on hospital matters, Mencken opened a letter of August 1945 with: "I certainly hope that those horrible pains have passed off. An infection in an incision is a really hellish thing. The silk sutures were really probably not to blame, for the same unpleasantness follows the use of gut." Very professional.

As World War II drew near, began, and then crescendoed, Mencken described many of its frustrations for the American civilian. He shunned references to armed conflict—for instance, Cleator noticed that he virtually ignored the assault on Pearl Harbor—but never to domestic hardships. In October 1942 he bemoaned the effect of the war on railroad travel and food supplies. "There is as yet no actual shortage of food," he added nervously, "but my cook tells me that it is already necessary to take what is in the market, not what one wants."

Although Mencken wished that the war would go away and turned his back on it whenever he could, the correspondence with Cleator kept it all too real. The story Cleator had to tell in his side of the correspondence shocked and dismayed Mencken. It's our loss that here Cleator prints only portions of that powerful and moving chronicle.

It starts slowly. In April 1939 Mencken is still betting that war won't come. By September he's wrong and by October he's writing Cleator, "I'm delighted to hear that you remain unbombed." Cleator and his wife are living in the Merseyside area, not far from his parents. By July 1940 they're enduring nightly raids by Hitler's bombers but with no damage in their immediate neighborhood. Then night and day bombing begins, and Cleator writes, "I have an average of 4 hours sleep out of every 24." The bombing comes closer, three bombs falling within thirty yards of his house. On the night of March 12, 1941, blasts from a string of bombs destroy the roof, ceiling, doors, and windows of the house. But far worse has happened to his parents. Their house has suffered a direct hit, killing them and their housekeeper. Nothing remains but a crater of debris. Cleator tells Mencken, "I found the bodies when daylight came, mutilated almost beyond recognition."

In July 1942 the bombers return in force. The fatalism with which Cleator has somehow reacted to prior bombing is another casualty of the war. Now, he confesses a letter of July 27, he finds himself having fits of uncontrollable shaking when the raids come. His nerves are in shreds. He tries to exorcise these fits by writing Mencken about some of the memories which have caused them. This letter is the most moving in the whole correspondence. Although he quotes only excerpts, they're unforgettable: "Dazed people, wandering aimlessly. . . . Staircases, majestically leading nowhere. . . . Passes for the emergency morgues. . . . Endless lines of mutilated dead. . . . The last minute realisation, through the evidence of a severed limb, that we'd identified mother as the housekeeper, and *vice versa*. . . . The blood-soaked earth where I found the bodies. . . . The search for somewhere to eat and sleep. . . ."

This is the climax of the correspondence. Thereafter the letters show that Cleator and his wife survived somehow and that Mencken's thoughts were often with them. They found a halfway decent place to live. They managed to feed themselves, making do with a meagerness which Mencken and his fellow Americans were spared. For example, since they had no cooking oil to fry their chips, they used medicinal paraffin. For baking they used petroleum jelly. For two years their house had only polyethylene windows instead of glass. They endured the discomfort of the constantly increasing government regulations, being forced to fill out a form for practically everything. With a nice irony they had to fill out their income tax form in the middle of warfare—and the form was longer than ever before.

Nor did things improve at the war's end. Cleator mentioned to Mencken, in passing, that he didn't have a decent shirt to put on his back, nor the ration coupons for one. Touched, Mencken wanted to replenish Cleator's whole wardrobe, but Cleator declined with politeness tinged with embarrassment. However, Mencken decided that the least he could do was to mail Cleator some new shirts, and this he did.

At home Mencken also experienced some postwar shortages, for which he cursed President Truman and his cronies, but they were nothing compared to Cleator's. However, Mencken had other and forbidding troubles: his physical condition was clearly growing worse. There were portents of the crippling stroke to come and Mencken knew enough medicine to realize it. He often remarked on his ails but did it so matter-of-factly that it could be lost in the rest of the things he was commenting on to Cleator, among them politics, the weather, his new books, and his other writing. Yet the comments were there.

Nevertheless, the correspondence proceeded as before. Both men were given to replying promptly, so their files thickened. Inevitably some patterns grew up in the correspondence. Cleator habitually enclosed clippings of new words and expressions from British newspapers. Mencken always replied with warm thanks. Both men promised to visit one another's countries; both came close to doing it. Mencken never did, however, and Cleator didn't cross the Atlantic till 1978. Mencken continued to offer aid and comfort to Cleator in the problem of placing his books with a suitable publisher. They continued to debate vigorously about which country was the dreariest to live in, Mencken stoutly maintaining that it was the United States while Cleator championed Great Britain. Mencken announced in a letter of October 18, 1948, "If I could only speak English I think I'd come to England. By all accounts, the state of affairs is considerably better there than in the United States." "All accounts" didn't include Cleator's.

Mencken wrote his final letter to Cleator two weeks later and three weeks after that had his stroke. For the final eight years of his existence, when he could neither read nor write, the correspondence became a mere exchange of polite notes between his secretary and Cleator. But the bulk of the correspondence remained and has been preserved for us. Both men saved the letters they received and now, thanks to Cleator, we have nearly all of Mencken's put in print. Through Mencken's letters and Cleator's helpful annotations we're offered a record of the meeting of two lively minds and the exchanging of two experiences. The record reveals a good deal about both men; it likewise tells us something about the relations of American and British cultures.

ACKNOWLEDGMENTS

This publication of Henry Mencken's letters to me can fairly be laid at the door of Professor Carl Bode of the University of Maryland, with whom I have been in friendly correspondence for some years, for he promptly responded to a proposal I made to him by suggesting that I tackle it myself. As the undertaking was originally conceived, this was not possible for several reasons, but it was his suggestion, nevertheless, which led to the appearance of the present volume. I am, moreover, also heavily indebted to its instigator, as Mencken's leading biographer, for his generous provision of answers to many of the numerous queries which arose as work on the book progressed, and to his ready (if somewhat rash) acquiescence in a request that he pen a foreword to the book when it was completed.

The decision to embark on the project necessarily required the finding of a sponsor for it, and an expression of interest was immediately forthcoming from Thomas Yoseloff, of Associated University Presses. Thereafter, agreement to proceed was reached during a discussion which took place between us in London, subject to the making of the necessary arrangements about copyright. As regards the Mencken letters, these rights are held by the Mercantile–Safe Deposit and Trust Co. of Baltimore, who administer the Mencken estate, and with whose Henry L. Meledin I had already been in touch. It was at this point that responsibility for reaching agreement with the estate devolved upon Thomas Yoseloff, who undertook to journey to Baltimore on our joint behalf, and my thanks are due to him for the successful outcome of the negotiations which followed. I am further beholden to Alfred A. Knopf, Inc., of New York, for permission to quote from H. L. Mencken's *Treatise on the Gods* and his *Menckeniana,* as noted under References. Two letters I received from Alfred Knopf shortly after Mencken's death also appear with the assent of the writer.

My indebtedness likewise extends to Jean R. McNiece, of the Manuscripts and Archives Division of the New York Public Library (who went to great pains on my behalf to identify and microfilm items missing from my Mencken correspondence as a result of enemy action during the war years); to Dianne Peacop, of the Edinburgh publishers W. & R. Chambers Ltd. (who similarly rescued details of records of mine destroyed in the bombing); to Elizabeth Scott, of the Reader's Digest Association (who diligently searched through records dating back more than a quarter of a century for details of a Mencken contribution relating to that remote era); to Dr. Louis Cheslock, of Baltimore (a former stalwart of the Saturday Night Club, who willingly provided me with information about some of the former members of that convivial assembly); to Jim Herrick, of the National Secular Society, London (for refreshing my memory in regard to contributions of mine to *The Freethinker* in the 1930s); to the BBC, London (for information concerning a leading light of one of their prewar programs); to Donald C. Yelton (whose painstaking scrutiny of the MS led to the adoption of not a few suggested additions and improvements); and to an anonymous army of librarians from half a dozen different establishments (who went to great trouble on my behalf to search for information of which I had need). As for the illustrations, these have been obtained from various sources, including Henry Mencken himself, as elsewhere acknowledged.

P. E. Cleator

ABBREVIATIONS FOR SOURCES
(See also References)

CB   Carl Bode
CJ   *Chambers's Journal*
HLM   H. L. Mencken
JBIS *Journal* of the British Interplanetary Society
NYPL New York Public Library
PEC   P. E. Cleator

EDITORIAL NOTE

During his lifetime, Henry Mencken was vilified and denounced by his opponents (and their number was legion) as a maggot, a jackal, a "pole-cat," a parasite, an intellectual nihilist, a dirty liar, an alphabetical mountebank, a disappointed, dishonest, distrustful, disgraceful, degraded, degenerate evolute of a species of fifty-seven varieties lower than a turkey buzzard—and as much else besides (HLM-1). He was also my friend.

This friendship extended over a period of twenty years, during which we corresponded with gusto and at frequent intervals. It has been authoritatively estimated that in the course of his career Mencken wrote at least one hundred thousand letters, some two hundred of which were addressed to me. Of these last, all those I received are contained in the present volume, together with copies of others, subsequently acquired, which were destroyed by enemy action. As to this, when, after a lapse of two decades and more, I came to examine the correspondence, it was to find that one of half a dozen files was missing. Its contents covered the early part of World War II, from September 1939, through 1940 to the end of January 1941, and they were presumably lost, along with the majority of my other records, during the heavy bombing of my home town in March 1941. However, after Mencken's death, letters he had received from authors, together with copies of his replies, were lodged with the New York Public Library, from whose Manuscripts and Archives Division I was able to obtain details of much of the vanished correspondence. But from various references contained therein, it was evident that at least eight, and possibly as many as ten, copies of Mencken's letters to me were not to be found among the NYPL documents, and as a painstaking search has since failed to reveal them, it must be assumed that they are now lost beyond recall this side of the Resurrection Morn. However, wherever a break occurs in the continuity, I have noted the fact in parenthesis, and added such information as is available about the contents of each of the missing items. By way of compensation, the NYPL records proved to contain transcripts of several of Mencken's wartime letters which had been lost in transit, and so had not previously been seen by me. They thus came as a veritable message from the dead.

In presenting the correspondence, I have closely followed (more or less out of necessity) the essentials of the arrangement by Carl Bode in his *The New Mencken Letters,* itself a model of what such a compilation should be. Which is to say, the Mencken material is assembled in chronological order, exactly as written (apart from the correction of an odd spelling error), and inclusive of any pen-and-ink alterations made by the signatory himself. Each item is accompanied by annotation which provides an explanatory comment, an interpretation enlivened on occasion by extracts from my own letters. Here again, these excerpta are quoted verbatim, with the exception of a single instance in which I was unable to resist the urge to rearrange the wording of a particularly flagrant example of slipshod phrasing.

Notwithstanding that the Mencken letters appear strictly in order of date, from time to time it will be found that after mention has been made of a particular subject, any further reference occurs only after an interval, during which there is no allusion to it. The explanation of this intermittence is simply that both Mencken and myself were compulsive letter answerers—on the day of receiving a dispatch, if circumstances permitted, as they often did. As a result, if, while awaiting a response to a previous note, one of us sent the other some item of interest—a book, a magazine, a newspaper clipping—its acknowledgment would promptly set in motion a secondary exchange of communications, so that as time went on, two, three, and even four separate streams of messages would be flowing between us. This circumstance also accounts for the fact that, despite the delays attendant upon the then customary surface postal service, many of Mencken's letters were mailed within days of one another—during October 1936 on the first, the twelfth, and the thirty-first; similarly, in December 1941 he wrote on the second, the twenty-third, and the thirty-first; while on one memorable occasion (April 20, 1938) he actually sent off two letters on the same day!

To my lasting regret, and this despite our long association, we never met—though it was not for want of trying. When Mencken visited England in 1935, and word of his presence in the British Isles reached me, I commissioned a London journalist associate of mine to track him down, but by the time I received word of the visitor's recent whereabouts, he was already on his way back home. My next move, in 1939, was to decide on a pilgrimage to Baltimore, but this plan also miscarried. At first, I proposed to make the journey in June, but on Mencken's recommendation (he had the climate in mind), I changed the date to late September. With my passage booked and accommodation in New York arranged, I was about to set sail when Hitler invaded Poland, thus causing the cancellation of the trip. Subsequently, toward the end of the conflict, Mencken announced his intention to pay me a visit as soon as peace broke out, but first there were difficulties about his obtaining a suitable berth, and then, as the months went by, overwork and ill health intervened. Again, in 1948, immediately after he had suffered the disastrous stroke which effectively brought his activities to an end, I resolved to board a plane to the U.S., only to discover that in those postwar times, a dollar travel allowance was impossible to obtain, and that I should arrive at my destination without a cent in my pocket. In the event, I did not reach Baltimore until 1978—more than twenty years too late. However, there yet remains one final assignation, thanks to a pact we long ago made to meet in the subterrestrial Hell of the Christians. Here, by all accounts, the warmth attending our long-delayed encounter promises to be considerable.

P. E. CLEATOR

PERSONAL PREAMBLE

Agnostic, sceptic and pacifist—a one-time idealist whose disillusionment is now complete. (JBIS-1)

For a full understanding of the contents of the pages which follow, it is necessary that I should enlarge upon the declaration noted above, and I begin by revealing among other things, I am also a humanist with socialistic inclinations. But this having been said, let me hasten to add that while I'm all in favor of a just and equitable society, experience has brought the realization that however desirable egalitarianism may be in theory, in practice it is likely to prove a dismal failure, human nature being what it is. Your militant left-winger, it would seem, tends to be high on his own rights and entitlements, but low on his obligations and responsibilities to others. Here in Britain, at all events, where we have now suffered from the malaise for a number of years, the results are becoming plain for all to see. What is in the process of being established is a scrounger's paradise, so overflowing with free governmental handouts, funded by penal taxation, that not only is there no longer any incentive to work hard, but there is little enough reason to work at all. What with the statutory unemployment payments, child allowances, debt remissions, rent rebates and other supplementary benefits which they now receive, many of the lower-paid members of the community are actually financially better off out of a job than in one—a circumstance that has not entirely escaped their notice.*

As for my steadfast opposition to war, this stems in part from a marked personal disinclination to plunge a bayonet into the

---

*Since these words were written, Britain's May 1979 general election has brought the reforming Thatcher administration to office, armed with a mandate to end such examples of misplaced legislative benevolence. But can these now firmly established perquisites ever hope to be abolished, endorsed as they are by a unionized labor force dedicated to the proposition that two or more persons shall be paid to perform the work of one? We shall see.

body of a fellow man, even though he, for some inexplicable reason, may be intent upon thrusting a bayonet into me. But my attitude also arises from a consideration of the senseless waste of resources, material as well as human, which armed conflict inevitably entails, not to mention the appalling suffering the undertaking inflicts upon innocent bystanders and participants alike—an undertaking, it seems to me, in which the inglorious role of the combatants is that of modern gladiators, set to slaughtering one another throughout the arena of Christendom for the edification of their political masters. But given the utter stupidity of the enterprise, who is there in authority who is both willing and able effectively to renounce such homicidal antics? Hardly the politicians aforementioned, whose inept handling of international affairs is one of the root causes of the bloodshed. And certainly not the practitioners of organized religion, who manage to preach the gospel of peace while at the same time catering for the demands of war—acting as service chaplains, sanctifying the instruments of mass destruction (God bless this atom bomb!), and uttering one-sided prayers for victory once the battle has been joined. Ultimately dependent as the Christian churches are upon the goodwill of the state, what their interpretation of the Sixth Commandment becomes, in effect, is this: Thou shalt not kill, *unless thy government calls upon thee to do so.*

For lone protestors such as myself, it is, of course, less hazardous to give expression to these misguided views in times of truce than it is to maintain them once there has been a resort to arms. Of this, I was promptly reminded when, at the start of hostilities, an ardent and uniformed World War II enthusiast saw it as his patriotic duty to liken me to a jellyfish which lacked the courage of a louse. But I move ahead somewhat.

I was born, of mixed Brythonic and Gadhelic (i.e., dual Celtic) stock (Cleator is a Manx name), on June 7, 1908, in what was then the Cheshire (now Merseyside) town of Wallasey. From my parents—my father was a constructional design engineer and a meticulous draftsman; my mother, in her leisure moments, a still-life and landscape painter of some merit—I inherited certain artistic leanings and capabilities, while from a paternal uncle I had never known, but who, by all accounts, was outstanding as a classical scholar, I received a posthumous gift in the shape of a collection of leather-bound books on ancient history, which he had amassed as prizes in the course of a brilliant but brief academic career.

In company with this uncle, I found myself acting as host to a virulent strain of the tubercle bacillus which had brought about his untimely demise, a circumstance which also made me a likely candidate for premature embalmment. That I managed to survive adolescence, I have to thank a now forgotten medical practitioner who urged that, instead of attending a place of learning, I should spend my childhood days out of doors, absorbing sunshine and admitting as much fresh air as possible into my scarified lungs.

I mention all this because of the profound effect the disability was to have on my later life. The loneliness imposed upon me by a convalescent boyhood served to enhance a natural reticence, and this, coupled with an inability to take part in any strenuous games (which unwonted activity left me gasping for breath), meant that I derived little enjoyment from the company of other youngsters, and none at all from the unaccustomed discipline of the classroom to which, at long last, I found myself subjected. All I can say about my subsequent period of servitude at the local grammar school, throughout which I inevitably lagged far behind my fellow students, is that I perforce endured it, though without enthusiasm or noticeable benefit. And at the end of it all, by general tutorial consent, any prospect of my qualifying for a university place about equaled the square root of minus one; it was at any rate hardly less imaginary.

The problem of a suitable vocation was eventually solved by my joining my father, a happy circumstance in that it left me free to continue to do much as I pleased. After due prayer and meditation, I decided to attempt to carve out a secondary career of my own choosing by becoming a writer, and my first effort in this direction produced a short thesis on the properties of hydrogen monoxide, appropriately entitled "Water" (CJ-1). The completed manuscript was posted to *Chambers's Journal,* an old, established scientifically inclined monthly magazine, now, alas, defunct. To my very considerable surprise and no little gratification, the response was a printed slip from the editor, intimating that my maiden piece had been accepted for publication!

Thus began a long and productive association which, from 1931 onwards, led to the appearance of a whole series of articles of mine in the pages of this highly respected periodical, items which ranged in subject matter from bacteria and anesthesia to combustion and the atmosphere, not to mention the prospect of man one day making his way to the moon. This last opus, "The Possibilities of Interplanetary Travel" (CJ-2), was written in 1932, and on my receiving notification of its acceptance, I dimly remember stressing the desirability of early publication, lest coming events in this fast-moving sphere of human endeavor should take place before my predictions found their way into print! Not to be outdone (and no doubt with his tongue firmly planted in his cheek), the obliging R. S. Chambers let the article take precedence over another of my offerings, then in proof, and used it in the January 1933 issue.

As it happened, my introduction to the idea of space travel had been by way of the cinema, rather than through a reading of the fictional accounts of Jules Verne and H. G. Wells. The precise year in which this introduction took place now eludes me, but it must have been in or about the mid-1920s. The film in question, a short documentary addition to the evening's program, concerned the discovery of, and the unusual properties exhibited by, the then wonder metal radium—of which one proposed application was its use as a nuclear fuel sufficiently powerful to convey man to the planets! The closing scene was of a rocketlike vehicle heading out into space, trailing a radioactive glow astern. I have no idea how other members of the audience reacted to this spectacular vision of the future, but it certainly made a lasting impression upon me.

In the event, the seed thus sown required half a decade or more to germinate, by which time reports about the experimental activities of members of the VfR (*Verein für Raumschiffahrt*—Society for Space Travel) in Germany had begun to appear in the daily press. This electrifying news was followed by word of the formation of an Interplanetary Society in America, with whose secretary I was soon in touch. Among other things, my correspondent expressed the hope that a kindred organization was about to make its appearance in the British Isles.

I was by no means averse to the suggestion, but the difficulties surrounding it appeared formidable: precisely how was a youthful nonentity such as myself to set about the founding of a movement dedicated to so improbable an achievement as the conquest of space? While pondering the question, it occurred to me that a possible answer might be found in my literary activities. Hence the *Chambers's Journal* contribution on the subject. And hence, to make a long story a model of brevity, the subsequent publication in a Liverpool newspaper of an appeal for members, which led to the birth on Merseyside of the British Interplanetary Society on Friday, October 13, 1933. If I remember aright, there were five of us at this inaugural gathering, at which we solemnly pledged ourselves to begin the monumental task of making the inhabitants of Great Britain rocket-conscious and astronautically minded.

In the meantime, thanks to the tardy development of an insatiable thirst for knowledge, I had become a diligent student of anything and everything that was to be found between the covers of a textbook, from the essentials of the Friedel and Crafts reaction to the mathematical implications of the Lindemann proof of the transcendence of pi. I was also a voracious reader of such dissentient scholars as J. G. Frazer, John M. Robertson, T. H. Huxley, Herbert Spencer, Andrew D. White, Robert Ingersoll, Winwood Reade, and Voltaire, to name but a few. But the two writers whose forthright opinions and superb prose style influenced me most were my fellow countryman Bertrand Russell and the American journalist and author H. L. Mencken. With the former, to my great loss, I at no time had any personal contact. But between Henry Mencken and myself there was maintained, from 1936 onward, a lively and uninterrupted postal rapport that ended only with his death.

It was from the works of these and other accredited unbelievers that I acquired my healthy contempt for professional theologians and their time-dishonored make-believe (in the guise, to quote Mencken [HLM-2], of "Trinities, Virgin Births, Atonements, and other such pious phantasms"). My disrespect for the advocates of this immemorial nonsense, I am led to believe, the perceptive among my readers continue to detect in my writings to this day—and they are no doubt right. My parents, at any rate nominally, professed to be Wesleyan Methodists, though their religious idiosyncrasies were never imposed upon me, apart from the fact that I unknowingly suffered the indignity of the then customary baptismal rites. It would seem, however, that the initiation failed in its purpose, for at no time in my life have I ever been conscious of being a member of the Christian community, or of entertaining any desire whatsoever to become one. Nor can I visualize the slightest prospect of my making a last-minute repentance, even though I have now reached an age when I find myself teetering on the edge of an open grave, into which I am liable to plunge at any moment. But it is not to be inferred from these remarks that I am an atheist, as has so often been suggested. For as long as I can remember, I have always proclaimed myself an agnostic—as one, that is to say, who is prepared openly to state what many others have the courage to acknowledge in private—e.g., that the supposedly sacred writings which compose the Old Testament record, far from being the word of some gaseous and improbable Divinity, are merely a jumble of early Jewish history and Sumero-Babylonian folklore, which man-made conglomeration displays all the fallibility of its human authorship.

As for my attitude toward the credibility or otherwise of a belief in the existence of a Supreme Being (not, of course, personally identifiable as Yahweh, Allah, Mazda, Zeus, Wotan, Thor, or what have you), I can do no better than refer once again to Mencken on the subject, as he expressed himself in a letter to his friend Marion Bloom as long ago as 1921 (CB-1). The following paraphrased extracts provide the salient points of his thesis:

1. No sane man denies that the universe presents phenomena beyond human understanding;
2. It is a reasonable assumption that these phenomena are directed by some superior intelligence;
3. Although this is as far as sound thinking can progress, all religions attempt to go further, in that they pretend to explain the unknowable; and
4. The objection to religion is that it represents an effort by ignorance to account for a mystery that knowledge simply puts aside as intrinsically impenetrable.

Here, Mencken states the case for agnosticism in a nutshell, and it was his ability to engage in critical and incisive discursions such as this, together with his unsurpassed clarity and trenchancy of expression, which attracted me to his writings from the moment I first encountered them. This was an event which took place somewhat belatedly, thanks, at any rate in part, to our difference in age—I was more than a quarter of a century younger than he. At all events, it was not until 1930 that I happened upon a copy of his newly published *Treatise on the Gods,* which I read avidly and with increasing wonderment and delight at the perspicacity of its contents. His six volumes of *Prejudices* then claimed my attention, as did as many of his other works as I could lay my hands on. Even so, it was not until six years had passed that I ventured to send their author a letter expressing my unbounded appreciation of his writings, by which time I was able, with due diffidence, to proffer him a book of my own.

Nihil Obstat
    Henricus Ludovicus Menckenius
        Censor Deputatus

Imprimi Potest
    Lucifer
        Ex-Archangelus

In Inferno Die, January 29, 1956

Letters from Baltimore

1
A Meeting of Minds
(1936–1939)

March 12, 1936

Dear Mr. Cleator:

Thanks very much for your letter of March 2nd. "Rockets Through Space" has not yet reached me, but I assume that it will be coming in shortly. Needless to say, I'll read it with the greatest interest and pleasure. It will be devoured also by my brother, who is an engineer.

You are kind indeed for what you say of my own books. I stopped the Prejudices series because I rather wearied of it and had other enterprises in mind. For nearly two years past I have been engaged on an enormous rewriting of my old book, "The American Language." A huge amount of new material had accumulated, and the new edition will be at least twice the size of the last one.

Sincerely yours,
H. L. Mencken

This was Mencken's prompt and amiable response to an unsolicited letter which began: "May I, as one of your best English customers, crave a little of your time? Having spent whole geological epochs reading, re-reading, and re-re-reading your *Prejudices* and other Christian works, I am rather hoping that you may care perhaps to waste an hour or so perusing a work of mine. . . ."

"'Rockets Through Space'": The unlikely title of the proffered book. It heralded the dawn of interplanetary travel, and had appeared earlier in the year under the imprints of Allen & Unwin (London) and Simon & Schuster (New York). I observe from a note among the Mencken records lodged in New York (NYPL) that in 1942 the book was presented by the recipient to the Enoch Pratt Library in Baltimore.

"For nearly two years past": Mencken's monumental *The American Language* was first published in 1918. The new and enlarged 1936 version was the fourth edition of the work.

"My brother": This was August, the youngest of the three male offspring of Anna Abhau and August Mencken, Sr.

March 26, 1936

Dear Mr. Cleator:

"Rockets Through Space" came in safely, and I have just finished reading it. Certainly you have made a most interesting book. I won't tell you that you convince me that visiting the moon is feasible but, nevertheless, it seems to me that you have made out a most plausible case. My best thanks for the chance to see the book. I am now passing it on to my brother, who is an engineer, and who will be greatly interested.

Sincerely yours,
H. L. Mencken

This second letter of Mencken's gave notice of a change of address—on the heading of his notepaper, the words "704 Cathedral St." had been crossed out and "1524 Hollins Street" added. The move was occasioned by the death of his wife Sara in May of the previous year, an event which now led to his return to the family abode where his brother August remained in residence.

"I won't tell you": In thus giving expression to his lack of conviction about the likelihood of man ever making his way to the moon, Mencken was, of course, being polite. In the astronautical Dark Ages of 1936, there were few who displayed any interest in, much less subscribed to, the idea of space travel as a prospect of the foreseeable future, and nowhere was this obstructive indifference more in evidence than among accredited members of the scientific hierarchy. Here in Britain, the author of what was contemptuously dismissed as "a somewhat premature book on the possibilities of using rockets for interplanetary travel" encountered nothing but derision and abuse from the learned of the land.

April 6, 1936

Dear Mr. Cleator:

I am sorry indeed to hear that you are booked for some serious surgery. Console yourself with the thought that surgeons, when they cure, usually do it quickly and completely. There is nothing of the long drawn out agony that so often accompanies medical treatment. The very best of luck to you.

I wish I could undertake the collaboration that you suggest, but unfortunately it would be a sheer physical impossibility. I am booked to devote most of this year to the political campaign, and after it is over I'll probably go to Germany or Russia on a newspaper enterprise. Thus it will be out of the question for me to undertake any serious writing during 1936.

I abandoned the Prejudices books simply because they began to tire me. Six volumes seemed enough. If I do any books hereafter they'll probably lie rather far afield. One of the things I have had in mind for years is a small volume of advice to young men. All of the existing tomes on the subject seem to be written by suburban curates and Y.M.C.A. secretaries. What is needed by the young is a treatise stating, not the desires of Yahweh, but the actual practises of decent men. It is curious that no one has ever thought to write such a book.

"The Canker" seems to me to be very effective stuff. You make an excellent point in it, and you present it with skill. Unluckily, it is hard to induce editors to print anything that deals adversely with religion. I could do it for so many years simply because I had a magazine of my own. Now that I have no magazine, I am in the same difficulty that faces all other skeptics.

The best of luck with the enterprise. My brother says that your book is grand.

Sincerely yours,
H. L. Mencken

Mencken had long ago observed (HLM-3) that he had yet to meet an author who was not a hypochondriac, and in making mention of some impending surgery, I inadvertently introduced into the correspondence a subject in which, as was soon to become evident, he evinced an abiding personal interest: the multitudinous maladies which the high gods, in their inscrutable wisdom, see fit to inflict upon a defenseless and long-suffering mankind. His own wide assortment of ailments, high among them a regular recurrence of the miseries of hay fever, in association with what were destined to be my all too frequent sessions upon the operating table, inevitably gave rise to a steady exchange of health bulletins in the days ahead. But levity, rather than morbidity, was to be their keynote.

"The collaboration you suggest": Over the years I had amassed an impressive collection of newspaper and other references to a profusion of national imbecilities, which I had intended offering to Mencken as the basic ingredient for more of his incomparable *Prejudices* books. On receiving the hard news that he had ended the series, I was brash enough to propose that joint use be made of the accumulated material by my first knocking it into some sort of shape, and he then adding the inimitable Mencken touch. In the face of such presumption, a lesser man might well have taken umbrage and given vent to his displeasure by terminating the correspondence forthwith. Mencken's more considerate response was deftly to parry the proposal by pleading other and more pressing commitments.

" 'The Canker' ": The title of a sample of my prose, written in what I hopefully imagined to resemble the Mencken manner, which I had submitted as a representative sample of my side of the proposed collaborative effort. The essay is now missing from my files, but the comments it engendered suggest that in it I sought to question the verity of some theological improbability or other.

"A magazine of my own": This was *The American Mercury,* launched in January 1924, as a successor to *The Smart Set,* a periodical whose destinies had been controlled by a Mencken-Nathan partnership from November 1914 until December 1923. As a joint Knopf-Mencken-Nathan enterprise, with Henry Mencken and theater critic George Jean Nathan as coeditors, the new publication was a phenomenal success, despite which its dual management soon led to irreconcilable differences of opinion. As a result, within little more than a year, Mencken emerged as sole editor, and he remained in control until, with the decline in circulation which followed the financial crash of 1929, he relinquished his post at the end of 1933. Thereafter, the once-color-blind magazine gradually changed in character and content to such an extent that in postwar times it became an organ of the radical Right, replete with racialist overtones.

April 18, 1936

Dear Mr. Cleator:

I surely hope that the operation has been a grand success, and that you are making a quick and comfortable recovery. It is at best a dreadful ordeal. There is simply no such thing as painless surgery.

I regret immensely that I offended the Christian people of Wallasey. My excuse must be that the reference books led me into error. All of them that I had access to spoke of Wallasey as a suburb of Liverpool.

Your *Chambers's Journal* article is very amusing stuff, and I am delighted to have a copy. When you tackle Appleton consider yourself quite free to speak of me as one doomed to Hell. I have a wide acquaintance among theologians, and all of them, up to and including archbishops, assure me confidently that my fate post-mortem will be very serious. I am certainly not one to question the professional judgment of such learned and virtuous men. Whenever I think of the matter at all, I assume as an axiom that I'll be a torch for all eternity, and that all the saved will rejoice to see me burn.

Sincerely yours,
H. L. Mencken

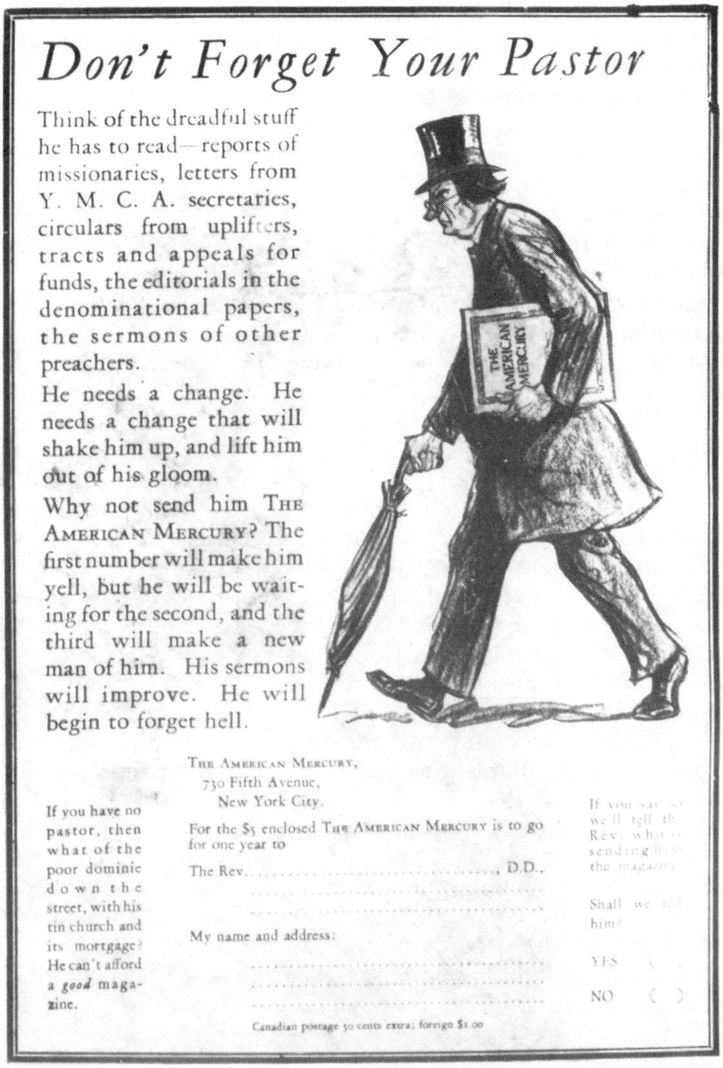

PLATE 1. Baltimorean buffooneries—1. This advertisement, extolling the merits of Mencken's magazine *The American Mercury*, appeared on the back of the jacket of his *Americana, 1926*. (*Photo:* Courtesy of Alfred Knopf, Inc.)

In an article in the *Yale Review,* Mencken had incautiously referred to my home town of Wallasey as a suburb of nearby Liverpool. Grave exception to this statement was taken by indignant residents of the borough, who promptly gave expression to their displeasure in the columns of the obliging Liverpool *Daily Post,* whereby the matter was brought to my attention. The two communities are actually located on opposite banks of the Mersey River, the one in what was then Cheshire, and the other in Lancashire. Under recent (1974) county boundary changes, both regions now form part of the conurbation known as Merseyside.

"Your *Chambers's Journal* article": As earlier noted, in the 1930s I was a regular contributor to this well-known and highly respected publication. Despite a careful search, I have failed to identify this particular item—unless the reference was to an essay which also finds mention in one of Mencken's subsequent letters (May 28, 1936).

"When you tackle Appleton": Professor (later Sir) E. V. Appleton was a distinguished British physicist whose experiments confirmed the existence of the Kennelly-Heaviside or E Layer of ionized gas in the upper reaches of the earth's atmosphere. He later demonstrated the presence of a higher or F Layer, which was named after him. This Appleton Layer was credited with a temperature of 1,000 degrees Centigrade, whereupon a London daily paper hastened to announce that the presence of such a heat barrier in the sky would make space travel impossible. In response to what I regarded as this ill-founded assumption, I penned a somewhat jocose essay entitled "Appleton's Inferno" (JBIS-2), which enunciated two propositions—(1) that because of the manifold sins of mankind, the traditional subterrestrial Christian Hell had become so full that to make room for H. L. Mencken and his followers, its location had been transferred to more commodious quarters in the empyrean; and (2) that as I did not believe in Hell, therefore the alleged threat of incineration from this source, supposedly faced by space voyagers, was nonexistent. Notwithstanding the slight logical imperfections of the argument, the conclusion to which it led was happily confirmed in later years by the exploits of Yuri Gagarin and his fellow cosmonauts.

May 5, 1936

Dear Mr. Cleator:

I am delighted to hear that the surgeons found you needed nothing worse than a deflation, and only hope that your recovery has been comfortable and complete. It is too bad, of course, that the article was spoiled. But don't forget that if the operation had gone through it might have appeared on the obituary page, and come from some other hand.

My plans about Russia are very vague. If I go there it will be on a newspaper enterprise. Needless to say, I'll be delighted to have introductions to Professor Rinin and Professor Perlmann. More of this anon.

I can imagine nothing pleasanter than a motor tour of England under your direction. But I greatly fear that it will be impossible, at least for this year. I was in London briefly last Summer, and if I get there at all in 1936 it will be only momentarily, on my way to the Continent.

I don't blame you for retiring from your journal. Editing with a pistol at your head would have been a sheer impossibility.

Sincerely yours,
H. L. Mencken

In the event, the threatened surgery, duly performed on an exploratory basis, had merely resulted in the draining of fluid, in the hopeful expectation (not fulfilled) that this might suffice to end the trouble. Meanwhile, an article I had arranged to write about the butchery had to be postponed.

"My plans": On learning of the possibility of his visiting Russia, I had offered Mencken letters of introduction to two correspondents of mine resident in Leningrad—Professor Nikolas Rinin and Dr. (not Professor) Jakow I. Perlmann.

"I don't blame you": A difference of opinion between myself and other members of the Council of the Interplanetary Society had led to my relinquishing the editorship of that organization's printed *Journal*. However, I continued to contribute an occasional article to the publication.

May 23, 1936

Dear Mr. Cleator:

I surely hope that the surgeons finally decided to let you go. Their ministrations, however beneficial, are always immensely unpleasant. It is a curious fact that they are, nevertheless, rather popular fellows, whereas dentists, who cause much less pain, are universally loathed.

I enclose a leaflet for your Sabbath reading, and under another cover I am sending you a pamphlet dealing with the same subject. Witchcraft is still in full blast in the Republic. There are mockers who profess to scoff at it, but every true American knows that the powers and principalities of the air still resist scotching.

Sincerely yours,
H. L. Mencken

"I surely hope": This expression of optimistic solicitude was fully shared by the victim. The fates, however, were to decree otherwise.

"I enclose": the leaflet here referred to concerned the Christian activities of the Reverend Celestine Kapsner, O.S.B., whose services in an execratory capacity were available to all who found themselves afflicted by witches and demons. The booklet, entitled *Begone Satan*, also dealt in a highly competent manner with the art of expelling evil spirits by adjuration and other means.

May 28, 1936

Dear Mr. Cleator:

Thanks very much for the copy of *Chambers's Journal*. I have read your article with great pleasure. For years past I have cherished a great yearning to raise whiskers. My poor wife in her time forbade it absolutely, but now I begin to toy with it again. It is many years since a bearded journalist has been known in America. The last one, I believe, was hanged in Massachusetts along about 1901.

Sincerely yours,
H. L. Mencken

The article, recording a personal experience, was entitled "On Giving Up Shaving" (CJ-3). After an unenthusiastic contemplation of the daily and never-ending routine of depilation which the dictates of the then prevailing fashion demanded of all adult males under the age of ninety, I decided to conform no more. That I acquired a healthy growth of beard in the process was merely incidental. And that I was eventually prevailed upon to shear it off was a sacrifice undertaken in the interests of world peace and domestic harmony.

June 5, 1936

Dear Mr. Cleator:

I am glad that you filed that caveat in my interest. It would certainly add a new terror to death if I believed that I'd be debarred from Hell. I have been looking forward for years to a meeting with its denizens, including incidentally my grandfather. He rejected every other Christian idea, but not that of Hell. He insisted on going there, and I like to believe that he had his wish.

At the moment, it would be a sheer impossibility for me to do anything for the *Journal*. I have taken a commission from my old paper, the Baltimore *Sun*, to go to both of the national political conventions, and they'll keep me jumping until the end of June. After that I must apply myself diligently to a history of the *Sun*, now under way. The paper will be 100 years old next year, and we are preparing to print a somewhat formidable volume on its services to God and country. The manuscript must be delivered early in the Autumn, and so I'll probably have to work hard on it during July and the better part of August. After that I'll be at your disposal.

Sincerely yours,
H. L. Mencken

"Caveat in my interest": Mencken had been vouchsafed a preview of the "Appleton's Inferno" article, wherein he found mention.

"At the moment": This comment was prompted by a plea that he might care to consider writing a short piece for publication in the Interplanetary Society's *Journal*. The hope he expressed of finding time to attend to the request in the months ahead was not realized, in part, it may well be, because with the ending of my editorial responsibilities, I did not pursue the matter as diligently as I might otherwise have done.

The suggested subject was the religious implications of space travel, and we are left to wonder what Mencken would have made of it. Given that throughout the universe there must exist countless solar systems akin to our own, some interesting theological speculations at once arise. Accepting the probability of the extraterrestrial presence of a multiplicity of different species of intelligent beings, are we then to suppose that these alien creatures are prone to commit the many misdemeanors associated with the daily activities of mankind? In which event, does their sorrowing Creator, on observing their transgressions, send a filial Redeemer to the rescue of the wayward inhabitants of each of these worlds in turn? And if so, can it be that their would-be Savior finds Himself condemned to an endless round of cruel and ignominious deaths in the familiar Calvaric manner? As an earnest seeker after truth, I pose these questions in all seriousness, though I here make no attempt to answer them, if only because the mind boggles at such a *reductio ad absurdum*.

June 17th, 1936

Dear Mr. Cleator:

The next time I come to England I'll bring you an American madstone to use on the archbishop. Unfortunately, sending it by parcels post is forbidden by American law, for it is extremely powerful, and is thus apt to singe the personnel of the postoffice. I always carry mine in an asbestos sack. I have seen one knock a policeman down and set him afire.

I have just returned from the Republican National Convention at Cleveland, and am planning to see the Democrats renominate Roosevelt at Philadelphia next week. Such shows are obscene, but they somehow delight me, and I have been going to them for many years.

Sincerely yours,
H. L. Mencken

Mencken's predilection for practical joking was diligently pursued throughout his lifetime, and one of his best known inventions was the Maryland Madstone, a powerful prophylactic reputed, among other things, to cure headaches, relieve impotence, combat hydrophobia, and pull teeth. The samples which he handed out to favored recipients supposedly came from a mine at Kitzmiller, in the foothills of the Allegheny Mountains, and in the present instance the designated target for the device's remedial influence was the redoubtable Dr. Richard Downey, the Most Reverend Roman Catholic Archbishop of Liverpool. His Grace had recently appeared in the news here by virtue of his denunciation of the growing use of contraceptives among the Faithful, a fulmination uttered in terms confidently those of one who was privy to the wishes and desires of the Most High in such procreational matters.

"I have just returned": Attending the national conventions was a quadrennial ritual which Mencken zestfully performed throughout his journalistic career, that he might regale his readers with firsthand accounts of the proceedings. In addition to his remarking upon the probity or otherwise of the candidates, he also ventured to predict the outcome of the various party meetings, an exercise in which, as he ruefully concedes in the preface to his *Making a President,* he was wrong more often than he would have wished.

July 1, 1936

Dear Mr. Cleator:

I returned from the two national conventions to find your two letters. Your account of "Appleton's Inferno" delighted me especially, for I have long held the notion that the human race will enjoy soon or late a revival of Hell. Its abolition by Unitarians and other such abhorrent shapes has done great damage to morals. Its revival will make the world happier and greatly improve humanity.

The two national conventions were inconceivably obscene. I have been going to such things for 32 years, but this year they reached depths of idiocy never before plumbed. At the Philadelphia convention of the Democrats there was a day on which no less than 57 speeches were heard. It sounds incredible, but it is a simple fact. In theory, these speeches were limited to five minutes each, but some of them ran to twenty minutes, and one ran to half an hour. I sat fascinated all day and all evening. There has been no such emission of imbecility since Apostolic times.

I'll do that article if my newspaper jobs permit. Whether they will or not I am not sure at the moment. I must go into the Middle West next week, and I'll probably be kept there for a month. It will be the battle ground of the coming campaign, and I am eager to look over the field and make the acquaintance of the principal champions. Landon, the presidential candidate of the Republicans, is said to be a complete idiot. If he is, then his election is certain.

Sincerely yours,
H. L. Mencken

"Landon": Alfred M. Landon, governor of Kansas. In preference to Franklin D. Roosevelt, Mencken favored Landon as the lesser of two presidential evils, the more so when he was agreeably surprised to discover that the candidate of his choice was by no means the idiot he was widely reported to be. In a letter (CB-1) to the Washington correspondent Henry Hyde, written a month or so later, Mencken confided that he had found Landon both a pleasant and a very smart fellow.

"That article": His proposed contribution to the Interplanetary Society's *Journal*.

July 8, 1936

Dear Mr. Cleator:

Thanks very much for the clippings, and for your pleasant note. I am leaving for Cleveland tomorrow, to attend the convention of the Townsendites. They are the nuts who propose to give every American over 60 years or more a pension of $200 a month. Their convention promises to be the largest collection of lunatics ever brought together in one hall in Christendom, and so I am very eager to see it. After it is over, I am going further westward to see Landon, the presidential candidate of the Republicans. Reports reach me that he is a complete idiot, but I suspect that they exaggerate the facts.

Sincerely yours,
H. L. Mencken

"The Townsendites": These were the followers of Dr. Francis E. Townsend, an independent presidential candidate whose convention found Mencken, as was his custom, in rapt if critical attendance. Although he did not hold with the policy of providing every American citizen over sixty with a requital of $200 a month (hence Townsend's sobriquet of "The Old Age Pension Man"), Mencken nevertheless regarded its author as an example of that great political rarity, an innocent and essentially honest man.

Years later (1943) in a letter (CB-1) of acknowledgment to Townsend, who had submitted the MS of his autobiography *New Horizons* to him for perusal, Mencken expressed his pleasure at the opportunity of reading it, and of its reference to him as someone who had regarded the pension proposals "with fairness, if not with favor."

July 30, 1936

Dear Mr. Cleator:

Thanks very much for your note, and for the cuttings. Mr. Hickey, of the *Daily Express,* has borrowed the terrible jargon of the American weekly, *Time.* It is a curious form of syncopated English, and it apparently has no use for articles at the beginning of sentences. I find it dreadful reading, but there are many Americans who appear to like it.

I have just got in from the Middle West. The temperature in Kansas a week ago was 114 degrees Fahrenheit. This sounds incredible, but I quote the official report of the weather bureau. Rather curiously, the heat was very far from unendurable. We had to keep out of the hot wind, but in the shade it was almost comfortable. Sleeping at night, however, was next to impossible.

Sincerely yours,
H. L. Mencken

"Hickey": William Hickey was the adopted name of what was to prove to be a succession of gossip writers whose column appeared (and still continues to appear) as a regular weekday feature of the London *Daily Express.*

August 19, 1936

Dear Mr. Cleator:

I am thoroughly convinced that the great events mentioned in the Book of Revelations are now upon us. The United States has been dreadfully ravaged for a year past by droughts, floods, hurricanes, locusts, grasshoppers, and other evidences of divine wrath. If the heavens were to split open tomorrow it would certainly not surprise me in the slightest.

I have just returned from the convention of the followers of

Father Coughlin, the radio priest, at Cleveland. The show was magnificent. Try to imagine 10,000 morons herded together in one huge hall, and bawling louder bawls that have ever been heard on earth since the day of Pentecost.

I surely hope that you don't proceed with your contempt of God Save the King. In this country the penalty for refusing to arise when the national anthem is played is burning at the stake.

Sincerely yours,
H. L. Mencken

"Father Coughlin": The Reverend Charles Coughlin, who delivered many of his sermons over the air, achieved a considerable radio following throughout parts of America in the early 1930s, but this popularity failed to carry him to the White House in the presidential elections of 1936.

"Your contempt of God Save the King": I had often observed, with no little amusement, the behavior of patriotic theater audiences during the brief lull between the ending of a performance and the customary playing of the national anthem. Invariably, those of His Majesty's subjects who found themselves within easy reach of an exit promptly scurried through it, leaving less advantageously placed members of the congregation unwillingly to tarry, and pay due homage while the overplayed tune ran its course. One memorable evening, by way of an experiment designed to highlight the hypocritical nature of the situation, I elected to remain seated while those around me were upstanding—to their great and mounting indignation. Such was the display of hostility, indeed, that only the lack of a suitable length of hempen cord, I incline to believe, saved me from an on-the-spot lynching.

There was, however, a salutary sequel to the episode. Some three months later, when a long-sustained conspiracy of silence on the part of the news media could no longer be maintained, a bemused and incredulous British public learned for the first time what the rest of the world had long been informed—that their revered and popular young monarch was having an affair with a twice married American lady, Wallis Simpson by name, and that he even contemplated making her his queen. As something of an antiestablishment man myself, I naturally applauded this challenge to the rigid protocol of Church and State, however much I might deplore the dereliction of kingly duty to which, if it were persisted in, such a course of action seemed likely to lead. At all events, it was in the midst of this constitutional crisis, at the conclusion of another evening's program of entertainment, that I deferentially rose to my feet and stood briskly to attention as soon as the opening notes of the familiar anthem sounded—only to be loudly hissed and booed by scores of King Edward VIII's erstwhile loyal citizenry, all of whom remained firmly rooted in their seats!

September 10, 1936

Dear Mr. Cleator:

The photograph indicates that you will have an exciting time in this great Republic. The women here are very susceptible to male beauty, and when they are thunderstruck by it they don't hesitate to make the fact known. My guess is that they'll keep you jumping. But if they bother you too much, I'll put one of my gunmen to guarding you and you'll be able to get some sleep.

I surely hope you don't bring your anarchistic antipathy to the national anthems to this country. The penalty over here for refusing to rise when "The Star Spangled Banner" is played is death by suspension from the nearest lamp post. One of my uncles was so hanged twenty years ago, and ever since I have been somewhat cautious—in fact, I rise when any music whatsoever is played, for many Americans believe that "Mademoiselle From Armentières" and "My Old Kentucky Home" are also national anthems.

Sincerely yours,
H. L. Mencken

"One of my uncles": As an essential part of the family ménage, Mencken maintained a rich store of imaginary relatives, not a few of them avuncular, and his worldwide correspondence was often enlivened by lurid accounts of their scandalous behavior and their well-deserved end.

October 1, 1936

Dear Mr. Cleator:

Umber-bloody-ella is magnificent, and I offer my best thanks. It goes into my files at once, and it will undoubtedly be embalmed in the next edition of my book. *Side-walk* seems to be a borrowing from American. It was used in England a century or two ago, then it went out. Of late it has been coming back, under the influence, apparently, of the American films.

I surely hope that Sir John Simon turns out to be right, and that you are restrained from risking your neck. Suppose one of your rockets really went off and you found yourself on the moon? What then? I have read your book assiduously, but your answer is far from satisfactory. I hope you stay on this earth for a while longer. It needs a few men capable of the now almost obsolete art of laughter.

Sincerely yours,
H. L. Mencken

"Umber-bloody-ella": This novel use of the so-called British adjective as an inserted intensive was encountered by a friend of mine in the wilds of Yorkshire, and I hastened to send word of the phenomenon to Baltimore. True to his undertaking, Mencken duly recorded its reported use in *Supplement I* of his *The American Language*.

"I surely hope": Would-be rocket experimenters stationed within the confines of the British Isles soon encountered serious and seemingly unsurmountable difficulties. The use of the more powerful liquid propellants favored by German and other experts abroad was expressly forbidden by the Home Office, of which Sir John Simon was then the titular head. The ban was imposed on the dubious grounds that the use of a liquid oxygen-hydrocarbon mixture would somehow contravene the Explosives Act of 1875.

October 12, 1936

Dear Mr. Cleator:

Thanks very much for your notes. They are valuable indeed, and I am delighted to have them. The chapter in my book dealing with the differences in current American and English usage gave me more trouble than all the rest put together. I submitted my final lists to a number of English friends, including H. W. Seaman—a very shrewd fellow, who has served as a journalist in both countries. The list, as it stands in the book, was passed by these experts, but ever since the book appeared I have been receiving corrections, additions and remonstrances. I begin to believe that concocting such a list is essentially impossible. There is a constant exchange between the two countries. I recall at least a dozen English locutions that have come into the United States during the past few years. As a rule, such importations disappear quickly, but some of them survive.

Ambulance-chaser is undoubtedly an Americanism, and it was probably seldom heard in England until a few years ago. But it is, obviously, so much better than *accident tout* that it is bound to prevail. In the same way, *speed-cop* is prevailing against *mobile police*.

The Republic is about to reëlect Roosevelt triumphantly. He is the worst quack heard of since Abraham Lincoln, and in consequence he is apparently unbeatable. I marvel that our Heavenly Father doesn't destroy all the great free democracies with a single blast of mustard gas. He'd do it, I am thoroughly convinced, if there were not so many Jews among us. He is naturally reluctant to assassinate His own people, and so the rest of us escape. It is a pity.

Sincerely yours,
H. L. Mencken

I had paused in the midst of a diligent reading of the fourth edition of *The American Language* to send Mencken my comments on his list of American terms and their English equivalents, thereby adding not a little to the existing confusion of tongues.

"H. W. Seaman": Mencken and the British journalist Herbert Seaman had been corresponding since 1921. When Seaman died early in 1955, if fell to my lot to convey the tidings to Baltimore, at a time when a sorely stricken Mencken had but another year to live.

"To re-elect Roosevelt": Although, over the years, Mencken had shown himself to be a far from reliable political prophet, this at least was one occasion on which his prediction came about. In November, 1936, Franklin D. Roosevelt was duly swept into power for a second term of office by defeating A. M. Landon, his Republican opponent, by no less than 524 electoral votes to 7.

"Mustard gas": the vapor from dichlorodiethyl sulphide, a vesicant introduced by the Germans during World War I. As a blistering agent, it caused many casualties merely by coming into contact with the victim's skin.

"So many Jews among us": There is undeniable evidence to show that collectively, Mencken regarded the Jews somewhat askance. But any suggestion that because of his Teutonic ancestry, openly proclaimed during and after World War I, he necessarily harbored anti-Semitic tendencies, does not bear examination, as the names of many of his publishing associates and intimate friends bear witness—Alfred Knopf, Isaac Goldberg, George Jean Nathan, Louis Cheslock, Philip Goodman, Israel Dorman, Louis Untermeyer. Indeed, so close was his relationship with members of the Jewish community that several of his enemies actually accused him of being a Jew himself (HLM-1). Moreover, whatever the extent of his pro-German sympathies, they did not altogether blind him to the persecutory activities of members of the Hitler regime, which maltreatment he consistently denounced during the 1930s.* As for his mock references to the "Jews of Hollywood"

---

*Although, as his published letters show (CB-1), Mencken was at first slow to appreciate the full extent of the Nazi persecution of the Jews, by the beginning of 1936 (January 6) he was replying to a correspondent from Frankfurt am Main as follows:

Dear Mr. Netzer:
  It goes without saying that that report is not true. Some time ago the Sturmer listed me as a Jew, thus adding one more to its immemorial repertoire of false reports. I should add that I am entirely out of sympathy with the method used by Hitler to handle the Jewish question. It seems to me that the gross brutality to harmless individuals must needs revolt every decent man. I am well aware that reports from Germany have been exaggerated, but am also well aware that intolerable brutalities have been practised. I don't know a single man of any reputation in America who is in favor of the Nazi scheme. As it stands, Germany has completely lost the sympathy it had during the years following 1920.
                                    Sincerely yours,
                                    (Signed) H. L. Mencken

PLATE 2. Mencken and George Jean Nathan, American editor and dramatic critic. (*Photo:* Courtesy of Thomas Yoseloff)

and to the "Jews of Wall Street," these utterances are no more to be taken seriously (and out of context) than are his periodic revilements of the Fatherland's World War I opponents ("May all Englishmen roast forever in Hell" was his reported remark to Theodore Dreiser in December 1914, as noted by Bode [CB-2]). Such sentiments, at all events, did nothing to cloud the Mencken-Cleator relationship throughout the period of World War II.

October 21, 1936

Dear Mr. Cleator:

You waste your time arguing with that holy man. The more proofs of his error you pile up, the more adamantine he will remain in his faith. There is a special kind of logic that such persons use. It has nothing whatever to do with ordinary common sense.

Thanks very much for the cuttings. I am always delighted to have such things.

I'll safeguard you against mob violence when you come to Baltimore, but if you'd like to see a little quiet lynching I think I'll be able to arrange one for some Sunday afternoon. If luck is with me, I may even manage to arrange a burning at the stake. Such burnings are now regarded with some hostility by the better sort of Americans, and so they have to be bootlegged.

Sincerely yours,
H. L. Mencken

"You waste your time": Currently, I was in the midst of a prolonged but friendly postal discussion with a young Catholic priest, who valiantly but unsuccessfully sought to make me see the error, if not of my ways, then at any rate of my views. He was Father Kenneth Meiklem, of whom I retain fond and appreciative memories. I last heard from him early in 1941, and if he chances to read these words, I should be delighted to have news of him.

"A little quiet lynching": It need hardly be said that despite his jocularity, Mencken was resolutely opposed to the mob violence which on occasion led to the summary execution of hapless (and no doubt often innocent) Negroes, or that he was equally loud in his denunciation of the travesty of justice which usually attended attempts to bring the perpetrators to book. See, for example, his letters on the subject to Walter White and George S. Schuyler, published by Bode (CB-1).

November 4, 1936

Dear Mr. Cleator:

Thanks very much for your letter, and for the cuttings. I am always delighted to have such things. "Appleton's Inferno" was very well displayed in *The Freethinker*. I am passing on my copy to a Christian friend. He still believes that Jonah swallowed the whale, but I gather that he has begun to doubt that Paul was really a great thinker. Such dubieties always afflict a Christian by degrees. He is a long time wobbling to the light.

Sincerely yours,
H. L. Mencken

"The Freethinker": As its title implies, this publication of the National Secular Society was (and still is) noted for the trenchant laicism of its contents. In one of its issues, the late Chapman Cohen, its then editor, had seen fit to reprint my "Appleton's Inferno" article.

"Jonah swallowed the whale": In these days of widespread dissent and disbelief, few theologians would be prepared to maintain that the anthropoid stomach, still less the human gullet, could accommodate an animal of cetacean proportions. That Mencken himself entertained doubts about the feasibility of such a gastronomic undertaking is to be found elsewhere in his writings, as when, in making reference to the suggestion that the hero of the Fifth Book of the Prophets really did swallow the beluga, he adds the proviso "or vice versa."

December 5, 1936

Dear Mr. Cleator:

My best thanks for the Post Office Guide. It is the sort of literature that I love, and I have been going through it with great pleasure. Some of the rules of the British post office turn out to be even more complicated and absurd than those of the American post office. The true bureaucrat is a man of really remarkable talents. He writes a kind of English that is unknown elsewhere in the world, and he has an almost infinite capacity for forming complicated and unworkable rules.

Thanks also for the quotation from the Pitkin book. It was printed in this country, but I never saw it. My opinion of Pitkin, I am sorry to have to add, is not too high. He has a sort of cleverness, but he seems to me to be intrinsically very shallow. However, he manages to amuse the customers, and certainly that is something.

The best of luck with the new book. My chaplain is instructed to pray for it.

Sincerely yours,
H. L. Mencken

"The Pitkin book": Walter P. Pitkin's *A Short Introduction to the History of Human Stupidity*.

"The new book": I had it in mind to gather together and collectively issue a series of articles of scientific import I had earlier contributed to sundry journals and magazines. In the event, the project came to nothing, thanks to a noticeable lack of enthusiasm for the enterprise on the part of my publishers.

January 5, 1937

Dear Mr. Cleator:

Thanks very much for your reminder of the holidays. I spent Christmas on my back in hospital, entertaining a severe throat infection. It is now passing off, and I am planning to go to Florida for a week or two. Florida is inhabited almost entirely by bounders and scoundrels, but nevertheless the climate is pretty good and I believe that a week in the sun will restore me to what Harding used to call normalcy.

Here's hoping that we are all lucky in 1937!

Sincerely yours,
H. L. Mencken

"Harding": William Gamaliel Harding, twenty-ninth president of the U.S. and arch exponent of the art of government by crony. The corruptness of his administration was matched by that attending his misuse of the English language, a perversion which gave rise to such expressions as "normalcy" and "betrothment."

January 7, 1937

Dear Mr. Cleator:

I am sorry indeed to hear that the surgeons have had you on the table again. It must have been a dreadful adventure. I only hope that they did a good job, and that you'll be out of their hands for a good while to come. The ingenuity revealed by our Heavenly Father in the invention of diseases is really worthy of a better cause. I am in constant contact with medical men here in Baltimore, and almost daily I hear stories of pathological conditions that make the most ingenious devices of Edison seem puerile. My own recent adventure was trivial, but nevertheless it included some very impressive details. I am still somewhat wobbly, and I am still hoping to get into the South for a week or two.

My best thanks for the telephone directory, and for the copy of the Royal Air Force magazine. I shall give hard study to both of them.

Poor Edward's adventure really made very little impression in Baltimore. It is accepted as an axiom that a Baltimore woman always get her man. Any Baltimorean can give you examples which make the snaring of Edward seem an almost childlike performance. It is not that Baltimore women are of extraordinary beauty, but simply that they are magnificent psychologists.

Sincerely yours,
H. L. Mencken

The need for further bodily deflation having become evident (and been undertaken), the exercise left the surgeon convinced that more drastic action on his part was now called for. My inclination was unenthusiastically to agree with him.

"The Royal Air Force": The publication was *The Halton Magazine and the Daedalus,* for which I penned an occasional article. It appeared twice yearly.

"Poor Edward's adventure": England's long-hushed-up constitutional crisis had at last come to a head. On December 5, Cosmo Gordon Lang, His Grace the Lord Archbishop of Canterbury, an implacable opponent of Edward VIII's matrimonial aspirations, had called for the saying of prayers in all the churches of the land, thereby to ensure that "God may in these momentous hours overrule the decisions of the King." When, despite these manifold implorations, the monarch declined to give way, and elected to abdicate instead, His Grace promptly berated the ex-king for his having "abandoned a trust so great," conveniently overlooking the fact that responsibility for the decision had earlier been transferred to another and higher Authority.

Mencken's views on the affair, although at the time he did not express them to me, have since become evident. From the contents of other of his letters (CB-1), it is clear that he considered the king to have behaved with the utmost irresponsibility and without thought to the consequences of his actions. Not only was it absurd for someone in Edward VIII's exalted position to have allowed himself to become enamored of "a highly oxidized double-divorcée," but it was stupid of him to have entertained the idea that he would be permitted to enter into a left-handed association with her, a *mésalliance* which would give promise of "two morganatic brothers-in-law hanging about the back door of the palace." As for Edward's abdication, this was an even worse act of folly. "Imagine what he gave up, and then look at what he got!"

January 30, 1937
Dear Mr. Cleator:

My best thanks for the clippings. They include some swell stuff for my files.

The book looks excellent, and I only hope that you make it plain that the troubles of mankind are all due to sin. If people would only follow literally the behests of Holy Writ there would be no woe and lamentation on this earth. If you adopt this thought you will have to rub it in pretty hard to make any impression on the customers. Nine-tenths of them incline to sin as naturally as a Congressman inclines to alcoholic intemperance.

A week in Florida restored me, and I am beginning to feel normal again. I have several large jobs in hand, and am eager to get at them.

Sincerely yours,
H. L. Mencken

"The book looks excellent": On a recent visit to London I had made arrangements to produce a work of fiction with extraterrestrial overtones. As things turned out, the undertaking came to nothing. The reason, if I remember aright, was that its intended publisher was inconsiderate enough to go out of business.

February 26, 1937

Dear Mr. Cleator:

Publishers who try to teach authors how to write their books are great pests but, unfortunately, the laws forbid shooting them. You'll thus probably have to grin and endure it. The specimens of your arguments that you send me recall the German saying,

> Himmel für Klima,
> Hölle für Gesellschaft!

In other words, Heaven for climate, but Hell for society.

My illness seems to have passed off. I am still a shade uncomfortable, but manage to get through a normal day. I have been amusing myself editing an English translation of a Latin book published in 1715. It deals with the quacks who flourished in that time, and it sounds curiously modern. It was written by Johann Burkhard Mencken, no ancestor of mine, but a member of my family. I have a painting of him showing him with a large wig and a noticeably red nose. I assume that he enjoyed himself in the barbaric fashion prevailing in that remote and unenlightened age.

Sincerely yours,
H. L. Mencken

"Publishers who try": I had been complaining that an outline of another book I had submitted for consideration had encountered so many proposed amendments that I was on the point of abandoning the enterprise.

"I have been amusing myself": The Latin book here referred to was *De Charlataneria Eruditorum,* a satirical exposure of some of the frauds perpetrated on their unsuspecting customers by the savants of the day. Gleefully, Mencken called upon Professor Francis Litz to prepare a translation of the work, to which he then penned a lengthy introduction and reissued it (in 1937) under the title of *The Charlatanry of the Learned.*

March 19, 1937

Dear Mr. Cleator:

Thanks very much for the clippings (or perhaps I had better say cuttings) of the Hickey articles. Hickey gives a really accurate picture of New York. What is more, he picks out very skillfully what is most interesting in the town.

I have been grinding away at some political writing of no importance. Once it is off my hands, I'll probably tackle another little book. On my retirement from the *American Mercury* I took an oath to write no more books. But such vows, of course, can never be kept. I'll probably carry a typewriter with me to the gallows.

The Post Office Magazine has not yet come in, but I assume that it will be arriving shortly. It goes without saying that I'll be delighted to see it.

Sincerely yours,
H. L. Mencken

Throughout our correspondence, I kept Mencken regularly supplied with cuttings, mainly of a philological nature, gleaned from newspaper and other sources, which items he identified as clippings. This difference between English and American usage was duly noted in his *Supplement I* of *The American Language,* in company with many other examples.

April 15, 1937

Dear Mr. Cleator:

I hope that by the time this reaches you you'll be out of the slaughter house and well on your way to recovery. Surgery is strictly no fun, despite the optimism of the surgeons. My own brief experience last Winter kept me very uncomfortable for several weeks. In a month or two I may have to tackle another dose of it. Let me hear from you by all means as soon as you feel like it.

My best thanks for the Hickey clippings. I have read all of them with the greatest pleasure. Thanks, also, for the extract from the *News Review*.

Sincerely yours,
H. L. Mencken

In a letter dated April 3, I had been able to announce that the long-threatened surgery was to take place two days hence.

"News Review": A weekly vendor of intimate personal material on well-known people currently in the public eye. The magazine subsequently became absorbed by *Illustrated,* another of the Odhams Press publications.

April 19, 1937

Dear Mr. Cleator:

Despite your graphic description of the pains of Hell, I assume from your letter that you are making good progress and so I hasten to offer my congratulations. It is really astonishing how uncomfortable the patient can be following major surgery. The chiropractors relieve him of all pain on the table, but once he is back in his room they hand him over to God and he suffers the usual barbarities.

The geography of Hell is more or less familiar to me, for my Uncle Julius is one of its principal inhabitants. I marvel that you didn't meet him during your brief tour. I hear from him occasionally through a talented spiritualist here in Baltimore. He tells me that he has got used to the extreme heat, and that the society of Hell is very amusing. When we get there together we must certainly look him up.

Sincerely yours
H. L. Mencken

This was Mencken's reply to a postsurgical note I dispatched on April 8, which began: "If what I've been getting during the past three days is a fair sample, you won't like Hell. I had it in mind to urge you to cast off sin, suffer a spiritual rebirth, and thus become a heavenly candidate. But alas, I fear it is too late. Yesterday, while making an informal tour of inspection, I accidentally happened upon your hellish quarters-to-be. You have been awarded one of the most modern of cells, with a private furnace at one end. It is simply furnished with a typewriter and a pair of tongs, suitable for pulling Methodist noses. Under the name on your door, incidentally, I noticed a scribbled note: Overdue.... I will say no more, except to mention that you are located in Bowel Buildings, Brimstone Lane, and are thus within easy reach of the Baptist and Christian Science Settlements."

"Uncle Julius": Yet another of Mencken's congenerous inventions.

May 17, 1937

Dear Mr. Cleator:

I am delighted to hear that you are fast returning to normalcy, and that the quacks failed in their second effort to convert you into an angel. My own troubles are trivial. I'll be up for some further repairs very shortly, but unless some accident happens I'll not be disabled.

Car Clinic is swell indeed, and I marvel that it was not invented in this great Republic. So far as I am aware, it is not used here. I shall certainly try to introduce it at once.

My best thanks also for the cutting of Herbert's article in *Punch*. Some of the novelties he lists are very amusing. Such things are manufactured in this country in enormous number. Fortunately, most of them pass out very quickly.

I have been engaged upon a somewhat elaborate investigation of the University of Maryland, a great rolling mill of learning supported by the taxpapers of my State. It turns out to be as costly as a dozen yachts. There are no less than 6,000 students on the roll, most of whom, I suspect, are of very low mental visibility.

Sincerely yours,
H. L. Mencken

"Herbert's article": A. P. Herbert was a well-known humorous writer of the 1930s and a frequent contributor to the magazine *Punch,* an old established and still flourishing purveyor of satire which celebrated its centenary in 1941.

June 16, 1937

Dear Mr. Cleator:

My most hearty congratulations on your escape from Hell. God knows I envy you that swing round the German circle. I can imagine nothing pleasanter. It is now seven years since I last made it, and I begin to feel that I'll never see Munich again. I hear that it has changed very little in late years. The beer is still good, the streets are still clean, and the waitresses still weigh 250 pounds.

The weather here has turned hot, and I begin to feel very comfortable. It is always easier for me to work when I am perspiring freely.

Sincerely yours,
H. L. Mencken

I had earlier written, "There seems to be little doubt that Europe is going to blow up shortly, and I'm determined to have one last look at it before God's next war to end war completes the destruction begun in the last."

The "German circle" referred to took in Ostend, Cologne, Munich, Garmisch, Mittenwald, Innsbruck, Buhrs, Zurich, Lucerne, Basle, Paris, and Dieppe, with frequent stops on the way.

July 5, 1937

Dear Mr. Cleator:

I certainly hope you don't forget to send me a copy of that article. It sounds immensely interesting. My best thanks, meanwhile, for the various enclosures with your last letter. The passport application form is especially interesting. It is even more complicated and idiotic than the American form.

The Stapledon book has not yet reached me, but I assume that it will be in in a day or two. I'll go through it with the greatest pleasure.

Yesterday was the 4th of July, the anniversary of the day on which this great free Republic threw off the yoke of the British Hun. The day was a Sabbath, and hence the pious patriots postponed the celebration until today. Baltimore is rocking with the explosions of fireworks. I hear from the *Sun* office that 40 head of patriots have already been taken to hospital. It is certainly good news, and I only hope that the total for the day runs to at least 10,000.

Sincerely yours,
H. L. Mencken

When giving notice of my impending departure for the Continent, I had been able to announce that the account of my recent dissection was to appear in a forthcoming issue of *Chambers's Journal*.

"The Stapledon book": Olaf Stapledon's *Last Men and First Men*.

July 28, 1937

Dear Mr. Cleator:

My best thanks for the cuttings, which, as always, are superb. The effects of Munich beer are not immediately visible. After three or four months you will begin to swell, and at the end of a year you'll have put on at least forty pounds. Such additions are extremely solid. They resist starvation, acute infections and even conscience.

The Stapledon book is here, and I am hoping to read it very shortly. I have been horribly beset by necessary work, and hence have fallen far behind in my reading.

Sincerely yours,
H. L. Mencken

On my return from Europe, among a mountain of mail awaiting attention, was Mencken's earlier note of July 5, in making answer to which I had commented on the excellence of the Munich beer. This mention evidently awoke fanciful memories, for his response was to warn of the latent effects that might be expected to follow a liberal consumption of this delectable but potent brew.

August 18, 1937

Dear Mr. Cleator:

Once you take to the air you'll be incurable. It is a disease of a powerful virulence. I got a touch of it two or three years ago, and came near perishing before I threw it off. I only hope that you say nothing against our holy Christian religion. It is a dreadful thing to shake the faith of people who look confidently toward sprouting wings post-mortem. They will be disillusioned soon enough.

I promise to read "Rome's Gift" if my eyes hold out. They have been horribly overworked of late, and begin to protest.

My very best thanks for the budget of cuttings. As we say in this great Republic, some swell ones are among them.

I heard yesterday a good story from Hollywood. It concerns a Jewish movie producer who was very pessimistic about one of his new pictures. "God knows," he said to a colleague, "how we'll come out of it. It ain't much—in fact, its only colossal."

Sincerely yours,
H. L. Mencken

The BBC had recently telephoned me from London, with a request that I prepare and deliver a brief discourse on rockets.

Rome's Gift was the title of a book by A. T. Sheppard which had come my way. I had threatened to send Mencken a copy of it for his edification and Sabbath reading.

September 9, 1937

Dear Mr. Cleator:

Old Moore's Almanac really delighted me. We have one here in Maryland that is somewhat similar. It is called the Hagerstown Almanac, and it has been coming out uninterruptedly since Colonial times. It predicts the weather for every day in the year. We used to have a colored cook who followed it religiously. One day when it had predicted fair weather there was the worst snow seen in Baltimore for years. She was, however, undisturbed. She simply fell back on the theory that the Almanac predicted country weather, not city weather. I give you this as a specimen of human reasoning at its best.

Sincerely yours,
H. L. Mencken

"Old Moore's Almanac": An English astrological annual justly renowned for the accuracy or otherwise of its prognostications concerning the year's forthcoming events.

"Hagerstown Almanac": Maryland's answer to the above, first issued in 1797. Essentially, it consisted of a calendar loaded with astronomical and astrological data. As Mencken notes, it also specialized, with varying success, in making advance weather predictions for each day of the year.

September 15, 1937

Dear Mr. Cleator:

"Rome's Gift" came in this morning, somewhat damaged in transit but still recognizable as a book. I shall fall upon it the first chance. This is the hay fever season in the United States, and though I have been cured by vaccines I am still somewhat irritated, especially in the eyes. Thus I read as little as I can while the curse is on me. I ascribe this infliction to the personal hostility of one of the Twelve Apostles—a gentleman I have always disliked. When I get to Heaven at last I shall seize the chance to give him a good beating.

Sincerely yours,
H. L. Mencken

This letter contained Mencken's first—but by no means his last—reference to the curse of hayfever which periodically assailed him. His ascription of this visitation to the personal hostility of one of the Twelve Apostles was not accompanied, alas, by information enabling the culprit to be identified. Can it be that he was the Paul to whom Mencken makes reference in his letter of November 4, 1936?

October 4, 1937

Dear Mr. Cleator:

My best thanks for the cuttings. As always, they are immensely amusing. I am ready to believe at once that Aldous Huxley wrote that quatrain—in fact, I am so convinced that he did that I am having a hundred copies struck off and shall send them to the principal religious papers of this great Republic, each of them with his name appended. This will set at least twenty thousand clergy to praying for his eternal damnation, and I'll thus be assured of meeting him in Hell.

The United States continues to go from bad to worse. It now appears virtually certain that Roosevelt will have a third term. Twelve years of him will surely bankrupt the country, and maybe bring us a Mussolini.

Sincerely yours,
H. L. Mencken

I had reported that a reader of my piece "On Giving Up Shaving" had sent me the following lines, attributed to Aldous Huxley, the English novelist and essayist:

> Christ-like in my behaviour,
> Like every true believer,
> I emulate my Saviour,
> And cultivate a beaver!

"From bad to worse": Mencken had been an unrelenting opponent of America's thirty-second president since almost the day of his inauguration. Although he had supported Roosevelt in the 1932 election on the grounds that the then prevailing Depression had been caused by the extravagances of the hapless Herbert Hoover administration, he soon withdrew his allegiance when it became evident that the New Deal legislators were intent upon spending their way out of trouble. Mencken also found objectionable the highly forcible propaganda which accompanied governmental exhortations in support of the National Recovery Act.

November 1, 1937

Dear Mr. Cleator:

My best thanks for the clippings.

The news that you are of Manx origin is interesting indeed. I only hope that your forebears left the island after its inhabitants had abandoned cannibalism. My own ancestors were heathen until the Seventeenth Century. They were then converted to Christianity and for a little while were very pious, but during the Eighteenth Century they reverted to the primeval animism of the clan.

The news that Huxley is doomed to Hell is distressing but not surprising. I have, indeed, long reconciled myself to his probable damnation. He started out in the world with fair promise, but yielded swiftly to corrupt influences, and is now an active enemy of our holy Christian faith. I have remonstrated with him more than once, but to no avail.

You should come to the United States and see the greatest show on earth. The New Deal becomes more and more preposterous, and as it grows in preposterosity the plain people love it the more. My guess is that Roosevelt will be reelected for a third term in 1940 by an almost unanimous vote. I may even vote for him myself. He gives a swell show, and the United States really deserves him.

Sincerely yours,
H. L. Mencken

Mencken had recently sent me a copy of *The Charlatanry of the Learned,* and the ancestral information he provided in his introduction moved me to disclose my Celtic origins, with particular reference to the Isle of Man.

"Huxley": The aforementioned Aldous Huxley.

"The New Deal": No doubt in Mencken's eyes, a significant contribution to its growth in preposterosity was the levying, way back in 1933, of a tax of $5 a barrel on his favorite malt liquor.

"My guess": On this occasion, as once before, Mencken made a political assessment which was in due course to be confirmed by events. As time went on, however, he hopefully but mistakenly convinced himself that there were sound reasons for reversing his earlier estimation.

November 29, 1937

Dear Mr. Cleator:

The outline of the book sounds excellent, and I hope you are making good progress with it. I trust that you say nothing in it in contempt of Father Divine. He is a great and good man, and the Holy Ghost actually seems to have him by the ear. The charge that he is a mere swindler is simply not true. To be sure, he accepts a tithe running in some cases to 90% of his customers' total earnings, but he has divine inspiration for doing so, and I am certainly not disposed to question him.

I am still hoping to clear off a lot of trash and get to work on a book. Whether I'll be able to do so remains to be seen.

Sincerely yours,
H. L. Mencken

I had announced the making of a start on yet another literary project intended to question certain theological pretensions. Predictably, the book itself was not destined to appear in print, though extracts from it were subsequently used in a later work (PEC-1). More immediately, other excerpts graced the unhallowed pages of *The Freethinker,* at first in the form of a separate essay, entitled "Moonshine," and thereafter as the aphoristic contents of a weekly column headed "Satanic Soliloquy."

"Father Divine": A Negro extrovert who had gained prominence in New York by his claim to be Yahweh, the Lord God of Hosts, in an atramentous guise.

"Get to work on a book": In another note, written less than a month later (on December 23), Mencken again alludes to "that book" on which he plans to make a start. The probability would seem to be that in both instances he was referring to a long proposed dictionary of quotations, in regard to which a rare and informative outline of his plans for the book, sent for consideration to his publishers in May, 1936, will be found in Bode (CB-1).

December 17, 1937

Dear Mr. Cleator:

Thanks very much for Leonard Woolf's "Quack, Quack." The American edition passed through my hands some time ago, but I unaccountably neglected to read it. I shall apply myself to it at once.

Here's hoping that you are lucky in 1938.

Sincerely yours,
H. L. Mencken

" 'Quack, Quack' ": This example of Leonard Sidney Woolf's pungent prose had first been published in 1935.

December 23, 1937

Dear Mr. Cleator:

I am planning to take a little trip to the West Indies in January. As soon as I return I'll spit on my hands and fall upon that book—God being my guide and counsellor. I have been gravid with it for ten years, and it is begging to be born. It will probably be bad, but so are most books.

If ever I encounter a copy of "Damn" I'll certainly snatch it and send it to you. It is full of very young stuff, but one or two pages are fairly amusing.

Broadmoor asylum seems to be full of enlightened people. One of them, as I recall it, was a subscriber to the *American Mercury* in my day. Another is one of the most eminent of English Biblical scholars. Here in the United States the society in the lunatic asylums is the best in the country, barring only that in the Federal prisons.

I offer you all of the hollow felicitations proper to the season.

Sincerely yours,
H. L. Mencken

"That book": As already noted (my comment on Mencken's letter of November 29, 1937), this and the present mention would appear to be a reference to his long-planned book of quotations, an identification here supported by his accompanying remark that "I have been gravid with it for ten years." This takes the inception of the work back to 1927, though in the book itself, first published in 1942, the claim is made that the compilation of its contents required twenty-five years to assemble and complete, thus suggesting that it was first conceived in 1917. This earlier date would seem to be confirmed by a comment subsequently made in a letter dispatched on February 12, 1941, at a time when the work was nearing completion: "At the moment I am in the last stages of a book of quotations that has been on my desk off and on for twenty-five years."

"If I ever": This was Mencken's response to a lament on my part that *Damn—A Book of Calumny,* which appeared in 1917, was one of the few of his books I had been unable to locate.

"Broadmoore Asylum": I had reported receiving an application for membership in the Interplanetary Society from an inmate of this mental home for the criminally insane!

January 13, 1938

Dear Mr. Cleator:

My best thanks for the copy of *Chambers's Journal* containing the article. I have read "Operation" with the greatest interest, and was delighted at the end to find your generous mention of my Prejudices books. It interests me especially to observe the difference in procedure in the two countries. In the United States a man facing serious surgery would unquestionably go to a hospital, not to a nursing home. Nursing homes are reserved mainly for persons needing rest cures and other such minor treatments. All of the principal hospitals in this country have private pavilions for paid patients. Some of them are immensely luxurious and the fees run to fantastic sums. There are hospitals in New York which charge as much as $30 a day for accommodations. They are thus mainly patronized by economic royalists, and the fact that their death rates are high causes no public indignation.

I am played out by hard work, and am planning to take a little holiday in the West Indies. Unfortunately, it will have to be short. I surely hope that you have recovered and are once again saucy and full of sin.

Sincerely yours,
H. L. Mencken

The account of my recent surgical experience (CJ-4) ended with a mention of how I occupied myself while bedridden, and during the times I was not being subjected to the postoperative administrations of members of the medical profession and the nursing staff. The concluding words of the article referred to:

> My complete re-reading, for the nth time, of the irrepressible H. L. Mencken's six volumes of *Prejudices,* and the constant threat of suture-snapping to which his searching and ribald impudences gave rise.

February 6, 1938

Dear Mr. Cleator:

The last trip to the West Indies turned out to be a great success. I got brown and sunburned and also managed to get down a few barrels of prime malt liquor. I travelled on a German ship and came home with my waist line bulged at least a foot.

Sincerely yours,
H. L. Mencken

My best thanks for the cuttings!
HLM:MVW

The added postscript was in longhand. An unusual feature of the letter itself was that it had been typed on a strange machine by someone other than Mencken's resident secretary. Again, exceptionally, the reference HLM:MVW was appended. Enquiries have failed to reveal the identity of MVW, but concerning the use of the initials HLM, see below.

March 4, 1938

Dear Mr. Cleator:

I was delighted to have that landscape of you in The Astronaut. It comforts me to discover that you are a handsome fellow. Come to America with a suitable wardrobe and I'll get you a job in the movies.

I have not seen *Good and Bad English* by Whitten and Whitaker. Who publishes it? Please don't bother to send it to me. I have a credit balance with Heffer of Cambridge and I'll order the book against it.

My very best thanks for the clippings. I have taken over, temporarily, the editorship of the Baltimore Evening Sun and I am clapping one of them into its editorial page at once. The job is only temporary. I'll be back at my usual enterprises before summer.

Sincerely yours,
H. L. Mencken

"The Astronaut": *The Astronaut* was the official publication of the Manchester Interplanetary Society, a newly emerged local group which later joined forces with the national organization. The copy of the February issue featured my picture on the front cover.

"Good and Bad English": The publishers were George Newnes, of London.

"I have taken over": The temporary supervisory activity here referred to was confirmed by the fact that this and Mencken's next three letters were typed on notepaper bearing the insignia "*The Evening Sun*—Editorial Department."

March 31, 1938

Dear Mr. Cleator:

My best thanks for the clippings and for the chance to see the enclosed. It is a really horrible piece of drawing. My guess is that things of the same sort will begin to appear in this great Republic before long. A really formidable anti-semitic movement seems to be rolling up.

My most sincere congratulations on the company you are keeping. The lady is immensely charming. Tell her that I am

PLATE 3. This was the "landscape" of a youthful Cleator to which Mencken refers in his letter of March 4, 1938. The picture had been taken some five years earlier, on the occasion of the official opening of Speke Airport, Liverpool, on July 3, 1933.

PLATE 4. Cleator and his wife-to-be, Madelon Bermingham, who gained Mencken's instant approval ("The lady is immensely charming") when a sight of the above picture was accompanied by the intelligence that she had rashly presented her prospective spouse with a copy of *In Defense of Women*.

planning a new edition of "In Defense of Women" to be published posthumously. It will contain a great deal of valuable matter that I have been too shy to print in the editions brought out during my lifetime.

I hope our Heavenly Father relents and you are able to come to the Republic this summer. There is not much time remaining. In a couple of years it will probably execute all foreigners at sight.

Sincerely yours,
H. L. Mencken

The "really horrible piece of drawing" was an example of anti-Semitic Nazi propaganda which I had collected on one of my trips to Hitler's Germany. It was a lurid and grossly distorted caricature of a Jewish member of the community—a foretaste of other and far worse persecutory horrors to come.

"The company you are keeping": The charming lady in question was my wife-to-be. I had sent Mencken a print of a recent photograph of the two of us in order to correct any impression of excessive youthfulness that might have been conveyed by the *Astronaut* picture, which had been taken some five years earlier.

April 20, 1938

Dear Mr. Cleator:

Those heathen apothegms are swell indeed and they have given me some salubrious chuckles. My best thanks.

I read Foote's book many years ago, but have pretty well forgotten it. I'll make a search for it in my library. It probably still exists.

Needless to say I'll be delighted to read Uncle Lionel's treatise on sin.

My term of servitude here ends on May 7th and I am looking forward to my release with the hopeful air of a Christian in the condemned cells. It may be that I'll go to Germany for the Sun in June. I haven't been there for ten years and I am eager to find out just what is going on. The press association dispatches seem to me to be probably dubious. They are mainly written by gentlemen resident in the bar of the Adlon Hotel. Some of them can't even read German.

The Holy Ghost has been giving some unpleasant attention of late to my stomach and I feel somewhat rocky, but the Resurrection men tell me that all that will clear up as soon as I get a holiday. I have been working twelve hours a day here and at home and begin to wear out. Prayer has availed me nought.

Sincerely yours,
H. L. Mencken

"Those heathen apothegms": As embalmed in print in the weekly column I was writing for *The Freethinker*. Two examples:

Syllogism

Major premise: If Christianity is true, then I'm a Dutchman.
Minor premise: I am a British citizen by birth.
Conclusion: Therefore Christianity is false.

Philosophy At 2 a.m.

What if Christianity *is* true?
Ah! but what if it isn't!

"Foote's book": This was G. W. Foote's *The Bible Handbook,* published some forty years earlier, from which I had quoted some quizzical irreverence or other.

"Uncle Lionel": The late Lionel Gamlin, a highly respected member of the BBC staff who catered for the younger members of the Corporation's listening audience. He had recently fathered a tract entitled *The Children's Hour,* and in sending Mencken a copy I warned: "Be careful how you handle it, or the moralic acid will cause a painful burn."

April 20, 1938

Dear Mr. Cleator:

I enclose a curiosity for your pious collection. The Baltimore Afro-American is the organ of the local colored people. It came out on Good Friday with the enclosed. No ordinary newspaper would dare to print such a thing, but the colored brethren seem to care nothing for ordinary prudence. Neither do they pay any attention to the libel laws. Whenever the spirit moves them they print articles accusing some Negro bishop of gross immorality. I have never heard of a suit for libel being entered.

Sincerely yours,
H. L. Mencken

If my memory serves me right, the copy of the *Afro-American* in question was printed in a variety of colored inks and splashed on its front page was a detailed, minute-by-minute account of the Crucifixion, written in the present tense, as though the event were taking place in full view of the reporter. In my reply, after expressing astonishment at the aboriginality of its contents, I added: "The publication of such a sheet in These Christian Isles would, I firmly believe, precipitate the end of the world; or at any rate cause the Archbishop of Canterbury to choke to death."

Of course, these comments were made in a bygone age, and at a time when the Church of England still commanded respect and retained something of its authority as the spiritual overseer of the awe-struck masses. But in England's free-and-easy, multiracial, polytheistic society of today, it may be doubted that even the *Afro-American* style of reporting would raise more than a languid eyebrow among members of a largely disbelieving and religiously indifferent populace.

May 11, 1938

Dear Mr. Cleator:

Give your eye to the book of Genesis and you will find a more or less connected account of Yahweh's opinion of His handiwork. Apparently, He was in some doubt about it. I have long had it in mind to do the New Testament in American. Unfortunately, the job is a formidable one, and so I have never tackled it. It seems to me that a good translation might be useful in spreading our holy Christian religion in this great country. Many Americans have never heard of it.

My plans for the German trip are still very vague. What I fear is that I'll be put to work as soon as I get across the ocean. The chances are at least three to one that something or other will cut loose, and that I'll receive a prompt cable from the home office. In all probability, it will be impossible for me to get to England. When I start for home it will most likely be from Bremen.

My best thanks for the new instalment of the "Satanic Soliloquy." It is swell stuff indeed, and I have been reading it with great pleasure.

Sincerely yours,
H.L. Mencken

I had suggested to Mencken that for the benefit of the uncomprehending natives of his homeland, he might care to consider translating Holy Writ into the American vernacular, along the lines of his rendering of the immortal Declaration of Independence: "When things get so balled up. . . ." In defense of what many of his indignant countrymen regarded as a sacrilegious exercise, Mencken maintained that in its original form, the wording of this revered proclamation was no longer intelligible to ordinary citizens—and he quoted verbose extracts from it in support of this contention. His timely translation into the modern American idiom first appeared in the Baltimore *Evening Sun* on November 7, 1921, and was subsequently reprinted in the second edition of *The American Language*. More recently (1949) it was published as one of several "Buffooneries" in *A Mencken Chrestomathy,* a selection of his out-of-print writings.

June 14, 1938

Dear Mr. Cleator:

Your letter and the clippings came in after Mr. Mencken's departure for Europe. I shall hold them against his return, about August 1st.

                        Sincerely yours,
                        Rosalind C. Lohrfinck
                        Secretary to Mr. Mencken

July 29, 1938

Dear Mr. Cleator:

That censored epigram is swell indeed, and I shall circulate it privately in this great Republic, with credit to the author.

I had a very pleasant time in Germany, and covered a great deal of territory—in fact, I must have travelled at least three thousand miles within the borders of the country, nearly a third of them by automobile. Despite Hitler's reported animosity to our holy Christian religion, my daily devotions were not impeded. As usual, I went to Mass every morning. The police sometimes observed me narrowly, but on no occasion did they molest me. Unfortunately, the street services of the Salvation Army have been forbidden. This deprives a great many poor people of the consolation of faith. They seek consolation in the excellent malt liquor of the country, which has apparently not diminished in quality.

The weather here is infernal, and I begin to feel like work. I never work more contentedly than when the temperature is above 90.

                        Yours,
                        H. L. Mencken

"That censored epigram": This was an aphorism of mine which *The Freethinker* declined to publish, on the grounds, I can but suppose, that it threatened to contravene the high moral tone which it at all times strove to maintain. At the risk of giving offense to the unsophisticated, I print the banned item here, lest a sight of it be forever denied to a curious and frustrated posterity:

Meditation On Multiplication
The fundamental principle of Christian matrimonial mathematics is the postulate that two will not, must not, and shall not go into one.

August 24, 1938

Dear Mr. Cleator:

My best thanks for those marvelous souvenirs of the efflorescence of Christian Kulture in England. They go in a preferred place in my collection. I only hope that the learned justice did not sentence you to the gallows. In this country, as you probably know, justices of the peace are commonly low political hangers-on, and some of them are almost illiterate. It is not unusual for an indignant prisoner to rise up and smack one of them in the eye. In the wilds of West Virginia, in fact, it is a common practice to shoot them. Unfortunately, that practice has not gone as far as I should like.

"This England" has not yet come in. Needless to say, I'll read it with the greatest delight.

It is good news that you are still contemplating a trip to the Republic. I begin to be optimistic. In all probability, our Heavenly Father will not blow up this half of the world for another year or two. Nevertheless, I am convinced that in the long run a volcano will burst out under the city of Washington. As for New York, I have predicted for many years that it will succumb eventually to an earthquake. Unfortunately, earthquakes are not quite efficient; there are always survivors.

Sincerely yours,
H. L. Mencken

The souvenirs referred to included a document purportedly couched in genuine Olde English and a summons from the local *Polizei,* demanding my presence in court on a charge of exceeding the statutory speed limit, aided and abetted by a motor vehicle (automobile), while traveling along one of His Majesty's highways. The offense rated a monetary fine and a driving-license endorsement.

"This England": A booklet compiled and circulated by the *New Statesman and Nation*. It featured a collection of national idiocies, along the lines of Mencken's *Americana* annuals.

September 16, 1938

Dear Mr. Cleator:

"This England" entertained me all of a gloomy evening. I had seen it before, but I read it again, and with great joy. I begin to believe seriously that England has a genuine talent for imbecility. It is not, of course, comparable to the genius of this great Republic, but nevertheless it is respectable.

My best thanks for the clippings; and my congratulations on "Hymn to Progress." It is very amusing stuff. I can only regret, of course, that you introduced your lamentable infidelity into the discussion of a purely scientific matter.

The United States buzzes and bursts with politics. Even the international situation takes second place. Here in Maryland last Monday the unterrified plain people administered a tremendous rebuke to Roosevelt. He had come into the State in an effort to defeat an anti–New Deal Senator, but the Senator was returned by an enormous majority. What this signifies, precisely, I don't know. But it apparently shows that Roosevelt is no longer the holy saint that he was only a short while ago. There was a time, indeed, when he seemed about to join the Trinity, but that time is apparently passed.

Sincerely yours,
H. L. Mencken

" 'Hymn to Progress' ": This was the title of a satire on the attitude—past, present, and projected—of the foremost scientists of the land toward the possibilities of space travel, which I had published in a recent issue of the *Astronaut* (vol. 2, no. 1, February 1938).

"An anti–New Deal Senator": The name of this gentleman whose election to office gave Mencken such undisguised satisfaction was Millard Tydings.

October 10, 1938

Dear Mr. Cleator:

I came home from Germany convinced that there would be no war, so all the uproars of the past few weeks made very little impression on me. I found that the Germans were very far from ready for a bout with France. Their fortifications in the West were only a third finished, and their army still lacked company officers. In two or three years both sides may be ready for a really first-rate tussle. I shall give up the privilege of service at the front in favor of service as a rhetorician. I have already, in fact, drawn up several speeches describing the infamy of the enemy. Inasmuch as it is not yet quite certain who that enemy will be, I have left his name blank.

The efforts of Washington to horn into the late unpleasantness were really pathetic. Old Hull, the Secretary of State, is an honest Tennessee Methodist, but a complete jackass in foreign affairs. He is in the hands of a small group of wishful thinkers who estimate all things by their effect on Russia. If Russia is damaged, then they are evil. I have some doubt that this is a sound test.

There has been no talk of giving the plain people gas masks in this country. The air here is already so saturated with carbon monoxide from automobiles that no conceivable war gas could make it worse.

Sincerely yours,
H. L. Mencken

Germany's going to war was less than a year away, but despite his on-the-spot investigation, an unduly optimistic Mencken failed to find convincing evidence of it. In a letter dated September 27, to which the above note was a reply, I had reported that the latest Hitler-induced crisis was about to come to a head, with an outbreak of hostilities an immediate and distinct possibility. In the event, as is now a matter of history, the threatened clash was for the time being averted by the infamous Munich Agreement.

"Old Hull": Cordell Hull. He resigned as American secretary of state toward the end of 1944.

"There has been no talk": In the days preceding the Munich meeting, forty million gas masks were hopefully distributed among the inhabitants of the British Isles.

November 21, 1938

Dear Mr. Cleator:

You speak of sending me a packet of Christian literature, but so far it has not come in. It may be that the cheka at Washington has seized it. The United States is now completely Jewish, and we Christians must watch our step. I am making discreet inquiries at Washington, and hope to recover the packet.

Idealism got a dreadful beating at the recent election. Roosevelt lost more than eighty seats in the lower house of Congress, and nine or ten in the Senate. He still has a majority, but it has become precarious, and I am looking for a circus in the grand manner when Congress reassembles in January. At least half of the so-called New Dealers now sitting are frauds. They will desert Roosevelt at the first opportunity, just as the bogus prohibitionists deserted Hoover.

The session begins constitutionally the first week in January, but there is no limit on its duration. It may last into the Summer.

Inasmuch as July and August in Washington are infernal, a Summer session usually causes the death of six or eight members. Their funeral orgies are very instructive, and their passing is viewed with rejoicing by all philosophical men.

The New Deal is moving rapidly toward a kind of sleezy [*sic*] Fascism. Bit by bit the constitutional liberties of the people are being narrowed. If Roosevelt gets into serious difficulties during the last two years of his term, he will probably grow bolder. I am convinced that some form of totalitarianism is inevitable in this great Republic. Democracy has blown up. No one actually believes in it any more. The only whooping in favor of it that one hears comes from Communists and other such frauds.

Sincerely yours,
H. L. Mencken

No record as to the precise nature of the contents of the packet of Christian literature is to be found in my files, apart from the fact that it included a list of publications available from a Liverpool bookseller by the name of Martin A. McGoff.

"Hoover": Herbert Clark Hoover, the luckless aspirant who reached the White House on March 4, 1929, in time to witness the stock market crash which occurred in the following October, and thereafter to preside ineffectually over America's destiny during the years of the Great Depression which followed.

December 27, 1938

Dear Mr. Cleator:

Thanks very much for the clippings. Your stuff is excellent, and I have read it with great pleasure. I only hope you can induce Roosevelt to make the first trial trip in your first rocket. He'll accept if you approach him judiciously.

I am distressed indeed to hear that there is so much sickness in your house. My brother and sister and I had Christmas dinner together. My sister was in a wheelchair, following a fall, and I had just got out of bed. Fortunately, we are now all restored, and look forward with confidence to renewed and even worse mishaps in 1939.

The New Year, in fact, starts off in a magnificently Christian manner. Here in the Republic Roosevelt and his friends are whooping up war. They don't seem to know who, precisely, they are to fight, but they are all for fighting. If Hitler refuses to give them an excuse, they'll probably tackle the Japs in the rear. Altogether, I am looking for an extremely interesting twelve-month. It will see a great deal of bloodshed and many a new angel in Heaven.

Sincerely yours,
H. L. Mencken

"Your stuff": I had sent Mencken a copy of "Interplanetary Parade," the title of a somewhat critical feature article I was regularly contributing to the quarterly journal *Tomorrow*.
"My brother and sister": August and Gertrude Mencken.
"If Hitler refuses": Once again, Mencken's prophetic utterances on the subject of war proved to be wide of the mark. In the light of the subsequent Pearl Harbor episode, his reference to the possibility of the U.S. tackling the Japanese in the rear must be regarded as particularly unfortunate.

January 21, 1939

Dear Mr. Cleator:

I am distressed indeed to hear of your mother's illness, and only hope that she is really comfortable. My own mother, when her days came toward an end in 1925, faced the possibility of almost unbearable suffering, but her characteristic good luck held out, and she died suddenly of what appeared to be a trivial intercurrent infection. She is gone now thirteen years, but living once more in her old house I am conscious of her presence all the time.

I doubt that it will be possible to induce the Hon. Mr. Roosevelt to make that trip to Mars. To be sure, he will undertake soon or late the great task of policing and reforming the interstellar spaces, but first he must tackle Europe. His job in the United States is now almost done. The New Deal has brought peace and prosperity to every American. There are no jobless, taxes are low, and Congress is manned by patriots only. The hon. gentleman and his friends hope to clean up Europe within a year or two. Then they'll be ready for the stars.

If you are seeking other recruits for the first trip, I'll be glad to ship you ten head of bishops. They are all somewhat bulky, but maybe you'll be able to squeeze them in. If you want any lesser ecclesiastics, let me know. I have thousands of them in my pens.

Yours,
H. L. Mencken

"I doubt that": I had taken up Mencken's earlier suggestion that Roosevelt be prevailed upon to make a trip in our first space rocket, by undertaking to book a presidential passage. Now, it seemed, doubts had arisen that F.D.R. could be induced to embark on the journey. I accordingly offered to resolve the problem: "If the Hon. Mr. Roosevelt won't come to Mars, I'll arrange to bring Mars to him. In the meantime, I accept your offer of ten head of bishops. As ballast, they'll come in mighty useful. I'll see that they don't land anywhere near Baltimore when they are heaved overboard, though if you wish it, I'll reserve the Archbishop of Canterbury for the backyard of 1524."

March 10, 1939

Dear Mr. Cleator:

Those epigrams are swell, and I surely hope you proceed with the book. Most of those that I printed in "A Little Book in C Major" were later printed in the jazz Webster in "A Book of Burlesques." Those that were omitted were mainly very bad.

I have lately spent a week at the Johns Hopkins, having some minor repairs done. The chiropractors did a good job, and I begin to feel normal again. When I got to the hospital I found to my astonishment that four or five old friends were also laid up there. By the favor of the holy saints all of them were more ill than I was, so I enjoyed myself immensely. Thanks to prayer, they are all recovering.

I am trying to organize a party of Chicago gunmen to accompany Roosevelt on his return visit to London. I hear that he will make it before the end of the year. His guards are very fearful of English anarchists.

Yours,
H. L. Mencken

I had announced the making of a start of a lexicon to be entitled *A Dictionary for the Damned,* and listed a number of entries. Some random examples:

AUTHENTIC: not so patently faked as to be immediately obvious.
CANNIBALISM: a recognition of the fact that alive, man may be good for nothing, but that dead, he is at least good to eat.
CORPSE: a man looking his best—and knowing the worst.
HOLY OIL: oil.

"The Johns Hopkins": A hospital which commemorates the name of its founder and benefactor, one of several nineteenth-century philanthropists (Enoch Pratt, of library fame, was another) who during their lifetime made munificent gifts to the city of Baltimore in the shape of medical and educational facilities.

April 3, 1939

Dear Mr. Cleator:

I am still betting in the barrooms that there will be no war. Adolf can get nearly all he really wants without it, and once he is set the Czechs in his back-yard will give him plenty to think of. War scares make swell newspaper stuff. They are seldom to be taken seriously. When war really comes it usually comes stealthily.

It now begins to appear certain that Roosevelt will come to grief next year. His collapse really surprised me, for I believed until recently that it would be possible for him to get a third term. That now seems to be out of the window. The best he can do is to force the nomination of some candidate not altogether obnoxious to him. According to the experts, even that begins to appear difficult, if not downright impossible. In some way or other he must have sinned. Superficially, he looks virtuous, but our Heavenly Father has detected him in some kind of wickedness. If I find out any more about this I'll let you know.

Sincerely yours,
H. L. Mencken

Here yet again, and on no less than two counts, Mencken was allowing wishful thinking to befog his judgment, thereby maintaining his reputation of being what Bode (CB-2) has described as "a superbly bad political prophet." Concerning the prospects of peace, as they appeared to me at a time when the start of World War II was a mere six months away, I shared Mencken's hopes, if not his expectations: "I incline to agree with your remarks about Adolf. In fact, I do not doubt that he wants to avoid war. The danger is that he may go too far. I have just been entertaining a friend from Berlin (and hence locally am under a cloud of suspicion). His attitude is best described as fatalistic."

"Adolf": Adolf Hitler, alias Schicklgruber.

"It now begins": As for the outcome of the forthcoming presidential election in the U.S., not only was "Le Roi" Roosevelt duly chosen for a third term in November 1940, but four years later he once again managed to retain his throne. Mencken subsequently made a handsome acknowledgment of his limitations as a political seer when he inscribed a replacement copy of his *Making a President,* which he sent to me in 1946. His admission reads: "Every prophecy here turned out to be false—but so did all those made in Holy Writ."

April 21, 1939

Dear Mr. Cleator:

My best thanks for those epigrams. They are really superb, I only hope that you print the volume. You will also be rewarded post mortem for the cuttings.

I incline to advise you to come to this great Republic in September rather than in June. The weather here toward the end of June is apt to be infernal. I begin to fear, indeed, that the King and Queen will suffer dreadfully. His Majesty, I gather, commonly wears very stuffy uniforms, and I assume that the Queen, as a Scotch woman, runs to rather substantial clothing. If they strike one of the hot spells that often come in June, they'll suffer like missionaries in a cannibal's soup pot. By September the weather commonly moderates and the nights, at all events, tend to be cool. By the first of October we reach our most pleasant season. For three months thereafter the weather is balmy, with increasingly colder nights, and eating and drinking become possible again.

I'll be here both in June and in September, so if you come either time we'll certainly meet. I am looking forward to it with great pleasure.

Sincerely yours,
H. L. Mencken

Those epigrams: I had submitted a few more examples, the following among them:

NECK: convincing evidence that man was born to be hanged.
OPINION: something shared—or denounced.
PREDESTINATION: the theory that life is an inescapable gamble with God, and that the Divine dice are heavily overloaded.
PROOF: a demonstration of doubtful value and passing validity. No proof yet advanced has proved entirely foolproof.

"I incline to advise": Plans I had long entertained to visit the U.S. were on the point of realization. I had many friends there, most of them interested in rocket research, with whom I had been corresponding for years and now at last hoped to meet. Another primary concern was to catch up with Mencken—hence my query as to whether he would be available in June or September. In view of the disquiet he expressed over the well-being of Their Majesties on the occasion of their impending June survey of their lost colonial Empire, I arranged to delay my departure.

"Scotch woman": I imagine Her Majesty would have been more pleased had she been referred to as a Scotswoman.

May 12, 1939

Dear Mr. Cleator:

I am delighted to hear that you have decided to steer clear of July in this great Republic. It is really infernal, and I begin to believe seriously that His Majesty may find it unbearable. If he could make his tour in a bathing suit it would be comfortable enough, but inasmuch as he will have to wear heavy padded uniforms, I really fear for him. By September 1st the nights begin to grow cooler, and life becomes tolerable again. I'll certainly be in New York at about that time, and we can have what is called in this great country an executive session.

I am at work on a new book, and making heavy weather of it. It amuses me, but putting it together is somewhat difficult. I am hoping to finish it by October 1st.

Sincerely yours,
H. L. Mencken

I had responded to the meteorological report given in Mencken's note of April 21 as follows: "Thanks for the warning about the June weather contained in your second letter. I've decided to avoid it. Boats leave here (Liverpool) for New York on August 26th and September 1st. Failing an Act of God, I'll be on one of them."

Such were my plans. The Almighty, however, entertained other ideas.

"A new book": *Happy Days,* the first volume of an autobiographical trilogy.

May 31, 1939

Dear Mr. Cleator:

The new epigrams are quite as good as the others. I hope you go on with them, and make a book. God knows the world needs some fresh and incisive humor.

So far, I have received no invitation to meet Their Majesties, but I am expecting it momentarily. No doubt it has been overlooked by their secretaries. If they pass through Baltimore, which seems probable, I shall present myself at the railroad station and utter a respectable banzai as their train whirls through. I am eager to see how they bear the temperature of a Washington June. It is cold in Canada, and they have been seeing snow and ice almost every day. When they get to Washington they will find the mercury bouncing round 90, with high humidity. I only hope that His Majesty brought along some relatively thin underwear. Most of the great statesmen in Washington wear none at all from June to September. The hair on their chests is distinctly visible through their shirt-fronts.

Yours,
H. L. Mencken

The flow of epigrams had continued:

ARSENIC: a useful substance, fatal to man.
RELIC: give a dog of a Christian a bone, and he'll announce the discovery of a sacred relic.
DESIRABLE: an inevitable attribute of one's neighbour's wife.
LAUGH: among mere males, the only safe answer to a maiden's prayer.
PERSECUTION: the doing unto others as they would do unto you—if they had the chance.
TROUSERS: a symbol of male supremacy, chiefly worn by bachelors and wives; a family heirloom handed over from husband to wife.

"I have received no invitation": When the poet Edgar Lee Masters wrote to him about the royal visit, bewailing the fact that Mencken was not among the honored guests chosen to meet Their Majesties at the state dinner held in Washington, he replied (CB-1) with a jocular account of how he, his brother August, and Heinrich Buchholz, an intimate of the Saturday Night Club, had entertained the king privily in a nearby tavern. The monarch, it was confided ("This is for your private eye. I wouldn't have it known for the world"), after managing to give his attendants the slip, had come to Baltimore for an evening's quiet relaxation, in the course of which, urged on by his unofficial hosts, the royal visitor reportedly downed eleven or twelve steins of the local brew.

June 20, 1939

Dear Mr. Cleator:

My worst forebodings were realized. On the day Their Majesties reached Washington the temperature ran up to 94, and the relative humidity approached 100. I hear confidentially that the King suffered damnably. He had come to Washington wearing the usual woollen underwear of an English gentleman. Seeing him on the point of collapse, the Roosevelt boys got him a supply of gauze drawers and underwear, but it was too late. When he visited Mount Vernon, where Washington was hanged and buried, he was apparently on the point of collapse. Fortunately, the distilled liquors of this great Republic are better than the climate, and so he managed to get through what must have been the most horrible day of his whole career.

Her Majesty apparently bore the heat better. She was, of course, dressed in thinner clothes. The King's heavily padded uniforms were as much responsible for his discomfort as his collision-mat underwear. I send you all these facts confidentially. I know that as a British patriot you will keep them secret. The concept of a royal personage sweating is necessarily abhorrent to all decent people.

That piece of news from the *Bootle Times* is grand indeed. I shall pass it on to the old gentlemen at Harvard, and no doubt they will know how to adapt it to their purposes.

My best thanks for the cutting from *Punch*.

Sincerely yours,
H. L. Mencken

"That piece of news": The extract from the Bootle *Times* concerned an item of local, even national, historic interest:

EDWARD I BRONZE VESSEL ON BOOTLE GOLF COURSE
VISITORS FIND

A bronze vessel bearing a Latin inscription thought to date from the time of Edward I, was found on Bootle Golf Course by two Morecambe men who spent the Easter holiday in Litherland. The two men, whose names are Major W. C. Benn and Mr. A. Kermode are students of Cambridge who are interested in archaeology. . . . Careful cleaning has made the inscription on the bronze vessel almost legible. It appears to read:

ITI SAPIS SPOTANDA TINO NE

This is low Latin and not readily translatable. There are two possibilities. The first, "Except being emptied in wisdom, I hold not" is rather trite. More likely is, "But to the wise I hold not emptiness"—suggesting the use of the vessel for preserving some sacred commodity. Just such a vessel was catalogued among the crown jewels of Edward I. One may conclude from this that such vessels were highly prized, and this has no doubt travelled far before reaching Bootle, where its discovery and exhibition will redound to the credit of the Borough.

July 12, 1939

Dear Mr. Cleator:

Unless war actually comes and I am called to the colors, I'll certainly be in these waters in October. Let us keep in communication on the subject. You will be well advised if you postpone your trip until September is over. October in the Eastern United

States is a lovely season, but September is apt to be humid and hot.

His Majesty, I am informed, found the heat of Washington actually unendurable. On one of the nights of his stay he slipped away from the official ceremonies long enough to come to Baltimore and spend a comfortable hour in an air-cooled beer house. It happened to be my own usual refuge, but I missed him by a few minutes. This is for your private eye.

Have you done anything about printing a book of your epigrams? Certainly I believe they should be done. How many have you in hand?

Sincerely yours,
H. L. Mencken

"You will be well advised": In view of this injunction and its accompanying climatic report, I booked passage on a liner due to arrive in New York early in October. It was to prove a fatal decision, for I thereby missed the boat.

"On one of these nights": Here, it will be observed, Mencken varies somewhat the apocryphal account of King George VI's surreptitious visit to a Baltimore tavern, earlier referred to in my comment on his letter of May 31.

"How many have you in hand?": There was the rub. On reaching a total of some 10,000 words, I found I was running out of epigrammatic material, and that there appeared to be small prospect of my adding greatly to it.

August 30, 1939

Dear Mr. Cleator:

As I write the newspapers are full of inflammatory stuff and American Customs agents are searching all German ships for bombs, cannons and zeppelins. Nevertheless, I remain confident that there will be no slaughter and so I assume that you'll reach New York on schedule. It will certainly be a pleasure to see you. I am sure to be in New York soon after October 9th, so we can meet there without dragging you down into these wilds. However, if you go to Washington you must certainly stop off in Baltimore, which is on the way. It is the Pompeii of America. Most of the houses have already fallen in and those that remain are beginning to shake.

The newspapers here are filled with the most dreadful blather ever heard of on earth. The question of Danzig and the Corridor has been resolved into a proposition in Christian morals and it is labored as a backwoods Baptist labors such a text as "Thou shalt not commit adultery." The English papers, I assume, are also giving an obscene performance, but certainly it can't be as bad as the one on view here.

Yours,
H. L. Mencken

The above was Mencken's reply to a note I sent on August 22, in acknowledgment of an earlier letter from him, a copy of which is not to be found among the NYPL records. In it he complained that some unspecified malaise was delaying the completion of *Happy Days*. As I learned later, what he had suffered was the first of a series of slight strokes.

"Nevertheless, I remain confident": Even at this late hour, Mencken remained convinced that there would be no war. After the Munich fiasco, my own expectations were less sanguine, but I continued to act on the assumption that he might, after all, be right. In my letter of August 22, I was able to announce that I had booked passage aboard the S. S. *Synthia,* departing from Liverpool on September 29 and due to reach New York on October 9.

"The question of Danzig": By the Treaty of Versailles after World War I, the newly proclaimed Polish Republic received a corridor of land along the course of the Vistula, thus giving her access to Danzig and the Baltic Sea. This territorial strip separated East Prussia from the rest of Germany, and it was its forcible occupation by Hitler, in the face of dire warnings of the consequences of such an action made by Britain and France, which precipitated World War II.

On September 5, with Britain at war, I sent another note to Baltimore, to the effect that failing the calling of an immediate and highly improbable truce, my trip to the U.S. would have to be postponed. At the same time, I enclosed a few more extracts from the *Dictionary:*

BELIEF: an opinion passionately entertained, to the entertainment of others.
BRIDEGROOM: a ham, about to be strung.
COMMUNISM: the theory that if I have a 10,000 acre estate and £5,000,000, it's yours for the asking; and that if you have exophtalmic goitre and hypertrophic stenosis of the pylorus, I'm welcome to it.
CONVERT: a highly commendable action in the course of which, having shown a man the error of his ways, you succeed in blinding him to the errors of your own.
FALLACY: a fly, found in ecclesiastical ointment.
PARENTS: any two people who, having acted the goat, proceed to look sheepish.
REQUIEM: ashes to ashes, dust to dust, and a worm to the worms.

October 20, 1939

Dear Mr. Cleator:

I am delighted to hear that you remain unbombed and that your withers are still unwrung. Here in the Republic we have seen no sign as yet of enemy airplanes, but I assume that they'll be on us soon enough. Roosevelt seems to be determined to get into the war at the first chance. I am against it, but I should add frankly that I am seldom consulted in such matters.

I surely hope that you don't abandon your projected social history of the war. It will make magnificent reading in the years to come. I am only sorry that I abandoned my project for a similar history. Twenty-five years ago I had, in fact, an enormous accummulation of materials, but its very size appalled me and so I quietly got rid of it.

So far Wagner's music has not been prohibited here, but I assume that it will be done anon. In the last war even German Christmas songs were put under the ban. An effort was made to save Beethoven by starting the story that he was actually a Belgian, but it didn't work. He went down the chute with Wagner and Johann Strauss. I had a note the other day from a man named Regan, asking if I had heard from you. I assume that you'll want to communicate with him.

Sincerely yours,
H. L. Mencken

The above was a reply to a communication of mine dated October 4, wherein I acknowledged a letter Mencken had dispatched on September 20, of which there is now no trace. In it, apart from commenting on the possible duration of the war, he announced that he had finished the writing of *Happy Days*.

"Your projected social history": Far from being abandoned, this work, entitled *Sidelights on the Slaughter,* was in due course completed, though it still awaits an entrepreneur temerarious enough to place on record a compilation which (to quote from an Editorial Note),

> . . . begun in September, *anno Domini* 1939, was continued without serious interruption until the outbreak of peace nearly six years later. The national imbecilities thus rescued for the benefit of posterity from the obscurity of newspaper and other files, and here collectively embalmed in print, have one thing in common: all are offshoots of that supreme and ultimate imbecility of the human species, the criminal lunacy of war itself.
>
> The material is arranged subjectively under appropriate headings, the items in each section appearing in chronological order. Thus, the godless and barbarian hordes of the U.S.S.R., who overwhelmed the luckless Finns,

in due course emerge as our brave and gallant comrades in arms against the selfsame Finns—all of which, we may be sure, is as it should be in this unjust and divinely disordered world.

At the onset, I inclined to the view that the local weekly papers would prove to be the most fruitful source of exuberant nonsense, as the contents of an outsize order I gave to a newsagent will testify. But in this, I was sadly astray, for it soon became evident that it would require more than a mere world war to enliven the incredible dullness of their parochial contents. In the event, as the acknowledgements go to show, it was the national Press which provided most of the fare—and some of the choicest.

Needless to say, the perennial nonsense of the astrologers is fully represented. Present, too, is a superabundance of the eternal and idiotic edicts of officialdom—the red tape, the barefaced lies, the impudent denials, the belated admissions. Here, in brief, expressed in a hundred and one incredible ways, are to be found the multitudinous absurdities, the extravagant hopes, and the imaginary fears that ride along with a nation at war.

Is there a publisher in the house?

"So far Wagner's music": I had reported that Julius Harrison, conductor of the Hastings Municipal Orchestra, had decided to ban Wagner compositions from his programs because of their Hitlerian asociations. I added: "I wonder if the Minister of Transport is prepared to consider forbidding the use of the engine invented by Dr. Rudolf Diesel?"

"Regan": This was Dick O'Regan, a young journalist of my acquaintance whose prewar exploits in search of news often gave me cause to remember. On one occasion he roused me by telephone at three o'clock in the morning to say that he was stranded in some godforsaken spot or other, and would I kindly come to his rescue? Should he recollect the incident, I would have him know that although I acceded to his request, it was to the accompaniment of much muttering of a near profane and even blasphemous nature.

November 1, 1939

Dear Mr. Cleator:

It is excellent news that you are not neglecting your record. I have not begun one here, but I'll certainly do so if, when and as the United States enters the war. When that will be I don't know. Roosevelt is declaring solemnly every two or three days that he is determined to keep the peace, but I put very little confidence in his statements. Almost everything he promised in his first campaign for the Presidency has been repudiated since.

The American newspapers are flooded with news from both sides. It is always at variance and sometimes even one side sends out two or three antagonistic stories. This always happens in time of war. People blame the Information Office but the truth is that the brethren at the Information Office are often as ignorant of the truth as the rest of us. In war time generals do not spend much time sending bulletins home. They wait until the show is over.

Sincerely yours,
H. L. Mencken

"It is excellent news": On September 13, I had announced that the compilation of my unofficial history of the fray had been begun, along the lines of Mencken's *Americana* series. I append a few examples, culled from the national press and other sources:

1

Question without answer in the estimable *News Review:*
Why do soldiers spend hours peeling potatoes when the Food Ministry advises they be cooked in their jackets as an economy measure?

2

Subversive plot to foil the official "Save Waste Paper" campaign, outlined in a Sussex Parish Magazine:
The verger requests that his friends who must eat sweets in church will kindly eat the paper as well.

3

Brief and revealing extract from the Government's War Damage Bill:
For the purpose of the preceding paragraph of this part of this schedule the proportion appropriate as at any date to a tenancy which at that date had still to run any period specified in the first column of the table set out in part two of this schedule is the proportion specified in relation to that period in that one of the succeeding columns of the table which corresponds with the proportion which the rent payable under the tenancy bears to value of the land comprised therein.

4

Car priority label to end all car priority labels, *via* the distinguished *Manchester Guardian:*
The competition for priority signs on the windscreens of motor-cars has now reached its final point. A car emerged from a garage in Pimlico to-day with this sign:

ON SECRET SERVICE

November 24, 1939

Dear Mr. Cleator:

I begin to suspect that the war may last for years—indeed, it may turn out in the end that war is a permanent state of man. I have long suspected as much and many years ago argued that the

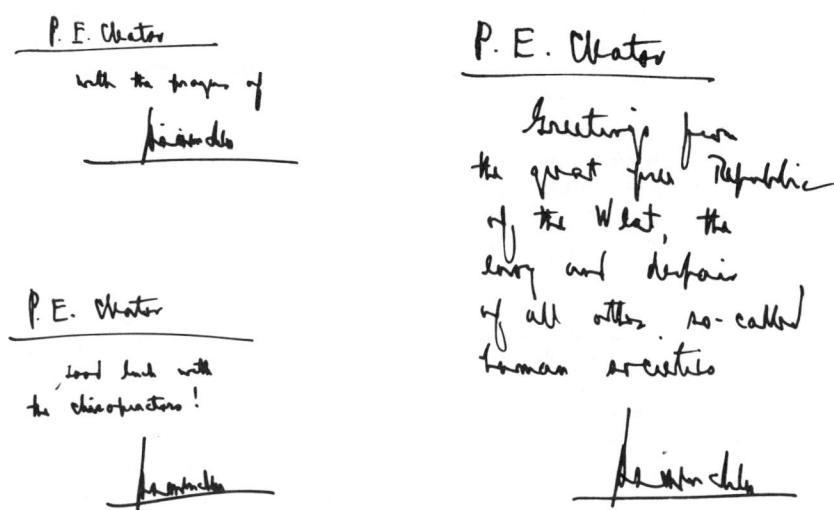

PLATE 5. The Mencken epigraphs—1. The *Days* books. A copy of *Happy Days*, dispatched at the end of 1939, though it escaped the U-boats, was later lost in the bombing of 1941. A replacement (fourth printing), together with copies of other contributions to the series, was received in June 1946. The three volumes bear the inscriptions shown above—*Happy Days*, top left; *Newspaper Days*, right; and *Heathen Days*, bottom left.

United States should declare war on Mexico and keep it up forever. As you know, I have always argued that the overwhelming majority of human beings hate peace. They enjoy themselves much more while war is going on and the fact that they deny it is irrelevant.

My new book will be out at Christmas or thereabout. Needless to say, I'll be delighted to send you a copy. It is trivial stuff and deals wholly with my first eleven years. Inasmuch as they were passed in comfort and even in a kind of opulence, I assume that the book will be denounced violently by all proletarian critics. Their authority, by God's inscrutable will, is much less than it was a little while ago. The Hitler-Stalin alliance really wrecked them.

I have been receiving pleasant notes from your friend Regan. He seems to be working on a newspaper in Philadelphia. So far I have not encountered him, but maybe I'll do so shortly.

Yours,
H. L. Mencken

The above would seem to be part of a secondary stream of correspondence from which two of Mencken's letters appear to be missing. On October 14, I sent an answer to the first of these lost items, expressing satisfaction at the news that he was about to tackle the writing of another book. And on November 10, I mailed a dispatch which was presumably sent in response to a second communication whose contents, however, find no mention in my reply.

"I begin to suspect": This philosophizing on the inevitability of human conflict was echoed years later in some reflections of my own (PEC-2):

> As became increasingly evident from the time of the Sumerians onwards, civilisation is inescapably associated with organised warfare. It is to be regarded, that is to say, as a way of life whose exponents find themselves more or less permanently engaged in a neverending series of armed conflicts, interrupted only by periods of relatively peaceful preparation for the next outbreak of homicidal strife. In the light of other and more worthy human activities, such a situation is as absurd as it is inexcuseable, and it arises, it may be supposed, from an innate bellicosity coupled with an excess of leisure and freedom from want which inevitably lead to boredom, and from boredom to altercation, and from altercation to bloodshed.

"My new book": *Happy Days* duly appeared early in 1940. My records show that I acknowledged receipt of the promised copy on January 6.

"The Hitler-Stalin alliance": In August, Germany's impending attack on Poland was preceded by the surprise announcement of a nonaggression pact with the hated Communists, whereby Russia was neutralized and a war on two fronts avoided—at any rate for the time being.

"I have been receiving": On my enquiring whether the encounter here envisaged took place, O'Regan replied (private communication, January 10, 1979): "I was a very negligent correspondent indeed as far as Mencken was concerned. I did not seek an opportunity to continue the 1939 correspondence, nor did I make an opportunity to visit the great man. I was too involved in trying to make my way on the Philadelphia *Bulletin*. I should have done so because I admired and respected Mencken. But I was too stupid—just a young reporter trying to make good."

2
My Kingdom for a Hearse
(1940–1945)

January 8, 1940

Dear Mr. Cleator:

I hope the lady you are marrying has been properly warned by her pastor against the risk of joining her fortunes with those of an infidel. Soon or late the Holy Ghost will floor you and she'll have to take part of the damage. I congratulate you most heartily but my felicitations to her must be ameliorated as aforesaid.

Certainly you must not stop your book because you have accumulated one volume. There is no reason whatsoever why you shouldn't bring out twenty. The material is rolling off the press at an enormous rate and it is your patriotic duty to gather it in and cherish it.

I haven't met Regan yet but I am hoping to get to Philadelphia very soon. I seize the opportunity to hope once more that you are lucky in 1940. Certainly you are starting out the year magnificently.

Yours,
H. L. Mencken

Records recovered from the NYPL show that the above was preceded by yet another lost Mencken letter. The missing item was posted on December 11, and told of the dispatch of a copy of *Happy Days*. In a reply sent on January 6, I was able to announce the book's safe arrival.

"I hope the lady": In a note dated December 9, I had given news of my impending marriage.

"Certainly you must not stop": With the war but four months old, I had already accumulated enough material about the fray to fill a book.

January 31, 1940

Dear Mr. Cleator:

Once you enter upon possession of that house you will begin to suffer from a series of dreadful headaches. There is, in fact, no more appalling career on this earth than that of the householder. I predict formally that the roof will begin to leak an hour after you move in, and that the plumbing will go on strike the next day. You will understand that I am naturally an optimist, but nevertheless the truth is the truth. I am living here in a small house nearly sixty years old. It has become actually senile, as a man becomes senile. The new ones are even worse. Their trouble is an offensive and preposterous sauciness.

My chaplain was instructed to pray that your marriage will be as happy as mine was. I assumed that he was at the business but, unfortunately, I discovered yesterday that he has succumbed to an attack of delirium tremens and is quite out of service. I am informed that the case is a mild one and that he should be quite well again within a month. It might be a good idea to put your own chaplain to work praying for him. Such international amities are always lovely to see.

The general impression here seems to be that the war on the Western front is a sort of political delusion. I only hope that it never turns to reality.

                                                   Yours,
                                                   H. L. Mencken

In my aforementioned letter of January 6, acknowledging the safe arrival of the copy of *Happy Days,* I also gave the news that I was about to desert the family home for matrimonial quarters not far away. It was a move that was destined to save my life.

                                                  March 25, 1940

Dear Mr. Cleator:

I accept your invitation not only with pleasure but with alacrity. The next time I am in England, which I hope will be soon, I'll certainly wait on you at Wallasey. By that time, I hope, you will have repaired the roof and got the plumbing to working. If not, I'll be glad to assist you, for I have had lifelong experience in house repairs. If any windows are broken let them wait until I arrive.

The dispatches from England in the American papers indicate that the war is nearly over. They show that Hitler is in a state of complete despair and eager only to escape with his hide. Now that all the German ships have been sunk and the people of Berlin are reduced to starvation, he must certainly yield before long. I ascribe this result mainly to the technical efficiency of the British General Staff but also in part to the intervention of the holy saints. I understand that Roosevelt is preparing to enter the war as soon as it looks completely safe.

Sincerely Yours,
H. L. Mencken

On March 9, while answering Mencken's letter of January 31, I also acknowledged receiving a second communication from him dated February 27, now missing.

"I accept your invitation": In my letter of March 9, I had expressed the hope that when he next visited England, Mencken would be able to spend some time with us as our guest.

April 24, 1940

Dear Mr. Cleator:

Needless to say, I'll be delighted to write a brief note for your book—that is, if you think it won't ruin it. I am seriously in doubt on that point. I may be clapped into an American Dachau the moment Roosevelt enters the war. I should see the manuscript before proceeding. If you haven't a carbon please do not trust the original to the mails in these days. My letters from Europe are constantly interfered with.

The dispatches printed in the American papers this morning indicate that Hitler is about to be thrown out of Normandy in the grand manner. Having lost his entire navy he is unable to send reinforcements to his army and so a débâcle is looked for almost immediately.

The news that Mrs. Cleator is a good cook is pleasant news indeed. Tell her that I am the most appreciative eater in Christendom. If, when and as I finally see you in Wallasey I'll probably settle down for the Winter. My very best thanks for the clippings. I am at work on a sort of supplement to my American Language and they are immensely useful. I have lately done a little piece for the Reader's Digest on English war slang. There is not much of it, but that little is very amusing.

Sincerely yours,
H. L Mencken

I had reported that as I had gone as far as I could with *A Dictionary for the Damned,* I proposed to seek a publisher for it. At the same time, I ventured to suggest that Mencken might care to consider penning an introduction.

"I have lately done": The little piece, entitled "War Slang, 1940," appeared in the May, 1940, issue of the *Reader's Digest*.

July 3, 1940

Dear Mr. Cleator:

In view of the general situation my publisher, Knopf, passed up your book of epigrams. What arrangements have you made for its publication in England? If I knew what they were I'd be able to proceed a little better. Let me know as soon as it is convenient, and I'll tackle some other publisher. I am still of the opinion that it would injure the book for me to do a preface to it, but that objection will not prevail after the present war is over.

We get a great deal of news here but nearly all of it is palpably false. The general impression seems to be that peace is not far ahead. I surely hope the rumor-mongers are right this time. I confess frankly that I enjoy wars as spectacles, but I believe that a year is long enough for any one of them to run.

I have just [got] back to Baltimore from Philadelphia, where the Republicans nominated a Wall Street gentleman for the Presidency. Rather curiously, it seems to be possible, though certainly not probable, that he may be able to beat Roosevelt. There is no telling what the people of a democracy will do. Their opinions change from day to day and in a really amazing manner. I know Willkie, the nominee, and have a pretty good opinion of him, though I am convinced that he is certainly not a messiah. Roosevelt I also know, and dislike. He has always seemed to me to be a shabby and hollow fellow.

I trust that no bombs have fallen in your vicinity and that the show will be over by the time these lines reach you.

Yours,
H. L. Mencken

The NYPL record of my correspondence shows that I replied to two letters sent by Mencken during June, copies of both of which are missing. The first, dated June 6, gave the news that the typescript of the *Dictionary,* after passing the censor and escaping the U-boats, had reached Baltimore. The second note, dispatched a week later (on June 13) announced that the MS had been submitted to Alfred Knopf for consideration.

"What arrangements have you made?": The answer was none, as I disclosed in a reply I sent on August 2: "By a strange coincidence, the supernatural significance of which has not escaped me, your letter of July 3rd announcing Messrs. Knopf's decision arrived by the same post as a printed note of regrets from Messrs. Cape. In the face of this double rejection, doubtless divinely contrived, I am all but tempted to call it a day."

"Willkie": Wendell L. Willkie. Unfortunately for Mencken's hopes, on the following November 5, the Republican nominee was defeated by Roosevelt, who retained the presidency for a third term.

July 10, 1940

Dear Mr. Cleator:

My very best thanks for the clippings. Some of the new words are really dreadful, and I am delighted to have them for my files. As I wrote to you last week, my own publisher, Knopf, has passed up your book but I am still hopeful that I'll be able to interest some other American publisher. Unhappily, they are all in a state of jitters and it is hard to interest them in an English book that is not being published in England. Have you any negotiations under way with an English publisher? If so, let me know precisely what they are and I can act more effectively.

The war fever seems to be diminishing here, but there is no telling when it will revive. I am going to Chicago tomorrow for the Democratic National Convention. Though it is less than a week ahead, not a soul knows at the moment whether or not Roosevelt will stand for a third term. If he does I incline to believe that he'll be re-elected and that he will take the United States into the war. If, on the contrary, he doesn't, any other candidate of his party is bound to be beaten by Willkie, the Republican. Willkie himself seems to be irresolute about the war. He is apparently in favor of giving England such help as possible, but his party platform rather inclines the other way. If there is peace before election day, which comes during the first week in November, Roosevelt and company will be left with their polemics down. Thus the result of the national election in this great Republic depends to a large extent on the issue of a struggle going on three thousand miles away.

I trust that you are in good health and full of sin, and that no bombs have come near you. Over here the Irish Republic brethren have taken to planting land mines and there is a considerable excitement. So far they have not undertaken operations in Baltimore, but I assume that they'll be along in a little while.

Yours,
H. L. Mencken

"I trust that": As it happened, there was reason enough for the concern Mencken expressed in this and his previous letter of July 3 about the bombing of Merseyside. In making joint reply to these two letters in the note I dispatched on August 2, I wrote that although we were experiencing air raids almost every night, thus far the damage in our immediate vicinity appeared to be slight. For imparting this information, my letter was returned by the censor with a reprimand, and with instructions to delete the offending passage.

August 3, 1940

Dear Mr. Cleator:

I am still convinced that it would be injudicious in the present state of affairs to bring out your book with an introduction by me. But I see no objection to the Nihil Obstat that you suggest. Very few readers would recognize me. Many, indeed, would probably assume that I was a genuine bishop. If I had my rights in this world I'd certainly be one. I have the figure for it and a pure heart. Unhappily, I find myself unable to subscribe to some of the ideas that bishops must preach.

The news here is that the proposed invasion of England has pegged out and that the end of the war begins to heave into sight. I surely hope that this is true. I am looking forward with great pleasure to crossing the ocean as soon as the show is over.

Yours,
H. L. Mencken

"But I see no objection": Subject to Mencken's approval, I had proposed prefacing the *Dictionary* with the *nihil obstat* that graces the present volume.

"The news here": Although the threat of a seaborne invasion of England appeared to have receded, there was little sign of an end to hostilities, as I reported when making reply on September 4: "Your note of August 3rd arrived about 10 days ago, *i.e.,* just before Adolf began his incessant day and night bombing of These Isles. Since its arrival, I have had an average of 4 hours sleep out of every 24. Hence I make no apology for the lateness of this reply. At this very moment I am almost asleep on my feet. And at this very moment a lone Nazi raider is streaking across the sky with three Spitfires on his tail."

On the following day I appended a footnote to the above: "We had 6½ hours of it last night—from 10 p.m. to 4.30 a.m. From the infernal din going on, one gathers that the entire district around is being laid to waste. But amazingly enough, the dawn reveals familiar surroundings untouched. Fearful damage has, of course, been done. But all things prayerfully considered, the havoc is comparatively slight. Usually, it is houses, schools, and churches which are hit. God knows that the Nazi aim is not beyond improvement, though here I may do the raiders an injustice: they may be heaving the stuff anywhere."

September 5, 1940

Dear Mr. Cleator:

Your censored letter came in safely yesterday, somewhat delayed but still not delayed unduly. I am delighted to hear that you are still in good health and spirits. The news printed here indicates that the Blitzkrieg on England has failed completely and there are hints that it will shortly be abandoned. I begin to hope myself that the war may be over in another six months. It has been a magnificent show but such things grow tedious after a while.

While the terror is on it will probably be impossible to find a publisher for your book in this great Republic. All of the Barabbases seem to feel that in such days it would be an indecorum to print anything so plainly in contempt of our holy Christian religion. I'll tackle them as soon as they change their minds, which will be within twenty-four hours of the conclusion of hostilities.

I am entertaining a magnificent attack of hay-fever and hence feel somewhat depressed, but I am still convinced that the Holy Ghost will conquer the human race in the end and bring in an era of sweetness and light. Let me hear your own opinion on that point.

Yours,
H. L. Mencken

It was comforting to learn from an independent source that the Blitzkrieg had failed and was likely to be abandoned. Comforting—but hardly confirmed by events. Earlier, I had reported that the nightly raids, once we had been roused by the wail of the warning sirens, usually found us making our way back to bed, secure (as we blissfully imagined) in the belief that, as a residential town, Wallasey would be a target for nothing more than a stray bomb or two. But by the start of September, the entire Merseyside area was being bombed incessantly, and our supposed immunity from attack was no longer a subject for convincing argument: "Under the personal direction of the Lord, I continue to survive. It is true that He permitted three bombs to drop within 30 lineal yards of me, but He quickly made amends by directing the blast to some place else. Other bombs have dropped very near, but not quite so alarmingly near.

"As might be expected, it is the younger members of the population who are most unconcerned. All boys everywhere tumble out of their shelters at the first sign of dawn, and search the streets for shell pieces and nose caps. They find plenty—at a rough guess, I'd say there's not a house within miles without at least one tile off. The splinters descend in showers. Another youthful trick is to stand behind some war-worn civilian, and emulate the unmistakable whistle of a rapidly descending bomb. Yes; the civilian reacts as desired. Which is to say, he whoops, leaps high in the air, and then falls flat on his face. It usually takes five minutes to convince him that he is still alive. Meanwhile, the cause of the trouble has chortled off."

"I begin to hope": Much as I should have liked to have done so, I was unable to accept Mencken's notion about an early ending of the war: "As to when this will be, I fear the slaughter is going to be prolonged. Substitute years for your six months, and you may have it."

September 25, 1940

Dear Mr. Cleator:

I think you are wise to postpone the book until after the present unpleasantness is over. If it came out today it would get very little notice and might, indeed, be denounced by the pious as an ignoble attack upon the Christian idealism of the time. Once the war is over, people will be ready for such things again.

I surely hope that the bombing attacks you mention have not brought you any harm. The newspapers here indicate that the German onslaught has failed completely and I gather from them that it is rapidly lessening. I can well imagine what a nuisance the loss of sleep must be. The only consolation I can offer you is that you and I will have millions of years in Paradise post-mortem and that in all probability there will be ample sleeping facilities for true Christian men.

I have been afflicted of late by hay-fever. I never sneeze and hence get no sympathy, but the malaise is really dreadful. The only remedy that seems to work at all is alcohol in aqueous solution. Unhappily, there are limits to the amount of it that one may take.

I am holding your manuscript until the uproar is over. When that time comes it should be quite easy to find a publisher in America, especially after the English addition is announced.

Sincerely yours,
H. L. Mencken

"I think you are wise": I had replied as follows to Mencken's views, earlier expressed, on the advisability of giving up attempts to find a publisher for the *Dictionary* until the war was over: "Your ideas on the book agree with my own: by all means let it wait until the Crusade is over, and not a single Hun remains alive to challenge our Christian Kulture."

In the event, once peace was declared, I became so involved with other literary enterprises that the abandoned manuscript remained forgotten in my files—where it lingers still.

December 4, 1940

Dear Cleator:

God knows I hope this infernal war is soon over, but I must add that I am not too optimistic. My guess is that Roosevelt will be in it by the end of the year and that will mean its prolongation indefinitely. I believe he could make peace if he wanted to, but there is no sign that he does. I hesitate to set myself up in judgment over such an inspired and immortal man, but nevertheless I can easily imagine more rational courses than the one he seems to be pursuing.

It is good news that you have escaped injury and that you have a secure bomb-proof. My brother is talking of building one here in Baltimore, but I suspect that he is really not serious. If the war ever moves to these shores I shall depart quietly for the wilds of the Middle West. In the great open spaces of that region a man is safe against everything except snakes, wolves and the police.

The new English words that you send me are swell indeed, and I am delighted to have them. The cutting from the Liverpool *Echo* is also very interesting. The author, Bernard Denvir is a new one to me. I am refreshing my pastor with a gift of a pair of pantaloons and so I am in hopes that he will renew his solicitations to the Higher Powers. Soon or late you and I will sit down to a drink and a palaver.

Yours,
H. L. Mencken

"It is good news that you have escaped injury": This was Mencken's response to a note I posted on November 11, announcing that a string of bombs had landed close to our house, which lost some of its windows in the process. We were at home at the time, and the vicious whistle of the missiles as they hurtled toward us tended to linger in the memory. It was this experience that convinced us of the necessity of investing in an underground shelter, the construction of which, cut out of the solid rock on which the house was built, I ordered forthwith.

"Bomb-proof": For this, read bomb-proof shelter. The term is, of course, a misnomer, as the structure was far too near the surface to have survived a direct hit. However, it afforded reasonable protection from missiles which landed only a few yards away, as subsequent events were to demonstrate.

February 12, 1941

Dear Mr. Cleator:

I replied to your letter of November 11th the very next day. No doubt my reply is lost somewhere in the interminable files of the censors. There was nothing in it of a subversive nature, but in war time even the most harmless words are sometimes under suspicion.

I have to report the sad news that the malt liquor in this great Republic begins to show deterioration. The best of it was made with Bohemian hops, and the supply seems to have run out. The American hops, though they are very charming to the eye, have an inferior flavor and beer made with them is deleterious to an elderly man. I have switched to Scotch whiskey. Large supplies of it are rolling in, and rather surprisingly the price is not greatly advanced. I am laying in enough to keep me over two or three wars.

My very best thanks for the war words. Some of them are extremely ingenious, and all of them are amusing. I'll probably do an article on the subject in the near future. At the moment I am in the last stages of a book of quotations that has been on my desk off and on for twenty-five years. It is a tremendously tedious job, and I'll be glad to see the end of it. Once it is off, I'll probably get to work on the supplemental volume to "The American Language."

I hope this letter reaches you promptly. If it doesn't, let me know confidentially and I'll send you a copy. This is an ancient Irishism, but it is still good for another turn round the track.

I sincerely hope that you are safe and have lost nothing in the raids. It is impossible at this distance to get any plausible picture of what is going on. Since the new entente cordiale began to flourish the American newspapers print rather one-sided dispatches. I used to receive German papers by way of Italy, but of late they have been coming in very seldom. God knows I wish the war were over.

Sincerely yours,
H. L. Mencken

The reply to my letter of November 11, referred to above, failed to reach me, and no copy of it is to be found among the NYPL records.

"I replied to your letter": Failing receipt of this reply, I dispatched another note on January 25, expressing the hope that all was well in Baltimore. I added that it had been officially announced that various consignments of Europe-bound mail posted in the U.S. during November had been lost as the result of enemy action, and that this no doubt accounted for the break in our correspondence.

"I'll probably do an article": As things turned out, the writing of the proposed article on war words, though it was eventually undertaken, was considerably delayed. (See Mencken's letter of March 12, 1943, and my comments thereon.)

February 14, 1941

Dear Mr. Cleator:

Your letter of January 21st, enclosing a carbon of your letter of December 19th, reached me precisely one day after the original of the latter. Obviously, the trans-Atlantic mails are in a somewhat chaotic state. I don't know, in fact, how they are transported, for the American Post Office refuses to give any information. I still receive occasional letters and papers from Germany, but how they reach me I don't know. The English mail comes in very irregularly. Sometimes I receive six or eight letters in a single day, and then no mail reaches me for ten days or two weeks.

I am in hopes that this infernal uproar will be over shortly. Roosevelt and his friends appear to be extremely eager to horn into it, but there is no evidence that they have sufficient means to do so effectively. Meanwhile, the waste of money in this great Republic has become almost incredible. Before the end of 1941 the United States will have spent more on the war than England, and maybe almost as much as all the belligerents put together. There is actually serious talk of increasing the national debt by thirty-five billions, or even fifty billions. I can see nothing ahead save inflation and a circus in the grand manner.

I am distressed indeed to hear that Wallasey has been bombed, and only hope that your own house has not been damaged. What a ghastly mess it is! Sometimes I wonder whether I'll live to see the end of it.

My best thanks for the additional cuttings. The new war words are amusing indeed, and I am delighted to have them.

Sincerely yours,
H. L. Mencken

The state of the overseas postal service was indeed chaotic. Until the simultaneous arrival of Mencken's letters of February 12 and 14, I had not heard from him for several months, though he had received and acknowledged the communications I had addressed to him in the previous November, December, and January.

"I am distressed": Although Wallasey was separated from the Liverpool docks and other strategic targets by the mile-wide Mersey River, in the constant raids made upon the area the town had suffered considerable damage from falling bombs, misdirected or otherwise. As I had reported in my letter of January 21: "Wallasey, it would seem, is classed as a military target of no little importance. Or so I judge from the Blitz which was turned on us a little while ago. Many thousands, alas, have been made homeless, and the damage has to be seen to be believed."

But far worse was soon to come.

April 18, 1941

Dear Mr. Cleator:

I am distrssed beyond expression by your postcard of March 21. I surely hope that you and Mrs. Cleator are quite well, and that you have now found a place to live. Your news brings the war much closer to me than anything I have encountered in the newspapers. I only hope that the horrible business is over soon, and that the world makes at least some progress back toward sanity and decency before I pass out.

I have been laid up in hospital—not seriously ill, but simply worn out. I am going to Cuba tomorrow, but shall be back here in a couple of weeks.

Sincerely yours,
H. L. Mencken

The ever-increasing frequency and intensity of the air raids reached a new peak on the night of March 12/13, when much of Wallasey was devastated. Our own dwelling, though the main fabric remained standing, was deprived of doors, windows, ceilings, and roof by a string of bombs which straddled it, one of them missing our underground shelter by a few yards. Although the place rocked as though smitten by an earthquake, we and half a dozen of our neighbors emerged shaken but unhurt. Less fortunate were hundreds of other citizens who were left either maimed, dying, or dead. A couple of hurriedly dispatched postcards informed Mencken (a) that we had been rendered homeless; and (b) of the address of the temporary accommodation we had been able to find out of town.

May 12, 1941*

Dear Mr. Cleator:

Your letters of March 27th and April 5th (they have just arrived together) are so dreadfully distressing that I can't make a sensible reply. Nothing that has reached me has made the war so close, or so horrible. When I think of your visit that ghastly morning to your old home I am simply struck dumb. I only hope that you and Mrs. Cleator are still safe, and that the end of the inferno is in sight. The human race is surpassing even itself in cruelty and imbecility.

You are to give no thought to those books of mine. Once there is peace again I'll see that you get every one you want. Some I have, and the rest I can find. I have been ill and out of service, but two more are at least under way, and they will reach you with the rest.

I wrote to you at least four or five times between November and February. Unhappily, the mails are now in a mess, and I am not sure that even this will reach you. Now and then I receive a letter from England very promptly, but usually they take weeks.

Let me have news of you.

Sincerely yours,
H. L. Mencken

In giving a more detailed account of the March 12 raid, I had to comfirm the news that among the many dead were my parents and their housekeeper. My old home had received a direct hit, and nothing remained of it but a debris-lined crater. I found the bodies when daylight came, mutilated almost beyond recognition.

Another grievous loss was my extensive accumulation of books, many of them signed copies, which had shared the same fate: "My library, completely blown to blazes, cannot be replaced now. But dare I ask you to keep a lookout for odd copies of your works, and to buy them on my behalf? My collection, all but complete, was mostly acquired from the U.S., only your newest works being obtainable here. Unaided, the task of replacement seems hopeless. Should you happen upon anything, please retain until the Crusade is over. The loss of one library is enough for any man."

Mencken's promised response to this plea, as immediate as it was generous, was in due course fulfilled.

"Two more are at last under way": Probably a reference to his forthcoming *Newspaper Days,* which appeared in the following October, and the aforementioned *A New Dictionary of Quotations.*

*Year added by the recipient.

H.L. MENCKEN ESQ.,
1524 HOLLINS ST.,
BALTIMORE, M.D.
U.S.A.

FROM P.E. CLEATOR ADRIFT   MARCH 21/41

Dear Mr Mencken,

The how family's gone; the Gamley's house gone; my own house has gone; all my papers have gone; my entire library has gone, including, so help me, about 500 irreplaceable volumes by your works; and God alone knows what else has gone. But Mrs Cleator & myself are somehow alive. More about it when we contrive to settle somewhere.

P.E. Cleator.

PLATE 6. Intimation of disaster. Facsimile of the card sent to Mencken on March 21, 1941, conveying tidings of death and destruction. Surprisingly, unlike earlier and subsequent references to the bombing of Wallasey, its contents were allowed to pass unmarked by the censor.

June 21, 1941

Dear Mr. Cleator:

Your letter of May 26th reached me today, which is certainly not bad running time. I am still dreadfully distressed by the tragedy that you tell me of, and I marvel that you bear it so philosophically. The war becomes more and more insane. If, as seems likely, Roosevelt gets into it, it will probably last for three or four years. I have always been of the belief that a reasonable peace could have been made after the first clash, and I still believe that it is not impossible. After all, the countries at war will have to go on living together in the future, and soon or late they must come to something approaching terms. The all-out plan was tried the last time and turned out to be extremely hazardous. But in such matters I have ceased to offer any advice to the powers that be. It is now no longer possible in this great Republic to practise anything properly describable as sane journalism.

My very best thanks for the clippings. I am now preparing to start work on the supplement to my "American Language." Your contributions to the new material have been extensive and valuable, and I'll certainly not fail to acknowledge them.

I surely hope that you and Mrs. Cleator are safe and well, and that the end of the horror is not far off.

Sincerely yours,
H. L. Mencken

So much of my American mail had been going astray that I decided to introduce a numbering system. My note of May 26 to Mencken had accordingly been designated No. 1.

"It is now no longer possible": Although he was no supporter of the Hitler regime, Mencken's pro-German inclinations, as during World War I, made his journalistic activities increasingly difficult and eventually impossible. As a protest against what he considered to be an editorial bias against the Fatherland, he had ended his weekly contribution to the Baltimore *Sunday Sun* earlier in the year, albeit when so doing he agreed to maintain his long association with the *Sunpapers* in a consultative capacity. Thereafter, however, he tended more and more to ignore the conflict, even when American herself later became actively involved in it (see below).

July 8, 1941

Dear Mr. Cleator:

Your letter of June 5th came in safely today, elegantly embellished with the labels of the censors. It shakes me once more to think of the fate of your library. Certainly I'll be at your service when the time comes to restore it. I'll begin by assembling my own books at once, and as soon as communications are safe the first lot will start for England. Some of them, of course, are more or less difficult to come by, and so it may take time.

I am still receiving regular instalments of war slang from Durrant, the press cutting agency. Some of them are very amusing, but I should add that the majority seem to me to be highly artificial. They are apparently mainly the products of what would be called newspaper copy-readers in this great Republic— that is to say, they are the products of journalists who at best rise to the third class. On this side of the water the war so far has produced precisely nothing. I have been asked by several magazines to write articles on its neologisms, but I have had to reply that there ain't none.

I surely hope that you are in reasonably good health and spirits, despite that food poisoning. It is the season for such accidents here. I seldom get through the Summer without one powerful dose of something or other. You are at least able to enjoy such visitations in reasonably decent weather. Here in Baltimore last week the thermometer reached 102, along with a high humidity. Rather curiously, I work best at high temperatures. When I am sweating as freely as an archbishop I really feel like industry.

The morning papers indicate that Roosevelt has gone into the war at last.

Sincerely yours,
H. L. Mencken

"Durrant": The London-based agency of Durrant's Press Cuttings, founded in 1880.

"That food poisoning": I had once again been laid low by the high ptomaine content of the wartime diet: "This time, it was meat. Last time it was fish. Pretty soon I'll be refusing to eat anything, on the grounds that death by starvation is more seemly, and not half so diarrhoeic."

"Roosevelt has gone to war": Presumably a reference to recent presidential activities designed to bring comfort to the enemies of the Fatherland, such as the state of national emergency proclaimed on May 27, and the closing of German consulates throughout the U.S. which was ordered on June 16.

August 22, 1941

Dear Mr. Cleator:

Your letter of July 15th reached me this morning, which is certainly very good running time. I needn't tell you that I am delighted to hear that you are in good health, and once more relatively comfortable. I surely hope that the new home is not troubled by the war.

The clippings are grand. I am supposed to get all such things from Durrant's Press Cuttings agency, but he invariably misses those that you send me. It is, of course, difficult in war time to make a thorough search of the English papers.

I note that "Americana 1925" and "Heliogabalus" survive. All of my other books will be at your disposal the instant the war is over. I have begun to assemble some of those that are out of print.

I am up to my ears in the proof sheets of my quotation book. They are running at a good speed, but the book itself is so enormous that they'll probably keep me jumping until November. My "Newspaper Days" is scheduled for October 20th. You'll receive a copy as soon as transportation is safe.

Sincerely yours,
H. L. Mencken

In making reply to this letter, I was able to report: "Thanks to the Russian interlude, we are enjoying a very quiet time at the moment. It would seem that the Nazi bombers are not unlimited in number after all. Meanwhile, I'm certainly not craving to hear them roaring overhead in a seemingly endless stream for an eight hour stretch, or to hear ten thousand shells scream skywards to miss them. Sometimes the shells fail to explode until they hit the ground. And sometimes they land quite close. There is a gaping hole thirty yards from where I sit."

"I note that": I had been able to impart the glad tidings that because they happened to be on loan, four of my books had survived the March holocaust: "One is Fowler's *Modern English Usage:* another, Ernst Toller's *No More Peace:* and the remaining two, I'm most happy to relate, your own *Americana 1925* and *Heliogabalus*—copy No. 1275!"

August 26, 1941

Dear Mr. Cleator:

Your letter No. 4 of July 26th reached me safely this morning, close on the heels of your letter of July 15th. The mail service seems to be somewhat irregular, but nevertheless it is apparently safe enough. I am delighted and horrified to hear that you and Mrs. Cleator are thinking of coming to this great Republic after the war. I am delighted because it will give me the chance to meet the two of you, and horrified because I am convinced that the United States is in for bitter days, and perhaps for serious constitutional changes. There is, of course, no question of proper supplies; the country is still bursting with food. But the financial condition of the government grows steadily worse, and I fear that when the tax burden really begins to mount there will be all sorts of uproars. I don't care much, for it is highly probable that I'll be an angel in Heaven before the circus reaches its maximum. I begin to suspect that the war may go on for years. There seems to be no disposition on the part of the Administration here to seek a way out of it—on the contrary, there is every indication that the prolongation of the butchery would be welcome. Whether or not the great masses of the plain people agree remains to be seen.

I have been hard at work for a couple of months past on a record of my newspaper experience. This record is not to be confused with my book, "Newspaper Days," which is scheduled for publication in October. The latter is mainly buffoonery; the former is a serious chronicle. It will not be published in my time, but it may conceivably be of some interest to historians of journalism in the years to come. In all probability, I'll deposit a copy of the manuscript in some safe bank in Oklahoma or Idaho and let nature take its course. There is nothing subversive in the story, but it deals rather freely with a great many of my contemporaries.

I am delighted to hear that you and Mrs. Cleator are in reasonably good health. I can only report that I feel like Hell. Hay fever has me by the ear, and the hot, muggy weather great[ly] exacerbates it.

Sincerely yours,
H. L. Mencken

After mentioning that we were considering visiting the U.S., perhaps for good, if we survived the war, I added: "Meanwhile, we are quite well, have almost enough to eat, and jump only three feet, instead of ten, into the air when a bomb lands within a quarter of a mile (of us). What more could we ask?"

"I have been hard at work": The record of Mencken's newspaper experiences here referred to was eventually completed and typed copies of it deposited with a trio of bibliothecal establishments—

Baltimore's Enoch Pratt Library, the New York Public Library, and the Dartmouth College Library. In each case, the MS (entitled "Thirty-five Years of Newspaper Work") was accompanied by instructions that it was to be withheld from the public gaze until the year 1991. The same procedure and conditions were also applied to another of his unpublished works, to which reference is made in a subsequent letter (February 5, 1943).

September 29, 1941

Dear Mr. Cleator:

Your letter of August 18th, along with the carbon of your letter of July 26th, reached me yesterday. The mails are slow, but nevertheless they seem to be sure.

Your mention of Lincke's waltz awoke very charming memories. I'll never forget the first time I heard it. It was in a restaurant in New York. When the band suddenly burst into it I leaped up as if prodded by the Holy Ghost, and demanded its name and address. Before the afternoon was out I had got the parts for my little orchestra here in Baltimore, and we have been playing it ever since. It is one of the loveliest waltzes ever written. At last accounts Lincke was still alive, though somewhat aged and decrepit.

My best thanks for the new words. They show all the heavy witlessness of newspaper inventions. Every one of the column brethren is imitating Winchell, and doing even worse than Winchell. In the supplement to "The American Language" I hope to devote a page or two to such ghastly inventions. The number of really good new words is always limited.

I am delighted to know that at least some of your books have survived. Once this insane war is over I'll send you a packet replacing some of those you have lost. I have already picked up a number of relatively scarce ones.

I put in a really unpleasant Summer, working hard and constantly uncomfortable. At the end of August hay fever struck me with the force of an avalanche. The vaccines used to give me considerable relief, but they have now worn out. Within the last week I have actually had several brushes with asthma. It has not been severe, but nevertheless it has been a dreadful nuisance.

God alone knows when the war will end. My impression is that the brethren in Washington are eager to carry it on at least until the end of the present administration.

Sincerely yours,
H. L. Mencken

In addition to the device of numbering my correspondence, that I might thereby keep track of its arrival or nonarrival at its intended destination, I had also adopted the plan of enclosing with each letter a carbon copy of my previous communication. This not only provided the recipient with a replacement in the event of the original going astray, but it also had the added advantage that, as often as not, the duplicate escaped mutilation at the hands of the censor.

"Lincke's waltz": Paul Lincke's *Beautiful Spring*. I had mentioned that while playing it, I had been saddened by the memory that it had been a favorite composition of my mother's.

"My little orchestra": Its members were Mencken's music-making companions of the Saturday Night Club, about which more in a moment.

"Winchell": Walter Winchell, a widely syndicated American newspaper columnist and gossip writer of the time.

October 6, 1941

Dear Mr. Cleator:

This is simply to notify you that the Saturday Night Club of Baltimore played "Spring, Beautiful Spring" in your honor last Saturday night, and afterward drank to your health in sound malt liquor. The members participating included one Czech, one Austrian, three Americans of old English stock, one Russian Jew, one American of pure German stock, two Americans of mixed German-British stock, and one English Jew. The Saturday Night Club has been in existence since 1904. It got through the last war without a riffle, despite the fact that an Englishman and a Belgian sat between two Germans every Saturday night. This time it seems to be doing quite as well. The members, to be sure, are now growing old, but not all of them, for we take in new ones from time to time. I am the only charter member still surviving. Along with a German, now sick and out of service, I ordinarily tackle the piano four-handed. While he is disabled I have to manage it with my two hands. One of the rules of the Club is that every meeting must end with the playing of a waltz. We have followed that rule faithfully for thirty-eight years.

Only recently we lost one of our most valued members, Dr. Raymond Pearl, professor of biology at the Johns Hopkins University. He was an amateur French horn player of great powers—in fact, when he let loose with a real blast the very building shook. He seemed destined to live to 90, for his family was very long-lived, but last November he died after an illness of precisely two hours. Such is the will of God. We object, but do not repine.

I hope that you are reasonably comfortable. If, when and as you honor this great Republic with your presence the Club, if it is still going, will stage an evening in your honor, followed by such a beer party as has not been seen since the days of the Romans.

Sincerely yours,
H. L. Mencken

"The Saturday Night Club": This convivial and now legendary institution had its beginnings at the turn of the century, when Mencken and a number of his friends and associates gathered together of an evening to play and sing, if on occasion somewhat raucously. The essential requirement of membership was the possession of a civilized attitude towards life, including a fondness for good liquor and a love of music. As Mencken notes in his letter, these attributes, even in wartime, combined to promote a fellowship in which racial discrimination and national hatreds found no part. To my lasting disappointment and regret, it did not prove possible for me to attend the bacchanalian orgy which it was proposed to stage on my behalf.

"Along with a German": Mencken's missing duettist companion at the pianoforte was Max Broedel, whose death occurred shortly after the dispatch of the above letter. At this late date, alas, I have not been able to identify all those who were present at the international gathering which drank to my health on that October night in 1941. Some valuable clues, however, have been provided by London-born Dr. Louis Cheslock, himself a leading member of the Club, and happily a surviving one.* In response to a query which I addressed to him, he referred me to a photograph which appears in his *H. L. Mencken on Music* (Alfred A. Knopf, 1961), taken at a meeting held in April, 1937. Apart from Mencken and himself, there were present Max Broedel (German), H. E. Buchholz (of German stock), Frank C. Purdom, E. Edwin Moffett, and Drs. Raymond Pearl and Franklin Hazlehurst (of British stock), Adolf Torovsky (Czech), and Israel Dorman (Russian). Dr. Pearl died in November, 1940, and Max Broedel, as already noted, in October of the following year, but it is reasonable to assume from the description Dr. Cheslock gives that several of the other members he lists were present at the 1941 gathering. However this may be, I take this opportunity to pay tribute to the memory of them all.

October 27, 1941

Dear Mr. Cleator:

Your letter of September 29th (No. 6) came in safely this morning, exactly one month in transit. Considering the fact that all trans-Atlantic mail has to go to Bermuda and is there held by

---

*But, sadly, no longer. Since the writing of the above, news has been received of Dr. Cheslock's death in 1981.

the censors, I think that it is not bad running time. God knows I hope that rational men will get together and put an end to the current infamy. It seems to me to be completely insane. On this side of the water, of course, all the favorite publicists are howling for war to the death, even if it means war forever. They seem to forget altogether that the burden will fall, not upon Americans, but upon Englishmen.

Dilutees is a swell word, and I am inscribing it on the roll at once—indeed, it is much better than nine-tenths of the others that have bobbed up during the war.

The news that you are at work upon a play does not surprise me. Every literate man does one soon or late. I only hope that it turns out to be scandalous and that, in consequence, you will make a fortune by it. I wrote one myself about twenty years ago. Unhappily, I made it a shade *too* scandalous, and so it never got to the stage. Meanwhile, the producers of Broadway kindly stole all the ideas in it, and today it seems almost as archaic as a play by Marlowe.

I trust that you and Mrs. Cleator are in good health and reasonably good spirits. As for me, I can only report that my disintegration continues. I am hard at work, but only as a desperate means of killing time.

Sincerely yours,
H. L. Mencken

"Dilutees": A term which first appeared in the London *Daily Mail* on September 25. It was coined to describe the semiskilled labor used to increase the working staffs of war factories.

"At work on a play": The offering, entitled *My Kingdom for a Hearse,* was a satire on war, the writing of which was inspired (if that is the appropriate word) by the death of my parents.

"I wrote one myself": This was *Heliogabalus,* described by its authors as a buffoonery in three acts. Mencken penned it in collaboration with his friend and business associate George Jean Nathan, the theater critic.

November 28, 1941

Dear Mr. Cleator:

Your letter No. 7, dated October 28th, reached me this morning. My very best thanks for the clippings, and for your observations on the new war words. Most of them, I should say, seem to me to be rather strange and artificial, but that is always the case when the newspaper columnists try to embellish and adorn the vocabulary. Their inventions are mainly puns, and most of them are bad puns.

I surely hope that you are comfortable, and in reasonably good spirits. The situation in this great Republic gradually worsens. It is, to be sure, in no danger of assault from without, but inside its bounds things are rapidly going to Hell. I believe that if a fair calculation were made it would turn out that the burden of taxes is already heavier than in England. Next year we'll face something hard to distinguish from confiscation. I care very little, for so long as I am on my legs, I can earn a living. Moreover, I have no children or other dependents, and am thus not bothered by concern for the future. If, on the day following my departure for bliss eternal, the whole Western world blows up with a bang I'll deplore it but hardly mourn it.

Sincerely yours,
H. L. Mencken

"In no danger of assault from without": To be fair, Mencken's confidence that the U.S. faced no threat of external attack was probably shared by the vast majority of his unsuspecting countrymen, even at a time when the Japanese bombardment of Pearl Harbor was a mere ten days away.

December 2, 1941

Dear Mr. Cleator:

Your letter No. 8, dated November 11th, reached me today. I begin to suspect that the mail service is becoming almost normal. Along with it came the carbon of your letter No. 7, dated October 28th.

The Provost "Intermezzo" is quite new to me. I am ordering a copy at once. It is probably published in New York.

My best thanks for the additions to my collection of fantastic and incredible war words. I am writing at once to Reginald J. G. Dutton asking him for details about his new language. It sounds even more preposterous than those that have preceded it.

I trust that you are reasonably comfortable and happy. As for me, I manage to get through my day, despite a long series of minor malaises. My brother-in-law, who is a doctor, advised me to stock up on vitamins. I replied that I already get down more than any other human being on earth.

I seize the opportunity to hope that you are lucky in 1942.

Yours,
H. L. Mencken

"The Provost Intermezzo": This composition by Heinz Provost was featured as a violin solo in the film *Escape to Happiness*.

"Reginald J. G. Dutton": The hopeful inventor of yet another universal language, intended to compete for popular support with Johann Schleyer's Volapük, Dr. Zamenhof's Esperanto, its offshoot Ido, and the rest.

"My brother-in-law": What began as a routine attempt to verify and enlarge upon this apparently factual statement quickly ran into unexpected difficulties. Secure in the knowledge that both Gertrude and August Mencken were unmarried, my enquiries centered on Henry's wife Sara and on Charles Mencken's spouse Mary, neither of whom, it transpired, was seemingly possessed of a brother. When I enquired of Louis Cheslock about the identity of this elusive medical kinsman, he not only questioned the fellow's existence, but added that, to the best of his knowledge, Henry Mencken had never taken vitamin pills in his life, and that, moreover, he was not above scoffing at those who did. On receiving this somewhat disconcerting intelligence, I then turned to Carl Bode for assistance in the matter. And he, in his biographical capacity, was also unaware of any such brother-in-law, but in my presence elected to settle the question by telephoning a niece of the claimant, in the person of Mrs. David S. Morrison, at her home in Lancaster, Pennsylvania.* In the course of the conversation which then ensued, I was able to obtain authoritative confirmation of the Cheslock theory that, as he had so often done during his zestful career, Uncle Henry in his letter to me had been writing with the fleshy organ of his mouth nestling alongside one of the lateral walls thereof.

December 23, 1941

Dear Mr. Cleator:

Your letter No. 9 of November 23rd reached me this morning. Along with it came a request from Dick Regan for your address. I am sending it to him by this post.

The news that you have finished a play and are hard at work on a book is excellent news indeed. I surely hope the play gets through to me safely. If you say so, I'll be delighted to turn it over to my old associate, George Jean Nathan. He is an expert in such matters, and he may be able to find a publisher or a producer for it.

---

*Mrs. David S. (Virginia Mencken) Morrison was the daughter of Henry Mencken's brother Charles, and my conversation with her came none too soon, for she subsequently died on September 20, 1980. Her son had earlier lost his life in an air crash, and with her death the Mencken line came to an end. Coincidently, HLM's unmarried sister, Anna Gertrude Mencken, died a few days later (on September 28) in the same year, at the age of ninety-three.

PLATE 7. H. L. Mencken and George Jean Nathan at the Stork Club in New York. (*Photo:* Courtesy of Thomas Yoseloff)

You don't say what the book is about. I surely hope it breathes a genuinely Christian spirit and contains something that will be an inspiration to young men.

My own news is scanty. I have been hard at work on a sort of record of my newspaper days—not the book published in October, but a more detailed chronicle for my own use hereafter. It is dull work at bottom, but nevertheless somewhat amusing.

My quotation book is now on the press, and I should see a copy in January. It will not be published, however, until late in March, for the publisher says he needs a couple of months to market it.

Good luck in 1942!

Sincerely yours,
H. L. Mencken

An infrequent correspondent, Dick O'Regan had lost track of us, thanks to our several changes of address in recent months. He had sailed for the U.S. soon after hostilities began, there, as earlier noted, to obtain a post on the Philadelphia *Bulletin*. After the war, he returned to Europe, where he acquired a wife and family. As chief of bureau for Associated Press, he was stationed for a time in Frankfort, where we staged a long-delayed reunion. He was later assigned to London, and at the time of this writing is resident in Geneva.

"You have finished a play": In part for Mencken's edification, but also in an attempt to ensure that it escaped the fate of other of my-manuscripts which were lost in the bombing, I had announced that I was mailing a copy of *My Kingdom for a Hearse* to Baltimore for safekeeping.

"Hard at work on a book": Here, Mencken would appear to have confused intention with performance. What my note actually said was: "I'm in the process of persuading myself to begin the writing of a new book. The answering of your letter [of October 27] provides an excuse as reasonable as any for evading the issue, at least for a while."

December 31, 1941

Dear Mr. Cleator:

"My Kingdom for a Hearse" came in safely, and I have read it with vast delight. It is swell stuff indeed, and if these were normal times I think it would be possible to get a producer for it, though I should add that, as it stands, it is rather too short for the stage. I am flattered by the dedication, and offer my best thanks. At the moment, of course, it would probably be hopeless to offer it. A great spiritual awakening is in progress in this incomparable Republic, and a kind word for Beelzebub would cause a painful sensation, and perhaps provoke riots. Some of the more alert critics in New York would undoubtedly charge that in praising the Devil you were thereby praising the Japs. To be sure, it wouldn't be true, but what is truth between friends?

The New Year opens beautifully—that is, from the standpoint of undertakers, jail wardens and the general body of public nuisances. I predict formally that it will be the worst the human race has seen since Noah escaped justice.

I hope you are well, and in reasonably good spirits. As for me, I can only report that my gradual deterioration does not seem to be accelerating. I am still able to eat and drink. The Baltimore *Sun*'s London correspondent reports, to my horror, that there is a shortage of whiskey in Fleet street. I can't imagine the brethren functioning without it. Over here, by the providence of God, there seems to be plenty, including a large supply of the best Scotch brands. The price is going up, but it is still within reach of a Christian man.

> Sincerely yours,
> H. L. Mencken

P.S. I'll keep the manuscript of the play until the present unpleasantness is over.

Mencken's comments on the play were encouraging, as was the news I was able to report having in the meantime received from another source: "You will be astounded to learn—as I was—that my Agents in London not only report favourably on the work, but actually want to try and have it produced. In this event, the dialogue will have to be increased considerably. But I shall probably not be bothered. Thanks to the conflict, there are tremendous difficulties in the way. Even publishing a work is becoming next to impossible, thanks to the acute paper shortage."

These misgivings proved to be well founded, and although I subsequently extended the wording of the work, it has since lain moldering in my files.

"I am flattered": The dedication here referred to took the form of the aforementioned *nihil obstat*.

February 4, 1942

Dear Mr. Cleator:

Your letter of December 3rd came in this morning. My very best thanks for the clippings, and especially for the one from the Rationalist paper. Such things seldom reach me through the regular channels. The newspaper cutting agencies seem to confine themselves pretty well to daily papers.

The Japs puzzle me, as they do you. I can't imagine what they are aiming at. They show a good deal more skill and enterprise than I thought they had, but in the long run, of course, they'll probably have a dreadful time of it.

I am ordering a copy of the Provost Intermezzo at once. It looks to be the kind of music that will go best when I am slightly in liquor. This happens now and then, despite the exhortations of my spiritual adviser. Despite all the wars and rumors of wars, the supply of sound liquor in this great republic remains almost infinite.

Another book of mine is waiting for you. It is an enormous

collection of quotations—the fruit of twenty-five years of more or less idiotic labor. It will start for your address the instant the war is over.

> Sincerely yours,
> H. L. Mencken

"Your letter of December 3rd": There was a mix-up here, not on Mencken's part, but on mine. For one thing, I had omitted the customary numbering (the missive should have borne the insignia 11, as the preceding and subsequent letters show). And for another, as my copy indicates, I had wrongly dated it December 3, 1942—i.e., almost a year ahead of its time. That this should have read January 3, 1942, rather than December 3, 1941, is confirmed, not only by the fact that letter No. 10 itself bears this earlier date, but also by the circumstance that my unnumbered eleventh missive contained a reference to the attack on Pearl Harbor, which did not take place until December 7. I had written, "Your letters of Nov[ember] 28th and Dec[ember] 2nd came in but a post apart—the latter this morning. In view of the assault on the Republic which has since occurred, I conclude that in the field of prophecy the Lord is not behind you. And indeed, why should He be?"

The letter continued, "I confess that the Japanese move somewhat bewilders me. I can conceive an ultimate Russian collapse, I can even conceive These Isles being swamped by sheer weight of numbers. But I cannot, for the life of me, conceive a Japanese victory over the Americas. Ultimately, she must fail lamentably. What, then, does she hope to gain?"

That until I posed this question, Mencken virtually ignored the assault on Pearl Harbor in his correspondence illustrates the extent to which he continued to hold himself aloof from the conflict. His letter of December 23, written a fortnight after the event which brought the U.S. into the war, made no mention of it whatsoever, while in his next communication there was merely an oblique warning of the inadvisability of "praising the Japs."

Despite this evident lack of interest, I nevertheless ventured to bring to his notice some of the inconveniences which he might expect to be called upon to face, now that America had actively entered the fray: "Meanwhile you are, I suppose, going through the early muddles of war which prevailed here—the edicts, counter-edicts, and counter-counter-edicts. As a motorist, I had to amend the car lights a dozen times in as many weeks before the now standard headlamp mask was evolved. I spent more time, in fact, altering the lighting than I did motoring. Towards the end I had to give up reading the papers, for every time I did so some new instruction hit me in the eye. As for the blackout itself, my condolences if you suffer from this widespread disease. It has caused more civilian deaths here, I believe, than all Adolf's bombing, and that's saying something."

I concluded with an offer of practical help: "Please let me know if I can assist by telling you what to do when a 2,000 lb. H.E. bomb lands on the dinner table. I am now something of an expert in such matters."

March 16, 1942

Dear Mr. Cleator:

I have read the first chapter with immense interest. It seems to me that it is both ingenious and amusing. Your argument gets on its legs instantly, and you push it along very effectively. I needn't tell you that I am in full accord with your lambasting of metaphysicians. They are worse curses to the world then even politicians, and if anything approaching true civilization is ever set up I am confident that they will be condemned to the mines. It is good news that there is a possibility of producing the play. It will need, of course, considerable fattening, but you can do it.

Your news about the whiskey situation is depressing indeed. Here in this great, free republic there is plenty of it left, but the price is gradually rising, and in a little while we poor people will have to go back to wood alcohol and horse liniment. I don't care much, for I have enough stored in my cellar to last a long while.

My best thanks for the cuttings. As always, they are very amusing, and I am delighted to have them.

I surely hope that you are pushing the book as fast as possible. It is grand stuff, and I see no reason whatsoever why you should have any difficulty in finding a publisher. To be sure there is now paper rationing—but this war can't last forever.

Sincerely yours,
H. L. Mencken

In view of the interest Mencken had earlier expressed in the new book I was planning, I sent a draft of the opening chapter to Baltimore, accompanied by a cautionary intimation that it was likely to be some considerable time before the next installment arrived. Thereafter, what with one wartime interruption and another, it seems unlikely that I ever completed the task, notwithstanding the high praise that was lavished upon the first episode. At all events, no sign of the typescript is now to be found among my papers, and it must be assumed that the world has forever been denied a sight of this potential masterpiece.

April 23, 1942

Dear Mr. Cleator:

Your letter No. 13 of March 18th, along with a carbon of No. 12 of February 4th, reached me this morning. I note that the running time grows longer and longer. I long ago gave up the use of the airmail. Only the other day I received a letter from England, coming by air, that took six weeks. It must have been sent by way of the Mediterranean, India, Australia and the South Pole.

So far there has been no paper rationing here, but it is threatened and it will unquestionably come. My publisher, Knopf, has just got his hands on sufficient thin paper to do a second printing of my Dictionary of Quotations. He is full of fears that when it is worked off he'll be unable to obtain any more. If so, my loss will be direct and serious, for the book seems to be catching on, and in normal times it would go through three or four printings the first year. The first edition shows some errors, and I am glad of the chance to correct them. Your copy will go forward the instant this cruel war is over.

My best thanks for the neologisms from the London papers. They seem to me, I must say, to be rather strained, but I assume that three years of war have pretty well exhausted the inventiveness of the brethren. In this country I am picking up next to no new war words of any merit. Indeed, the whole national attitude toward the war seems to be quite solemn. Americans are beginning to realize that they are in for a hard and perhaps long struggle. The supply of automobile tires is already running short, and the rationing of gasoline and sugar is announced. My guess is that there will also be shortages of tea, coffee and various other familiar commodities. It will do the American people some good to go on short commons. They have been living an almost fabulously comfortable life for years past. Even at the height of the depression there was always plenty of food and clothing. It is already announced that there will be shortages of wool and leather. Fortunately, I have enough clothes in hand to last me the rest of my life. At 62 it is prudent to assume that the holy angels have my name posted.

I note your change of address. I surely hope that you are in the best of health and reasonably comfortable. Good luck with the play!

Sincerely yours,
H. L. Mencken

"My Dictionary of Quotations": Exceptionally, the promised copy of this book, assuming it to have been dispatched, failed to reach me.

"I note your change of address": This, our fourth move from one temporary abode to another since we were rendered homeless, found us installed in a farm located in mid-Wirral, some twelve miles from devastated Wallasey. Piped water apart, the premises offered little in the way of civilized amenities, but as supplies of gas and electricity were about to be rationed, we were happy enough to make do with log fires and oil lamps. Moreover, the renting of two large empty rooms enabled us to bring our own furniture out of store, thus helping to create the illusion of a home away from home.

May 8, 1942

Dear Mr. Cleator:

Your letter No. 14, dated April 18, came in safely. Mr. Mencken is laid up at the Johns Hopkins Hospital, following a severe head infection. While he is recovering, he is still very weak and unable to transact any business. He'll write to you the moment he gets back to Hollins street.

Sincerely yours,
Rosalind C. Lohrfinck
Secretary to Mr. Mencken

May 18, 1942

Dear Mr. Cleator:

I have escaped from hospital, and seem to be making fair progress at home. I am still somewhat wobbly and have to take more rest than usual, but I have got back to a certain amount of work. What fetched me was a severe throat infection. It yielded quickly to the new sulfa drugs, but the drugs themselves almost floored me.

Thanks very much for the Prohibition literature and your notes on the new war words. The Prohibitionists begin to show signs of renewed activity here in this great republic, and I am thoroughly convinced that if the war goes on for three or four years longer they'll win again. Already, indeed, they have forced up the tax on liquors to such a height that bootlegging is reviving. I don't care much, for I have now in stock enough hard liquor to last me the rest of my life—in fact, I figure that there will be enough left on my departure to keep the pallbearers tight for a week at least. There is no surer way of being remembered pleasantly.

I hope that you are comfortable on the farm, and that you have luck with your crops. The blockade is making great changes in

American life. Here along the East coast there is a serious shortage of gasoline, and all over the country rubber is almost unobtainable. Thus the Americano who has been automobiling constantly for years past finds himself on foot again. So far the only food rationed is sugar, but I assume that tea and coffee will soon follow. I don't care, for my consumption of all these things is slight.

The best of luck with the book! As wobbly as I am, I am preparing to start a new one myself. after all, there is nothing else to do in war time save work.

Sincerely yours,
H. L. Mencken

The brief note from Mrs. Lohrfinck, earlier received, announcing that Mencken was in hospital, though it had been dispatched on May 8, did not reach me until June 17, by which time the patient was back home. In replying to his letter giving news of his escape from the Johns Hopkins ménage, I revealed that immediately on learning of his internment "I spent the day in fasting and prayer, and consider it not insignificant that you found it possible to dictate a letter the day following."

"Prohibition literature": This had been sent with an earlier note: "I'm enclosing some anti-drink literature for your prayerful perusal. I dropped in [at] the local Temperance Hall the other day to obtain some first hand information for literary purposes. The Secretary, I fear, completely mistook my intentions, and pressed me to join. I almost gave my name as Mencken, with an address in Baltimore, but thought better of it, and confessed that I was no Christian, and no abstainer. Apparently my honesty commended itself, for I received all [the information] I needed."

"I am preparing to start": Mencken's new book here mentioned was presumably *Heathen Days,* the completion of which is referred to later in the year (letter of October 16).

June 26, 1942

Dear Mr. Cleator:

Your letter No. 15 came in yesterday. I am distressed to hear that the play is making such heavy weather of it, but I am certainly not surprised. Up to a few weeks ago the literary business in this great Republic followed the lines of normalcy, but now it has suddenly begun to realize that the war is in progress. There is no actual shortage of paper, but simply of transport. The Canadian mills, in fact, are bulging with stock. What gives the newspapers pause is the problem of getting it across the border. It used to come by water, but that is now impossible—and the railroads are naturally worked to capacity.

I note what you say about rationing. So far in this country it has affected only sugar and gasoline, but various other articles will unquestionably go on the list in the near future. There seems to be no lack of supply, but once again, as in the matter of paper, transport presents difficulties.

My adventure in hospital left me considerably depleted, and I am still more or less shaky. However, I am able to sit up to my desk, and am devoting myself to getting my papers in order. I tackle them every two or three years, but they are quickly reduced to chaos again.

God help us all!

Yours,
H. L. Mencken

"I note what you say": As I replied somewhat wistfully to Mencken, his account of the rationing then in force in the U.S. read like a fairy tale. With us, by this time, apart from the air we breathed, everything in the way of consumer goods was either in short supply or impossible to obtain—except, perhaps, at fantastic prices on the black market. But the main concern was how to obtain a sufficiency of food that was palatable enough to eat. The amounts of butter, bacon, and meat, much of it of very dubious quality, which were allocated to each person, sufficed for no more than a couple of meals each week. For the rest, the staple diet consisted of bread and potatoes. And of these items, the so-called bread, a dirty gray in color, had a consistency and a taste reminiscent of cardboard. It also possessed the added characteristic that if left uneaten for much more than a day, it rapidly acquired a green sheen of mold. As for potatoes, converting these into something that was succulent and tasty required cooking fat, which was unavailable in anything like sufficient quantity for the purpose. However, some unknown genius experimented with medicinal paraffin, and found that this laxative formed an excellent substitute for lard when applied to the making of chips, whereupon there was a countrywide demand for supplies of the liquid. Puzzled government officials, alerted by the acute shortage of so unlikely a commodity which then developed, on enquiring into this cathartic phenomenon, discovered what was afoot. They then promptly set about discouraging the practice by announcing that, if persisted in, it would give rise to cholecystitis, perforation of the duodenum, and cancer of the stomach. True or false, the warning succeeded, at any rate for a while, so it was back to the unpalatable monotony of steamed spuds. And by way of encouragement, in a series of advertisements urging the populace to eat potatoes morning, noon, and night, the Ministry of Food was not above making such feeble puns as Show Your Potatriotism. There was even a reference to Tuber über Alles!

As for the rationing system itself, on occasion even this burdensome imposition was not enitrely devoid of unconscious humor, thanks to the ramifications of the procedure. Thus, not only was the weekly allowance of a given food strictly limited, but in the case of certain items, the place of purchase was also designated, a restriction which led to complications for persons who happened to be away from home. In such circumstances, Emergency Ration Cards were provided, and on Merseyside an enterprising firm of meat retailers, intent upon securing their share of migrant customers, caused the following notice to be displayed in their branch shops throughout the harbor area:

SEAMEN SUPPLIED WITH PLEASURE

July 14, 1942

Dear Mr. Cleator:

Your letter of June 17th has just come in. I got out of hospital safely enough, though I had a violent infection while it lasted. Unhappily, it developed that an old scrap of tonsil tissue was doing some damage, and so I returned last week to have it dug out. The operation was trivial, and I am already pretty well restored to normalcy. It turned out that the tonsil tag was full of pus, so I assume that it may have been responsible for the malaises that have been harassing me for two years past.

You say nothing about yourself. I surely hope that you are reasonably contented. The pressure of war begins to be felt in this great Republic. There is a very noticeable diminution of automobile traffic, and many common objects grow scarce. Fortunately, the brewers have been unmolested so far, though the Prohibitionists are reviving and threaten to start a new crusade. Excellent malt liquor is obtainable at a reasonable price here in Baltimore. As long as it lasts I'll continue to trust in God.

Yours,
H. L. Mencken

Mencken's homecoming was soon followed by a return to hospital, whereafter successive letters illustrated his abiding interest in the vulnerary aspects of his physical ailments. On my expressing due concern about his continuing need for medical attention, he at once responded, as between one amateur pathologist and another, by sending a more detailed account of his afflictions.

July 28, 1942

Dear Mr. Cleator:

Thanks very much for your letter #16, dated July 4th, which came in yesterday morning. My first illness involved a greal deal of discomfort, for I had a severe streptococcic infection in the upper nose passages. However, the new sulfa drugs disposed of it promptly, and I came out of hospital feeling fairly vigorous. Unhappily, it developed that a tag of old tonsil tissue was flourishing in a tonsil crypt, and so I had to go back to have it removed. The operation was trivial, and I am now fully recovered. If the weather were not so infernal I'd be hard at work. As it is, I languish in a temperature of nearly 90 degrees, with a relative humidity of nearly 100.

Casual travel in this great Republic has already become as difficult as in England. My sister has a farm thirty-five miles from Baltimore, and I'd like to spend a little time there with her. Unfortunately, getting to and from the place is almost impossible. The nearest railroad station is five miles from her farm, and it is quite impossible, in the town it serves, to hire any sort of conveyance. Thus she has to come in from her farm to haul me out, and that involves a serious depletion of her gasoline supply.

The papers this morning announce that fuel oil for the heating of houses will be very short during the coming Winter. Inasmuch as five houses out of six in Baltimore are now heated by oil, this will mean much serious discomfort. The shortage, of course, is due to the activity of U-boats along the coast. Most of the oil for the Eastern seaboard comes from the Gulf of Mexico by sea.

Good luck with the play! I surely hope you are not discouraged by the fact that the first three entrepreneurs failed to take it. I have known good plays to go the rounds of dozens before they finally landed.

It looks impossible, at the moment, to foresee the end of the war. It may end suddenly, but on the other hand it may go on for years. I am planning to start a new book, but I suspect that by the time it is finished the publishing business in America will be virtually suspended. There is no shortage of paper in Canada, but printing costs are going up enormously, and transportation is becoming more and more difficult.

I surely hope that you are in good health and reasonably lively spirits.

Yours,
H. L. Mencken

"My sister": Gertrude Mencken, whose farm, "Choice Parcel," was located near Westminster, Maryland.

"I am planning to start a new book": Confirmation that this was a reference to *Heathen Days* is to be found in Mencken's next letter.

August 28, 1942

Dear Mr. Cleator:

Your letter No. 17, of July 27, has just reached me, exactly one month on the way. I can well understand your feelings about these air raids. It is simply impossible to get used to such an assault. Here in this great Republic the war continues to be a show far away. To be sure, a few young Americans are being killed, but the number is trivial when compared to the population of the country, and so the dangers and hazards of the business still fail to strike home. Even the sinkings of merchant ships along the Atlantic coast seem far away to the people on shore. They have never seen an enemy airplane or heard a bomb go off. Moreover, I am in some doubt that they ever will. The only consolation I can offer you would disgrace Polonius. The thing is horrible, and that is the beginning and the end of it. Soon or late, of course, it will have to finish, but I begin to fear that it may yet go on for a long time. It will probably take a couple of years at least to clean up the Japs in the Pacific, if, indeed, it can be done so quickly, and while the business is going on the war spirit here will not abate.

I have no news to offer. Hay fever has me by the ear, and I am middling miserable, but nevertheless manage to get in a certain amount of work. I am engaged upon a third volume of my idle reminiscences. It is, of course, trivial and even puerile stuff, but it somehow entertains me in war time. If I were more energetic I'd tackle the proposed supplement to "The American Language." Unhappily, I am almost paralyzed with alarm every time I look at the accumulated material. It runs to many pounds, and is stacked up to the ceiling of my office.

God help us all! The human race, I begin to suspect, is insane.

Yours,
H. L. Mencken

"I can well understand": Toward the end of July, after a long lull, I had to report the return in force of the enemy's nocturnal bombers—and a disconcerting reaction on my part to the visitation. In the past, successive raids night after night had come to be regarded, if not exactly with indifference, then at any rate with resignation and an outward display of calm. I well recollect that if, when the warning sirens sounded, we happened to be at the theater, or driving across town, we remained in our seats until the end of the show, or continued on our journey, as the case might be, notwithstanding that this last undertaking might well entail continuously dodging a hail of bombs and a rain of shrapnel in dual descent. Alternatively, if the start of the raid found us at home, we retreated to our subterranean shelter, from which we periodically emerged to make sure that the house was still standing, or to extinguish a shower of incendiary bombs, or to carry to our place of refuge a neighbor's child from across the way. So much for our almost carefree attitude toward the early attacks, a response sustained to some extent by the fatalistic theory that if a missile had one's name on it, then it would inevitably find its mark. But now, in the aftermath of the events of March 1941, and even though I was lodged in the comparative safety of a house in the country, I found myself subject to a fit of shaking, which I sought in vain to control, at the mere thought of the death and destruction that was being meted out to those at the receiving end of the bombardment. Without my having realized it, my nerves, it seemed, remained in shreds. As I wrote to Mencken, in an attempt to rationalize the situation:

"The trouble is, I think, that the sound of bombers and guns is associated in what remains of my mind with a picture I'd give five years of my life to forget—Roads blocked everywhere . . . Houses partly demolished, houses half demolished, houses completely demolished . . . Thousands homeless . . . Dazed people, wandering aimlessly . . . Time bombs everywhere . . . Continuous explosions . . . No gas, no water, no electricity . . . Buildings still ablaze . . . Staircases, majestically leading nowhere . . . A house with a pane of undamaged glass in it . . . Instructions to boil all water . . . The queues for the water carts . . . The mountain of debris that was once my old home . . . My people, strewn about the back garden . . . Passes for the emergency morgues . . . Endless lines of mutilated dead . . . Chloride of lime . . . My brother's confidence that he'd know mother's face anywhere . . . His discovery that there *was* no face . . . The last minute realisation, through the evidence of a severed limb, that we'd identified mother as the housekeeper, and *vice versa* . . . The harassed custodian's promise to switch the numbered discs . . . My subsequent wondering if he bothered . . . The congress of shocked relatives . . . The hastily summoned gentleman of the cloth . . . His valiant efforts not to lay the blame on God, and yet maintain the fiction of His omnipotence . . . The tattered remains of a world-wide correspondence, littering the entire block . . . The thought that hundreds of the letters were written in German, Italian, and Russian, and that some idiot would be sure to denounce me as a spy . . . The blood-soaked earth where I found the bodies . . . The search for somewhere to eat and sleep . . .

"*Was wird das Ende sein? Wer gewinnt aus allem? Wer weiss . . .*"*

*"What will the outcome be? Who gains by all this? Who indeed . . ."

PLATE 8. The architecture of war. "Houses partly demolished, houses half demolished, houses completely demolished. . . ." Before the air attacks made upon it, Wallasey was a residential town of some one hundred thousand inhabitants. *(Above and below)* This was Lancaster Avenue. (*Photos:* Courtesy of Wirral Borough Council Leisure Services)

September 18, 1942

Dear Mr. Cleator:

Your letter No. 18, dated August 10th, came in today. I am naturally enormously interested in that chemical investigation. My own knowledge of chemistry, of course, is very slight, but nevertheless I am still interested in the subject, and know at least enough about it to understand what you are driving at. If you solve the problem you'll make a really first-rate contribution to knowledge. I offer you the only help in my power, which is, of course, the praying capacity of my chaplain. He is already on his knees, and he is instructed to stay there until I hear favorable news from you.

I have just got over hay fever, and feel somewhat ragged. The season here was extremely severe, but I managed to get through it with very little discomfort. I ascribe my relative immunity to the fact that I took no treatment whatsoever. After twenty-five years of struggling with vaccines, I resolved to throw them out of the window. The only medication I have had has been an occasional dose of calcium gluconate and a few shots of vitamins A and D. My guess is that they did me no good whatsoever.

I am delighted to hear that you are busy. The only real anodyne for the horrors of the time is hard work. I have just put in two dreadfully busy days in New York, but actually feel refreshed.

Yours,
H. L. Mencken

Mencken's youthful interest in chemistry was coincident with a first love of my own, and at the time I was engaged in a reexamination of D. I. Mendeleev's classic arrangement of the elements, the apparent periodicity of which nevertheless continued to present, in Frederick Soddy's challenging words, "a completely unsolved riddle, the meaning of which seems scarcely hidden beneath the surface, and yet perpetually eludes the grasp."

My approach entailed a consideration of proton-neutron ratios, a mathematical appraisal which revealed a specific relationship between the short and long periods of the Mendeleevian table. But the pamphlet I published on the subject in 1950 *(The Periodic Problem)* was greeted with a deafening silence in scientific circles, from which I was left to draw the conclusion that either my analysis was (a) worthless; or (b) of unrecognized merit. My natural modesty restrains me from indicating which of these alternatives I incline to favor.

October 16, 1942

Dear Mr. Cleator:

Your two letters, No. 19 of September 5th and No. 20 of September 24th, have just reached me, simultaneously. Why No. 19 should have taken so long in transit I simply can't tell you. We live in astonishing days, and all sorts of marvels are everyday occurrences. There is now some talk of rationing railroad travel in the United States. Inasmuch as I have to make frequent trips to New York, this will probably inconvenience me immensely. Nevertheless, I submit as a Christian and a patriot. The fast trains between Washington and New York are so heavily loaded with government officials that it is already difficult for the common run of us to get accommodation.

If you actually decide to spend a few weeks in jail, I predict formally that you will enjoy the experience. It is now 16 years since I last had the pleasure of being incarcerated myself. What I remember of the adventure is that it gave me a chance to do some earnest reading, and brought me into intimate contact with a number of interesting and worthy policemen, warders and so on. One of the cops actually presented me with a quart of very excellent American rye whiskey, but this, I should add, was as I left, not while I was in his custody.

By the direct intervention of SS. Agatha, Charles Borromeo and Ignatius, I have managed to finish my book. It is to be called "Heathen Days," and is a sort of catch-all for material left over from "Happy Days" and "Newspaper Days." I had a lot of fun putting it down, although I was uncomfortable physically during the whole time. It is trivial stuff, but nevertheless it will probably please the customers.

Now that it is off my desk, I am devoting most of my time to some legal business of journalistic nature. It is, of course, tedious, but nevertheless there is some amusement in it. When it is finished I hope to fall to work on the supplement to "The American Language." Thanks to your kindly aid, I have accumulated a really enormous mass of interesting war slang from England, and I certainly hope to give it a large and florid chapter. Most of the new phrases, of course, are strained and ineffective, but here and there a really good one is hidden among them.

The war has already begun to interfere enormously with the routine of American life. I have mentioned its effect on railroad travel. There is as yet no actual shortage of food, but my cook tells me that it is already necessary to take what is in the market, not what one wants. I am planning, if the worst comes to the worst, to resort to the Southern American bill-of-fare, which is based on fat hog meat, meal made from maize, and the cheapest sort of molasses. It lacks vitamins, but I hope to supply them through the use of malt liquor, which is reported to reek with them. God help us all!

Yours,
H. L. Mencken

"If you actually decide": The indications were that my long if futile opposition to mankind's predilection for fraticidal strife was about to engage the attention of the authorities.

"Since I last had the pleasure": Mencken ran foul of the law in 1926 over a ban on the sale of the April issue of his magazine *The American Mercury,* which featured a contribution concerned with prostitution. He challenged the interdict in person by selling a copy of the magazine on the streets of Boston, whereupon he was arrested and taken to the Pemberton Square police station. After being detained for some hours, he was eventually released on bail.

"By the direct intervention": Of the sanctified trio here mentioned, and with no disrespect either to the erstwhile Archbishop of Milan or to the founder of the Order of Jesuits, it seems reasonable to suppose that as a candidate for Hell, Mencken derived most help from St. Agatha of Catania, one of the blessed dead justly revered for the protection she affords against danger from fire, lightning, and (by extension) the atom bomb.

December 30, 1942

Dear Mr. Cleator:

My very best thanks for your letter No. 21, and the enclosures. I could match that wireless form with 10,000 worse ones here. It is really incredible how fertile the wizards at Washington are in devising such nuisances. The other day the Baltimore *Sun* printed a dispatch showing that a department store in Washington was confronted with instructions running to no less than 13,000 printed pages. The manager of the place had been forced to set up a whole new department to handle this balderdash. There were large sections of it that were completely unintelligible. Curiously enough, after the *Sun* printed the story it received a great many letters denouncing it for interfering with the war effort! The psychology of the human race in times of public excitement is really almost fathomless.

I hope and pray to God that "Heathen Days" will be the last of the series. I have now got down 240,000 words of my reminiscences, and that certainly seems enough. My publisher is eager to have a fourth volume, to be called "Magazine Days," but, fortunately, I can plead honestly that writing it would be impossible. It would have to deal with a great many men and women who are still alive, and treating them in anything approaching a realistic manner would break their hearts. As a humane man and a professing Christian I am forbidden to do this.

I surely hope that you are reasonably comfortable and contented, and that no one has yet really proposed to jail you. Things here gradually grow more disturbed and onerous. Until a few months ago there was no serious rationing, but now it impends. I don't care much, for if I can't get a sufficiency of human food I'll rob the horses of their oats and the dogs of their horse meat. In my early days in journalism I trained myself to eat whatever victuals were set before me. I found that the art was really quite easy, and I have practised it ever since.

God help us all!

Yours,
H. L. Mencken

"That wireless form": I had forwarded this item with the comment: "I send it as an example of what this country suffers from most of all—an infinity of Forms. What used to be the simplest of actions, such as the buying of an egg, or the purchase of a hundredweight of coal, or the acquiring of a piece of timber six inches long by two inches wide, or indeed the buying of almost anything, requires that the requisite Form be duly filled, signed, and delivered. As for more complicated actions, such as making a change of address, or changing one's job, or obtaining a gallon of petrol, there is no end to the form filling involved. I myself am still busy over the change of abode we made six months or so ago, and the end is not yet in sight. I question, indeed, if there is an end. And the purpose of the Form enclosed? This document, sealed, signed, and delivered, is the first step towards the acquirement of a wireless valve—radio tube to you. Just how many months the entire process requires I don't know, for after taking one look at the Form I decided it would be easier to do without the radio.

"I am now beginning to see why it is that I am not yet in jail; why it is, indeed, that since September I have not heard another word: someone, somewhere, is filling up forms."

"I hope and pray": Mencken's wish was realized, for *Heathen Days* proved to the last of the *Days* series. His mention of Alfred Knopf's call for a fourth volume, to be entitled *Magazine Days,* was prompted by a somewhat more ambitious entreaty on my part: "*Heathen Days,* from its very title, sounds vastly interesting, and the news that it is ready for the press is news indeed. It will soon be followed, I hope, by *Unrepentant Days,* and so on right down to *Baptist Days,* when you finally manage to throw off sin."

February 5, 1943

Dear Mr. Cleator:

Your letter No. 22 of January 7th, along with the carbon of No. 21 of November 29th, reached me safely yesterday. I am delighted to hear that your work is going ahead so prosperously, and I surely hope that you publish it without delay. There is no telling in these horrible times how long any of us will last. I am putting in some hard work on a record of my magazine days—not for immediate publication, but for the delight and edification of posterity. It is conceivable, if I live long enough, that I may boil it down into a printable book, but it is rather more likely that I'll leave the manuscript to some library and invite the nascent Ph.D.'s of the future to do their damndest.

It is a curious fact, but nevertheless a fact, that the word *bugger,* like the word *bloody,* has no indecent significance in this country, save among a small class of sophisticates. When I was a boy my father used *bugger* as a general term of endearment, especially for his sons. It has rather gone out, but nevertheless it is still occasionally encountered.

The whole question of forbidden terms ought to be investigated at length. So far it has got very little attention. Even the more fundamental question of indecency has been passed over far too lightly by the psychologists. Most of them, of course, are idiots, and the rest have the general mental constitution of Methodist parsons.

My best thanks for the cuttings. They are full of amusing stuff. I had hoped to get to work long before this on the projected supplement to "The American Language," but various other jobs have intervened, and so I'll probably not tackle it until the end of the year.

Sincerely yours,
H. L. Mencken

The delight here expressed at the progress I had reported making concerned my aforementioned investigation of the periodicity displayed by the chemical elements.

"I am putting in some hard work": The record in question was entitled "My Life as Author and Editor." As Mencken anticipated, copies of the completed manuscript were subsequently deposited with the three libraries of his choice, to which reference has already been made (my comment on his letter of August 26, 1941).

"It is a curious fact": Mencken's dissertation on the use of forbidden terms was occasioned by some remarks of mine about life on the farm. The local alphabet, I had reported, contained only twenty-five letters—aitch was missing. Thus we lived in a world of 'eifers and 'orses, in which the participants were continually being asked to "lend an 'and." Another endearing facet of rustic speech was its occupational profanity: "The word most commonly used is *bugger,* closely followed by *bloody*. These two prime favourites, not normally heard in polite company in These Isles, are used on every possible occasion. Everything, unless my ears deceive me, is a *bugger*. I've even heard of a *bloody bugger,* though the occasion was a special one."

March 12, 1943

Dear Mr. Cleator:

I hope that the move back to your reconstructed house is made safely, and that you are reasonably comfortable. If it takes you less than thirty days and thirty nights to make out the necessary forms, you should congratulate yourself that you are not a citizen of this great Republic. The bureaucrats here have gone on a veritable spree of questionnaires. I receive them daily, and in enormous quantity. Nearly all of them have to be attested before a notary public, which means that I must pay 25¢ every time I communicate with the rulers of the land. A few weeks ago one group of them actually forced me to make oath to a simple request for a hearing. There was no statement of fact in the request, and I don't know to this minute what I swore to. All such things must be made out in triplicate, quadruplicate or quintuplicate, and the State Department in many situations demands six copies. Inasmuch as questionnaires are printed on extremely thick paper, it is impossible to make so many carbons. As a result, the secretaries of the country are working day and night.

My very best thanks for the cuttings. I am hoping soon or late to do an article on English war slang. A good many brief pieces on the subject have been printed over here, but nearly all of them have been inadequate. I have now, thanks mainly to your generosity, accumulated a really enormous mass of material.

At the moment the curse of God is on this house. I am taking my brother to hospital in an hour, to be treated for a really

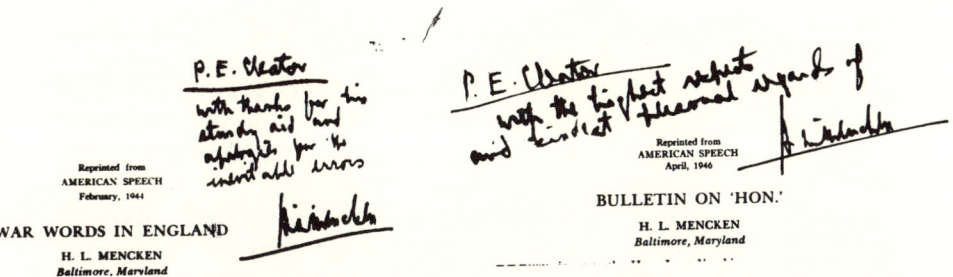

PLATE 9. The Mencken epigraphs—2. Reprints of articles from *American Speech*. A reference to British restaurants in the February 1944 issue serves as a reminder that early in World War II the manager of one of these governmental establishments found that he was losing knives, forks, and spoons at an alarming rate. To deter the light-fingered among his deprived customers, he imposed a refundable deposit of half a crown for the use of each such item. A month later he made the interesting discovery, not only that the pilfering had ceased, but that his stock of cutlery had risen tenfold, and that it consisted mainly of battered instruments whose worth was considerably less than the sum he had paid out for them!

severe head and throat infection. Meanwhile, my own sinuses have run amuck and I feel like a drowning man.

The news in the papers here is extremely optimistic. Apparently, the end of the war is only around the corner.

Sincerely yours,
H. L. Mencken

After a delay of nearly two years, repairs to our home in Wallasey had been begun, to the extent that it could now boast a permanent roof and real glass (as opposed to polythene) windows. But a permit for internal work, such as the provision of ceilings, was almost impossible to obtain, and I had reported finding myself adrift in a sea of officialdom. To these grumbles about the arbitrary edicts of a despotic bureaucracy, Mencken replied with an ululation of his own.

"I am hoping": The proposed article, entitled "War Words in England," duly appeared in the issue of *American Speech* for February, 1944.

April 9, 1943

Dear Mr. Cleator:

I am delighted to hear that you have got home at last. However formidable the job of cleaning up, it will be at least a pleasure, and I hope you'll be settling down comfortably in a little while.

It is curious that the word *bloody* has never had any unpleasant significance in this great Republic. It is seldom used, but when it is heard no one winces. *Bugger,* of course, is more dubious, but even *bugger* is not really scandalous.

I trust that you are in reasonably good health and spirits. I have put in a really wretched Winter, with constant infections and many other malaises. The weather, taking one week with another, has been almost unendurable. Here on the edge of the South, it is common for winter to be a mild season, but this year we had a great deal of snow and sleet, with many strong and bitter winds. All last week, indeed, a violent Northwestern gale was blowing.

I am in hopes that when the sun comes out at last I'll be restored to normalcy. Meanwhile, I am at least getting a few licks in on my book—that it, on my record in preparation for a book. Whether or not I'll ever finish it I don't know. That question is in the hands of our Heavenly Father. His will, not ours, be done.

Yours,
H. L. Mencken

"It is curious that": On the subject of forbidden terms, in making reply to Mencken's letter of February 5, I had commented on the comparative freedom of expression which seemingly prevailed in the U.S.: "The terms *bloody* and *bugger,* as I mentioned, are not normally heard in polite society in These Isles. Pre-war, both were absolutely taboo. Hence the public excitement over Shaw's "Not bloody likely!" in his *Pygmalion*. And hence the expression "Not Pygmalion likely." The word, by some miracle, was allowed in the film version, and I've heard tell of scores of folk who sat through the thing several times simply and solely for the pleasurable business of being mildly shocked. Since the war, however, *bloody* has become tame enough. The affair is, indeed, a bloody one, and even the pure and holy B.B.C. occasionally describes it as such.

"But *bugger* retains its ban. General Montgomery may have given Rommel a bloody nose, as indeed it was recently reported, but it is unlikely that he will ever finish the bugger off."

In the above reference to the BBC, I observe that I referred to the Corporation as being pure and holy—and so it was in those far off days when it languished under the sabbatarian dispensation of the late lamented Sir John Reith. His idea of Sunday entertainment for the masses was a succession of church services, followed by an organ recital featuring such lively refrains as "Nearer My God to Thee" and the "Dead March," interspersed with prayers and exhortations to throw off sin. But the era of this Presbyterian force-feeding did not long survive the war, since when the aethereal diet has changed out of all recognition. Whereas in the broadcast I made in 1937, I was not permitted to say "imprecations"—even the mere suggestion of profanity was then strictly *verboten*—nowadays, much of the language heard over the air, both on radio and television, is so highly charged with hitherto unmentionable four-letter words that even dockers have been known to blush on hearing them, at any rate in the presence of their wives and daughters, if not in the company of their mistresses. For my own part, while I'm all for freedom of expression, I tend to regard a surfeit of pointless obscenities as no more desirable than an excess of pious platitudes, and I am just as likely to switch off the one as I am to turn a deaf ear to the other.

"My book": Another reference to the projected *Supplement I* of *The American Language*. It eventually appeared in 1945.

May 21, 1943

Dear Mr. Cleator:

Your letter No. 25 of April 19th came in this morning. The censor had relieved it of one sentence, but he let pass the two specimens of bureaucratic imbecility. I refuse to make any attempt to choose between them: they are both completely perfect. However, I should warn you that the American bureaucrats, though they have had less experience, are already showing a magnificent talent. I receive notices and commands almost every day that are completely unintelligible. Fortunately, the laws of this great Republic are seldom enforced with any energy, and so it is always safe to throw such things into the fire.

I note what you say about the bomb-proof [shelter] you are building. If the war ever comes to close grips with this coast, I'll probably dig one in my backyard. It is not large, but I am informed by high authority that the ground under it runs all the way to China. There was a time when I was a diligent and talented operator with the pick and shovel, and though that time is now long past, I believe and hope that I'll be able to recover my gift.

My very best thanks for the cuttings. As always, they are superb. I had hoped to get to work long before this on the supplement to "The American Language," but various other jobs have interfered and so I'll probably not tackle it until the end of the year. The accumulation of new and first-rate material is really immense—in fact, I have almost a camel-load of it.

The rationing now in force here is a nuisance, but not really onerous. There seems to be a shortage of meats, but fish are still plentiful and so I get enough to eat.

Sincerely yours,
H. L. Mencken

"I refuse to make any attempt": Of the two specimens of bureaucratic imbecility above referred to, one was a spoof, invented by an enterprising journalist in the pay of the London *Daily Express,* the other a typical example of the genuine article:

Determined not to be surprised by peace, the Committee which is considering various schemes for pooling smoked glass for eclipses after the war has announced that it is proposed to consider as a user of smoked glass any person or persons who may or might be said to be actively or passively engaged in using, whether temporarily or otherwise, for the reasons outlined in leaflet 734 C (91) el. (b). 126 (42) 71. (H) 318, a piece or bit or slab or circle of smoked glass. Officials will be empowered to enter houses at discretion to gather informaton from the householder.

In calculating the points available for use with deposit slip PP2 for ration period number 9, a deduction will be made equivalent to 10 per cent. of the points deposited by retailers in the PP1 envelope in respect of ration period number 7. Thus the number of points available for use by retailers in period 9 will be the sum of the points carried forward from the deposit slip for ration period 8, and the points value of the coupons received during period 8, less 10 per cent. of the points deposited in PP1 envelope for ration period 7. The deduction will be entered as a *minus* quantity at (C) of part A of the deposit slip PP2.

"I note what you say": Repairs to the house, which were going on around us, included work on the air-raid shelter, which was being extended—downward: "This heavy labour has been undertaken after a somewhat critical examination of several places nearby where landmines fell—places where twenty or more houses have been swept into nothingness in one split second precisely. Nothing on the surface can survive in such a circle of destruction. But deep down, there's at least a chance."

As the NYPL records show, it was my reference to the cause of the destruction which was deleted by the censor. The so-called landmines, which added a new horror to the aerial bombardment of towns and cities, were massive metal containers, packed with high explosive, which floated down by parachute. From a reasonably safe distance (as luck would have it) I witnessed the descent of one of these monstrous blockbusters while standing at the entrance to our air-raid shelter, on the lookout for incendiaries. As the thing landed, there was a blinding orange flash, followed a few seconds later by a blast of air which swept me off my feet and flung me backward and down the shelter steps.

"There was a time": A photograph providing evidence of Mencken's bricklaying capabilities is to be found in Carl Bode's *Mencken* (plate 17).

July 12, 1943

Dear Mr. Cleator:

Your letter No. 26, dated June 11, reached me yesterday. I needn't tell you that I am delighted to hear that you have at last got your house in habitable shape. I can well imagine your difficulties. Even here in this great republic all sorts of building operations are now seriously impeded. There is no actual shortage of materials, but they are needed for military and other enterprises, and so the private builder fares badly. He has to make out endless forms in order to undertake the simplest repairs. In my own house at the moment a wooden beam holding up three courses of brick has broken through, and I am trying to get a small steel ell beam to replace it. My brother has already put in four or five days on the enterprise, but the ell beam is still non est. If we are lucky we'll probably get it by the end of the war, which, according to local opinion, will probably come about August 1.

My very best thanks for your notes. They are, as we say over here, swell indeed, and I am delighted to have them.

The heat for a month past has been infernal, but I have nevertheless managed to do a reasonable amount of work—as a matter of fact, I am always more comfortable when the temperature is above 70 than when it is below. The one thing that fetches me is high humidity. Unhappily, we have had plenty of it of late.

Yours,
H. L. Mencken

I had been able to announce that the elusive building licence which I had been diligently seeking for the past eighteen months had unexpectedly been granted—after three point-blank refusals: "As a result, the house is swarming with artisans and labourers, and the crash of falling ceilings smites my ears as I type. The dust is indescribable. We are, in brief, in one Hell of a mess. As for my time, it is mostly spent in carting furniture about from room to room, with hordes of wreckers in close pursuit. God knows when we'll be straight again. But I suppose it *is* possible. . . ."

In the meantime, Mencken's account of his own trials and tribulations in effecting even minor repairs had an all-too-familiar ring.

September 2, 1943

Dear Mr. Cleator:

Your letter No. 27 arrived safely this morning, along with an unmolested carbon of letter No. 26. The censors, I suppose, occasionally change their minds. In this great Republic the whole business of putting down false ideas seems to be in chaos. I frequently receive letters from officers who appear on the envelopes as their own censors! Not infrequently they actually do a little censoring inside—in a waggish spirit, of course.

I have decided not to build a bomb-proof [shelter] here in Baltimore. For one thing, it seems highly improbable that any of the current enemies of the country will ever be able to land explosives on the town. For another thing, I have been given access to the caves of a brewery not far from my house, and they promise to be not only quite safe, but also extremely comfortable. More than two thousand barrels of prime malt liquor are stored in them at this minute. How long that stock would last in case of serious air raids I don't know, but I assume that it would last at least a few weeks.

I surely hope that your own building operations are going ahead with reasonable dispatch, and that you are as comfortable as any one can be in such times. That questionnaire you sent me could be matched very easily on this side—in fact, I only lately filled one out myself that was at least twice as long. Its purpose was to find out whether I had any talents that would be useful to the government. After examining it with some care, I concluded rather sadly that I hadn't.

Hay fever has me by the ear, thanks be to God, and I am middling uncomfortable. The usual new and infallible cures appeared this year and I have discovered, also as usual, that they are frauds. I am now taking no treatment whatsoever, and feel fairly well. At all events, I am able to get in some hard licks on my projected supplement to "The American Language." When the time comes to deal with war words, I'll certainly make heavy use of your contributions. Our Heavenly Father will reward you for them in the life to come.

Sincerely yours,
H. L. Mencken

Apparently not all mail was scrutinized; or, if it was, it would seem that individual censors entertained different ideas on what constituted information likely to assist the enemy.

October 14, 1943

Dear Mr. Cleator:

Your letter No. 28 reached me safely yesterday, along with the carbon of No. 27. My very best thanks for those really marvelous clippings. As it happens, I am putting them to work instantly, for I am now in the midst of my projected supplement to "The American Language." Getting to work on it was incommoded by a bad attack of hay-fever, but I am now restored to normalcy and making fairly good progress. There is a really enormous accumulation of new materials, and I hope to make an amusing book.

The Churchill speech gave Basic English a tremendous lift in this great Republic. In the past it had been the toy of a small sect of pedagogues, and the great masses of plain people had not so much as heard of it. But now the newspapers are full of it, and I assume that the public schools will soon be teaching it to their poor victims. My own view of it is rather dubious. I believe that Ogden's verb scheme is really harder to master than the normal verb scheme of the language, and that writing intelligibly in Basic is actually very difficult, at least for the foreigner. However, we shall see.

I am grieved to hear that the enemies of democracy are at large in Britain. On this side of the water they have been driven into the sewers and free government prevails throughout the land. A citizen has but one duty, and that is to obey all official orders. When two of them happen to be contradictory he is supposed to obey both. We have a new income tax scheme that involves an amount of bookkeeping fit for a large bank. Last week I actually put in two whole working days trying to get my own accounts in order.

I certainly hope that you are in good health and spirits. Hay-fever this year was extraordinarily vicious, and so I am still a bit shaky. Nevertheless, I survived it, which is certainly something in these times.

My book will take me about a year, so I hope to bring it out in the Spring of 1945, God willing. Your prayers are solicited.

Sincerely yours,
H. L. Mencken

"The Churchill speech": Britain's Prime Minister Winston Churchill, acting in conjunction with America's President Roosevelt, had recently announced the setting up of a governmental committee to investigate the vocabularian possibilities of Basic English. This concept, the brainchild of the linguist Charles Kay Ogden, consisted of 850 selected words, including 18 simple verbs, 600 nouns, 150 adjectives, and a number of phrases. In later years, the story went the rounds that when Churchill's famous wartime speeches were thus represented, his well-known reference to "blood, sweat and tears" emerged in translation as "blood, body water and eyewash"!

"I am grieved to hear": I had announced a serious breach in the democratic process which had recently occurred in the City of Liverpool. Under a new governmental scheme, it was proposed to introduce a Block System for fireguards, as opposed to the existing arrangement under which office and other workers spent one night in eight guarding their own place of employment against aerial attack. Locally, those concerned received notice to attend a meeting to discuss the matter, in the course of which various objections were made to the suggested change. It was accordingly agreed to put the question to a vote, whereupon, without a single exception, those present decided *against* the new scheme. At this, the official who had called the meeting decreed that, the voting having gone against the plan, he would be forced to invoke the powers invested in him and make it compulsory. And so it came to pass.

November 29, 1943

Dear Mr. Cleator:

Your letter No. 29, dated November 8th, arrived this morning. That envelope enclosed is interesting indeed, and I shall certainly add it to my collection of souvenirs of the great struggle to save humanity.

My best thanks for the cuttings which, as always, are immensely interesting and useful. I am now knee-deep in my new book and making fair progress, despite a long series of petty illnesses. It will run to the length of "The American Language," and so I assume that it will keep me hopping until the end of 1944. I have so much new material accumulated that it is really appalling. There has been a large amount of writing on the subject in the Republic during the past five or six years, and I must somehow manage to digest it.

I had my worst hay fever season since 1869. Some of the brethren at the Johns Hopkins Medical School suggested that ascorbic acid might be helpful. I took it in truly enormous doses, running beyond a gram a day, but it did me no good whatsoever. The season was made especially horrible by the fact that there was a drought. As a result, the air was loaded with pollen. I managed to get through the horror by dint of earnest and even indignant prayer. Moreover, I employed a couple of colored clergymen to help me. The fact that I didn't perish was certainly not due to the medical brethren, so I am inclined to give full credit to those of the ghostly faculty.

The general view here seems to be that the war is now over—indeed, there is talk of getting the boys out of the trenches by Christmas. I am not quite so optimistic, but I am in hopes that it will not last for more than a few years longer, at least in Europe. In the Pacific it seems doomed to go on almost indefinitely, for as soon as the present round is over the Chinese will probably launch a civil war.

I trust that you are in good health and spirits. Despite my malaises, I continue to maintain a certain equanimity. My refuge in the beer cellar is waiting for me, but now the brewers have cut down their production enormously, and sound malt liquor actually grows scarce. This is something that never happened during Prohibition.

Yours,
H. L. Mencken

"That envelope": This was one of Mencken's own covers, addressed to me at Wallasey, which, at the first attempt, the postal authorities had been unable to deliver for the reason stated thereon—it bore the ominous inscription "Bombed."

"The general view here": A growing popular belief that the end of the war in Europe was in sight was not confined to the U.S., though, like Mencken, I found it difficult to entertain such unduly hopeful expectations. As I said in reply to his letter: "But for myself, I don't know. There were high hopes that it would be over last year, and the year before that. On the other hand, it hardly seems possible that any people can long endure bombing such as the German people are being called upon to endure. The bombing we had, God knows, was bad enough—200 tons, say, in the course of an eight hours' raid. But compare this with the 2,000 tons being dumped on German towns in 30 minutes! Knowing what we went through, it makes me sick at heart even to think about it. But protests such as mine are of no avail. The good work goes on. . . ."

December 24, 1943

Dear Mr. Cleator:

Your letter No. 30, dated November 23rd, reached me yesterday. My hay fever is now gone and forgotten, but it will return infallibly next Autumn and put me to the torture again. I ascribe all such afflictions to the personal enmity of the heavenly hierarchy. I have refused to put any money into the poor-box, and as a result I am persecuted.

The best of luck with the book! This is a good time to get such things together. After all, the war can't last into infinity, and soon or late there will be a search for lively and iconoclastic manuscripts. I am preparing one myself, and only hope that our Heavenly Father spares me long enough to complete it.

My best thanks for the additional clippings. I am always delighted to have them, and they are always useful. An enormous amount of your material has gone into my book already, and more will follow. At my present rate of progress I'll probably finish the job by the end of 1944.

I hope you are lucky in the New Year.

Sincerely yours,
H. L. Mencken

"The best of luck with the book!": This was a reference to my account of the fray, my notes for which had by this time reached astronomical proportions. I had reported making a start on the work: "I recently hurled a preliminary editing of it at my publishers, and am still awaiting their verdict. As it deals with the current slaughter, I shall not be surprised if they wisely decide to leave well alone, and so escape the Tower and the noose. Incidentally, I carted the MS. to London personally—my first visit since the war. Raid damage, generally, appears negligible—far less than is to be seen here. The explanation is the inconceivable vastness of the place. I ran slap into a raid when I was down there, but heard or saw little of it."

"I am preparing one myself": The news that Mencken himself was making a start on the compilation of a wartime *Americana* was not followed by any further reference to the project, and it would appear that it foundered somewhere along the way.

February 21, 1944

Dear Mr. Cleator:

Your letter No. 31 of January 26th reached me this morning. The surname of your Jewish friend from Vienna was cut out by the censor—on what ground I do not know, for it would have been meaningless to me. I certainly hope that the news you get from his son is not altogether bad. These are truly horrible days, and I hear constantly of disasters to old friends.

The general opinion in this country seems to be that the war is now in its last phase. I am not quite so optimistic, but I begin to believe that it may end soon or late. Unhappily, there will be uproars afterward, and they'll probably continue for years. I begin to wonder what the state of the American taxpayer will be when the total cost is reckoned up. The outpouring of money in this war makes that of the last war seem trivial.

I continue in relatively good health, and manage to get in a lot of hard work on my book. It has already gone to nearly 200,000 words, but inasmuch as it will run to at least 350,000, I still have a lot of work to do. The actual writing is not the worst of it. The hard part is the arranging of the materials. If all goes well, however, I should finish the job by the end of 1944. By that time, alas, my publisher will probably be out of paper. But I do not repine. We are all in the hands of our Heavenly Father, and must submit to His will and judgment. The book won't spoil. If it is not printed in 1945, it may very well lie over until 1946.

My best thanks for the cuttings. As always, they are extremely amusing and interesting. You will get florid credit in the preface to my book for all your valuable contributions to it.

Sincerely yours,
H. L. Mencken

"Your Jewish friend": He was a prosperous businessman and an amateur astronomer, who entertained some highly unorthodox notions about the conditions which existed on the lunar surface.* Though it perplexed me at the time, doubtless his surname was deleted in case of possible (if somewhat unlikely) word of it leading to repercussions within the confines of the Third Reich. If so, the good intentions of the censor were thwarted by the carbon copy of my letter which subsequently reached its destination unmarked. In it I had written: "Before the war I was in touch with a certain Josef Weisberger—by accident of birth a Jew, and an inhabitant of Vienna. When Adolf marched into

*He expounded these views at length in a paper entitled "The Riddle of the Earth-Moon Double Planet," but his thesis was ignored by professional astronomers as undeserving of serious attention. On his complaining that no one could be found who was prepared even to comment on his ideas, let alone attempt a refutation of them, I undertook their ventilation in the printed pages then at my disposal (JBIS-3). Sadly, Weisberger did not live to see his expectations dashed when America's Apollo XI mission landed on the moon in 1969, for he had perished a quarter of a century earlier in the Nazi extermination camp at Auschwitz.

Austria, Weisberger fled with his family to Prague. There, alas, he was subsequently swallowed up. The last I heard from him was a pathetic request to assist, not himself, but a lady secretary he'd been forced by circumstance to leave in Vienna. She spoke, it seems, eight or nine languages. The [immigration] laws of These Isles being what they are, I finally arranged for the lady to come here as a domestic servant. But before she contrived her escape, war came. I've often pondered her fate.

"The question may now be answered. For last week came a letter from one Emil Weisberger, a son of Joseph, and stationed with the Czechoslovak Forces here. He's spending a leave with us next month. . . ."

Emil Weisberger, who had obtained our address from my publishers, duly arrived, and I was afterward able to report: "He and his brother, it seems, escaped from Czechoslovakia by 'underground' to Egypt, and joined the Forces there. About his family, he has little news. His mother, he knows, is dead. His father, when he last had word of him more than a year ago, was seriously ill. His sister has been deported to Germany. And about his father's late secretary—the Fräulein Weiss I tried in vain to save—he knows nothing, but fears the worst. In brief, a tale almost too distressing to contemplate."

Although those members of the Weisberger family who remained entrapped in Europe did not survive the war, Emil and his brother Edouard did. Both now reside in Israel, where there have been several reunions between us on the occasion of visits we have made to the Middle East. Yet another happy sequel was news of the survival of Fräulein Weiss, who subsequently married and who still lives in Vienna.

"Work on my book": *Supplement I* of *The American Language*.

April 15, 1944

Dear Mr. Cleator:

Your letter No. 32, along with the carbon of No. 31 and the packet of newspaper cuttings, reached me safety [the] day before yesterday. What you tell me about Unwin and the book doesn't surprise me in the slightest. The publishing situation in this great free Republic is almost as bad. I was in New York a week ago, palavering with my own publisher, Knopf, about my projected supplement to "The American Language." He tells me that he'll have to give his printer at least six months to set it up, and that at the moment there seems to be no prospect whatsoever of getting it bound. However, he is still full of trust in our Heavenly Father, and so he hopes to finish the job one way or another. I have already accumulated more than 250,000 words of

PLATE 10. P. E. Cleator and friends. *(Above)* With Emil Weisberger *(right)* at the Cleator home in the Wirral Peninsula, sometime in the 1950s. What remark caused Cleator to close his eyes and throw back his head in mock repose is not now remembered, but it brought a smile to the face of his guest. *(Below)* With Mencken authority Carl Bode *(left)* in the garden of his residence at College Heights, Hyattesville, Maryland, in 1978.

manuscript. Some of it will probably have to wait for a second supplement in 1946—that is, if I am spared so long.

The newspapers here report that the war is virtually over, but I am still not altogether optimistic—in fact, I begin to suspect that it may last until the end of the year. There is no apparent food shortage here, and in the department of clothing everything is readily obtainable save a few items. Nevertheless, life grows more and more inconvenient. I receive questionnaires almost every day, some of them from government agencies, but the majority from volunteers banded together to annoy their neighbours. My waste-paper revenues become substantial. Needless to say, I always consecrate them to pious works.

My very best thanks for the cuttings, and for that circular in German. All such things are enormously interesting to me. Since the beginning of the war I have been collecting its literary oddities and passing them on to the New York Public Library, which is gradually amassing a really enormous collection. They will be valuable to the historians of the future—that is, if the laws permit historians.

I certainly hope that you are in good health and spirits. My own deterioration continues, but I yet manage to eat, drink, and work.

Yours,
H. L. Mencken

"Your letter No. 32": In it, I had conveyed the news that Allen & Unwin were unable to consider bringing out my *Sidelights on the Slaughter,* one compelling reason for their decision being an acute shortage of paper.

"That circular in German": This was entitled *Luftpost*. It was a propaganda leaflet, then being scattered over Berlin and other cities by the Royal Air Force. I had been given a copy of it by Arthur C. Clarke, at the time an officer in the RAF, who was spending a period of leave with us. With the prospect of peace looming, he, the late R. A. Smith, and myself were in the midst of planning the resurrection of the Interplanetary Society, which body had, of necessity, remained dormant since the start of the war.

May 15, 1944
Dear Mr. Cleator:
Your letter No. 33, dated April 5th, reached me this morning. The mails of late have been more regular than in the past, but there are still unaccountable delays. Whether or not they are

caused by the censors I do not know. It may be that the Post Office itself is remiss. Certainly it is doing very bad work in this great Republic. Sometimes it takes three or four days for a letter to reach me from New York.

I certainly hope that the military decision that you are unfit for field service does not mean that you are actually ill. If I were of draft age the American Army doctors would certainly turn me down, for my stomach is a wreck and my kidneys are mere shells. Nevertheless, I manage to eat, drink and be merry, and even to get a certain amount of work done.

In New York last week I encountered a large number of old newspaper colleagues, gathered there for the annual meeting of the Associated Press. I discovered that nine-tenths of them believe that the war is in its last stages. One offered to bet me that it would end by July 4th. The most pessimistic of them fixed the date of the armistice in November. I refuse to make prophecies, for I am not a gypsy.

I am still somewhat rocky, but still manage to get in a few licks on my book. It is about half done, and if all goes well I should be able to finish it by the end of the year. It is an extraordinarily tedious job, and I sometimes stand aside from it for a few moments and marvel that any man presumably sane would waste his time upon it. All the same, it holds me, and I really enjoy some of its worst pedantries.

Sincerely yours,
H. L. Mencken

"I certainly hope": The imminent prospect of my being jailed because of my anti-war stance had suddenly receded. I had received a summons to attend a medical center, and as an otherwise law-abiding citizen, I duly presented myself for a physical examination whose criteria, though by no means outstandingly high, I failed to satisfy.

Regarding the concern Menckin expressed about my general health, I was able to reply: "Despite the verdict of the medical fraternity, I contrive to get along and around. I have positively no wind—but then, I never have had, not since the day the Almighty let me loose on this ball."

"The war is in its last stages": Although the signs were that the fighting in Europe seemed likely to come to an end in the foreseeable future, putting a date on the outbreak of peace remained a hazardous enterprise which tended to be unduly tinged with optimism, here as in the U.S.: "I hope you took that bet about the current Crusade coming to its divinely appointed end by July 4th. At this end of the Universe, tales reach me of a Hebrew gentleman touring the country with a ten-to-one offer that all will be over in Europe before the end of September next. It may be that he has information of a private nature from On High. If I happen to catch up with him, I'll risk fifty dollars for each of us. For I think he's wrong—and I'd gladly expend a few dollars to find that he's right."

June 30, 1944

Dear Mr. Cleator:

Your letter No. 34 dated May 25th reached me this morning. My very best thanks for the additional war words. Some of them are even feebler than the earlier ones. The same thing is to be said of the neologisms produced in this great Republic. For some reason unknown, the brethren seem to be unable to invent anything really pungent. I leave the problem to the psychologists.

As an American, I am really astonished by that English income tax form. Compared to our own, it seems beautifully simple and clear. The document sent to taxpayers last year was really appalling—in fact, it was so appalling that Congress had to pass a special act in an attempt to simplify it. Any taxpayer in this country is free to go to the income tax office and get the assistance of one of the staff experts. Various wags went to six or eight experts in order, and all of them reported that no two agreed as to the amount of tax due. My own return was guesswork and nothing else. I put down what seemed to me to be reasonable and fair and am now waiting for a visit from one of the inspectors.

I note further that the English income tax makes allowances that are quite unknown on this side—for example, for insurance premiums, for dependents who are not children, and for children who are in school. Also, the penalties listed for errors and omissions are much less severe than ours. It is perfectly possible for an American who overlooks an item to be sent to prison for as much as five years. Moreover, it has been done.

There is no actual shortage of food in the United States, but the quality of the victuals offered seems to be deteriorating. It is now really difficult to get sound meat, and most of the canned things are decidedly inferior in quality. I don't care much, for I can eat anything from oats to fried rats.

My book is making slow but steady progress. My publisher already has a small part of it in hand and is fevering himself with calculations about paper, printing costs and so on. The temperature at the moment is in the 90's with a relative humidity of nearly 100. Thus I assume that he is doing some sweating.

Sincerely yours,
H. L. Mencken

"I am really astonished": The copy of the income tax form I sent to Mencken was intended as a curiosity. How, in the absence of the necessary document, I managed to render unto Caesar an account of my financial affairs for the year recently ended, I do not now remember.

"There is no actual shortage": This reference to the food situation which existed in the U.S., as was to be expected, compared very favorably with that prevailing in the British Isles: "Most of the things which I used to enjoy, and upon which I used more or less to thrive, have been unobtainable for years. We exist on a curious mixture of cardboard and bread, and on potatoes. Much of the stuff sold at fabulous prices as cake is uneatable. Even the water is not the same, for the softening process has been discontinued."

July 4, 1944

Dear Mr. Cleator:

Your packet of temperance tracts reached me safely and I have been going through them with the greatest interest and, so I hope, a considerable edification. One thing I note at once, to wit, that the English Prohibitionists are considerably less ferocious than their American colleagues. In this great Republic the crusade against rum was almost wholly a crusade against brewers, distillers and their customers. It was immensely vituperative. I can testify to this as a frequent victim. I had a lot of fun with the brethren by paying them back in their own coin. Also, I occasionally invented bogus statistics to match their own. The battle went on here from 1910 or thereabouts until the final overthrow of Prohibition in 1932. There was never a minute during these 22 years when it lagged.

The Prohibitionists are now attempting to revive the holy cause, but without much success—that is to say, there seems to be but small prospect that Prohibition will be restored to the Constitution. But I should add at once that some of its worst practical effects are already achieved. There is an enormous shortage of distilled liquors and sound beer is becoming scarcer and scarcer. The Methodists are now trying to get through an act prohibiting the sale of even the mildest beer on military reservations. Some of their leaders tell me that they have genuine hopes of success. Certainly I'd not be surprised myself if they scared Congress into giving them what they want. American politicians are the worst cowards on earth. They always follow the bandwagon.

I have been enjoying my usual rocky health and making somewhat slow progress with my book. I am hoping to get a week's holiday beginning next Sunday. Whether or not it will buck me up remains to be seen.

Sincerely yours,
H. L. Mencken

The temperance tracts I showered upon Mencken evidently brought back vivid recollections of the twelve years, ten months, and nineteen days of the Prohibition horror (as he termed the hiatus, in his *Heathen Days*) which afflicted the U.S. from 1922–33.

"I have been enjoying": Ominously, the slight stroke Mencken had suffered in 1939 was repeated in 1942, and again in mid-1944, in addition to which the condition of his heart was also giving cause for concern.

August 2, 1944

Dear Mr. Cleator:

Your letter No. 35, of July 11, along with the carbon of No. 34, reached me this morning. My very best thanks for the clippings: they are, as we say in the Republic, swell indeed. You detect many interesting items that elude the otherwise excellent Durrant. I begin to suspect that his service may be incommoded by the troubles of the times. On this side the clipping agencies are in a state of suspended animation.

So am I, thanks to various misfortunes. My secretary, with me for 14 years, is seriously ill, and my office is in chaos. I fell down stairs a couple of weeks ago, and am still sore. All my old war wounds hurt, and there is a revival of malaises quiescent since the 80's. Finally, the weather has been infernal for weeks past, with high temperatures and even higher humidity. At this moment the mercury stands at 94, and there are squeezes of rain every few minutes. Thus my book is shelved, and I pant and complain. But Jahveh is deaf.

Barring some incredible and irrational act of God, Roosevelt will be reelected in November. I shall vote for him on the ground that the American taxpayer deserves him. Dewey is a worthy man, but lacks the power to inspire the proletariat. Some one habitable. God knows I hope there will be no repetition of the bombing. The newspapers here indicate that the war will probably end tomorrow or next day.

I have finished my first volume of my projected supplement to "The American Language." Unfortunately I have had to postpone all discussion of war words to the second volume, which will follow in about a year. Volume 1, if all goes well, should be published in the spring. I'll see that you get an early copy of it.

Mrs. Lohrfinck has been discharged from hospital at last but she is still somewhat weak and I fear that it will be a month or more before she can return to full-time work. She had a really desperate illness and her recovery seemed hopeless until her doctors put her on Penicillin. It produced an almost miraculous effect.

Hayfever this year was the most dreadful seen in America since the days of Columbus. I am still somewhat dilapidated but nevertheless manage to work. I am certainly looking forward to seeing you in England as soon as the war is over. I'll be a passenger aboard the first ship that sails.

Sincerely yours,
H. L. Mencken

"I'll be aboard": Mencken's declared intention of taking the first ship bound for England as soon as peace was declared sounded promising. But in the past, plans to bring about a meeting between us had developed a habit of miscarrying, and this latest proposal was to prove no exception.

October 30, 1944

Dear Mr. Cleator:

This is the first letter that Mrs. Lohrfinck has written since her return to work. She became ill in July and has been out of service ever since. Save for a lingering weakness, she now feels perfectly normal.

I have just finished the first supplement of "The American Language." Unhappily, the paper shortage will make it impossible to bring out the book before January 1st. The galley proofs are already running, but the Index and the horrible list of Words and Phrases are still to be done. I faltered so often I doubt that the book would have ever been finished if it had not been for the prayers of my pastor. He is a man of high talents, and when he settles down to wrestle with the Holy Ghost there is usually a happy result.

My best thanks for the cuttings. I am delighted that you are once more aided in your night-prowling by street illumination. Here in this country the craze for blackouts lasted but a short while, but during that time Baltimore was in a state of chaos.

I began to realize that the war is in its last stages. If all goes well, it will end in three or four years at most. That will take up very neatly into Roosevelt's fifth term. As I write, it seems likely that he will be reelected with a substantial majority. There is, to be sure, a movement toward Dewey, but unfortunately it is not sufficient to elect him. There, again, I see the hand of God.

Sincerely yours,
H. L. Mencken

"Your night-prowling": The reference to this activity was occasioned by my intimating that "the one piece of news from this part of the world is the triviality that the street lamps are actually to be seen lit at night. After five years of complete blackout, you've no idea what it means to walk along a lighted street once more. And in keeping with this indication that the slaughter in Europe is nearing its end, I've decided to omit sending copies of previous letters. . . ."

December 6, 1944

Dear Mr. Cleator:

My best thanks for those clippings. The numberings on your letters somewhat resemble those of my check book. Every now and then I get into such confusion that I must begin the numerations with a new 100.

Mrs. Lohrfinck is now completely recovered. I am myself in the last stages of a severe head infection. It floored me for four or five days, but the proofs of my new book were running and so I entertained myself with making the two indexes.

The bagpipe cure for asthma is well known to the American faculty. Unfortunately, a local law in Maryland forbids the possession of bagpipes. The penalty is ten days in jail, and for a second offense ten strokes with a birch. This is a refined community, and such disturbances are not tolerated.

It is difficult even in this great Republic to get hold of necessary clothes. Silk socks, which were my one luxury, are now completely unavailable, and those that survive in my wardrobe are a mass of darns. I may have to turn to wool or cotton in the near future. It is a dreadful prospect. Shirt-tails are short and it is hard to get material for shirts. I figure that my supply will last until Spring. After that, if necessary, I'll go naked.

The first volume of my Supplement is now finished, but the two indexes remain. They present extraordinary difficulties and they'll probably keep me jumping until the end of the year. Why a sane man should engage in such pedantries I simply can't tell you. It is the will of God, and I don't repine.

Sincerely yours,
H. L. Mencken

"The numbering of your letters": I had found it necessary to draw attention to an inexplicable mathematical mix-up: my two previous communications had each been given the number 37!

"The bagpipe cure": I had come across a report of this infallible remedy in the columns of a newspaper, and hastened to pass it on: "Your mention of the hayfever epidemic reminds me that a sure and certain cure was published in the *Sunday Express* for November 5th. It was from a reader. I quote: 'A friend who suffered from asthma started to play the bagpipes, and has had no symptoms since, 24 years ago.' True, it is asthma that is specifically mentioned. But the effect on hayfever, I suggest, should be no less desirable. The rest of Hollins Street, I daresay, will without dissent petition that the cure is most certainly worse than the disease. And so it would be—for them."

"It is difficult": This was Mencken's contribution to an exchange of laments on the then prevailing clothing situation. My own jeremiad: "I myself am wearing pre-war socks that are more darn than original sock. New socks not only require clothing coupons for their purchase, but are useless when bought. Thanks to a Board of Trade ruling, they reach to the ankle, and no more. The shopkeepers, I imagine, sell very few socks. I've yet to meet a self-respecting man who wears the utility article. It is much the same with other garments. Shirts? Three times-prewar price, one quarter the quality of material, no double cuffs, and a tail that would shame a Manx cat. Shoes? I've just had a pair soled and heeled. The soles leak. And no wonder, for they're made of what appears to be rather poor quality cardboard. Tailor-made suits? Beyond my pocket and patience. Three months wait and a price that produces a gasp—for comparative trash. But enough, I could fill pages with such complaints."

January 25, 1945

Dear Mr. Cleator:

Your letter of December 9th has just come in. I am especially touched by your good offices in the matter of the Wallasey Fire Guard Association. I needn't tell you that I greatly appreciate the honor of membership. When, as and if I get to Wallasey at last, it will be a pleasure to address the Association on the issues of the hour.

Thanks very much for the additional cuttings. My debt to you now mounts to astronomical proportions. My book is finished, but the business of seeing it through the press remains. The two long indexes probably run to a hundred pages in fine type. Preparing them was dreadful indeed. Fortunately, I was sustained throughout by the heavenly powers, and have emerged from the job with no more damage than after returning home after seventeen years' service in the trenches.

God help us one and all.

Sincerely yours,
H. L. Mencken

"Wallasey Fire Guard Association": If I remember aright, when exhorted to join this worthy body, I resisted the temptation and diverted the membership application form by express post to Baltimore.

February 19, 1945

Dear Mr. Cleator:

Your unnumbered but always welcome letter of January 14th came in safely yesterday. I needn't tell you that I am delighted to have the additional notes on war terms and other such novelties. The first Supplement to my "American Language" is now in the hands of the printer. All discussion of slangs and argots have had to be postponed to Volume II, which is not due until next year. I am in hopes of having a copy of Volume I by the end of April. It will be dispatched to you at once. You will note by the Index that my debt to you is extremely heavy. You are mentioned over and over again, and in many places your excellent material is used without any mention.

Now that the war is over, we are promised better food service in this great Republic. Unhappily, this has not begun. Meats are extremely scarce along the Atlantic Coast. Also, there is a great shortage of materials for shirts. This last doesn't bother me much, for I still have two excellent shirts in stock, and while one is being washed I wear the other. But there are various victuals that I crave powerfully, and I'll be delighted to see them again.

Despite my advanced age and long life of sin, I seem to be holding up pretty well. I am putting in some hard work on my accumulated miscellaneous notes. They fill many drawers of a large chest. I am hoping to reduce them to printable form and at some future time may try to assemble them in a volume or two.

They include much saucy stuff, some of which would probably be indiscreet in war time.

Yours,
H. L. Mencken

The reference above to my letter of January 14th was a typographical error, presumably on Mrs. Lohrfinck's part. For 14th, read 15th.

"Now that the war is over": Here, Mencken was anticipating somewhat. At the time he wrote, the fighting in Europe had yet to continue for nearly three months, and in the Pacific for as long again. Even so, the early ending of the prevailing food and other shortages may have been in sight in the U.S., but in the meantime I had expressed a malign satisfaction on learning that the situation was still far from normal: "I'm delighted to learn that your socks are also a mass of darns. I'd be even happier to learn that you too are restricted to 2½ pounds of potatoes a week. With me, the potato restriction is something of a calamity, for I've been living on potatoes for years. There remains the lawn, and thereafter the worms beneath. When those are done, I shall be really stuck."

"Despite my advanced age": Although Mencken claimed to be holding up pretty well, his medical history shows (CB-1) that by this time his series of slight apoplectic attacks had adversely affected his mental capabilities, and that he was also troubled by double vision.

April 2, 1945

Dear Mr. Cleator:

You don't mention precisely what that surgery was. I certainly hope and pray to God that it is not of a scandalous nature. I hope, also, that by the time these few lines reach you will it be all over and half-forgotten. Let me hear about it when you feel like writing again.

Now that the war is over, its burdens in this great Republic seem to grow heavier than while it was in progress. There are shortages of various foodstuffs—not really serious but still sufficient to be a nuisance. I do not care much, for I am one of those fortunate persons who can eat absolutely anything. So far I have not tried cannibalism, but I assume that if I ever confronted it I'd swing into it without a qualm.

My book has been set up and electrotyped for weeks and months, but so far my publisher has been unable to obtain the necessary paper. He is in hopes of procuring it by July. If he succeeds he'll bring the volume out early in the Autumn. If not, it may have to go over until 1946.

I am planning to leap aboard the first passenger boat that sails for Liverpool.

> Yours,
> H. L. Mencken

When making reply to Mencken's earlier letter of January 25, I had mentioned in passing that I was booked for some more surgery ("nothing unduly serious"), and in a subsequent note supplied some of the pathological details, in anticipation of his expression of curiosity and concern: "The trouble? An outsize specimen of the feminine of hisnia, to wit, hernia—got, I suspect, by too lusty a bawling of 'Onward! Christian Soldiers' to the tune of 'John Brown's Body,' in tango tempo."

"I am planning": In the acknowledgment above referred to, I also reverted to the question of Mencken's forthcoming visit to Merseyside, and to the eternal problem of what he would find to eat when he arrived: "When your ship finally docks in Liverpool, I'll have the Wallasey Fire Guard Association pump the Mersey dry in your honour, that you may walk across dry shod, and so reach these parts troubled neither by Ferry nor Underground (Subway?). The signs are that the European slaughter will reach its divinely appointed end at any time now. And thereafter, we certainly hope to see you soon. What you'll eat it would be unwise to predict. There *may* be a potato or two left in the land by the time you reach here. Of a few things, indeed, there's actually a surplus—dried egg powder, for example. The Ministry of Food spends thousands of pounds a year in a laudable endeavour to persuade people to use it—if possible, with every meal. Alas, it remains in the shops, musty and unmourned."

(Chromatic note: Unlike the customary white of the writing paper he had invariably used in the past, Mencken's epistle of April 2 was pink in color, concerning which I commented: "Your new notepaper is certainly a wow, and owes its inception, I assume, to the Russian victories in the hated Fatherland. It caused a blink or two when I first opened your letter [of April 2nd] this morning. But it is now evening, and I'm able to peruse it without fear of dazzle.")

April 20, 1945

Dear Mr. Cleator:

It doesn't surprise me to hear of your post operative troubles. The butchery for hernia is always represented by the chiropractors as a simple thing, but actually it throws the patient into a very uncomfortable state. Fortunately, its discomforts pass off eventually, and by that time the victim has a tight hull and begins his second time on earth. I certainly hope that the hemorrhages have quit and that you are beginning to return to normalcy. When, as and if we ever meet, I shall give you a long and intricate account of my own adventures with suppressed functions. The climax was really very dramatic.

My very best thanks for the cuttings. My debt to you mounts to truly astronomical heights. You will find some acknowledgement of it in my Supplement I to "The American Language"—that is, if the book ever actually comes out. It has been in type since Christmas, but my publisher has been unable so far to obtain the paper he needs to print it. He is full of hopes that he'll get it during the Summer and that he'll thus be able to publish the book by the end of August. But I am not too sure.

So far Roosevelt's will has not been published, but I doubt seriously that he has left me anything. More anon.

Sincerely yours,
H. L. Mencken

This was Mencken's reply to a postoperative report which, as in duty bound, I had earlier submitted for consideration and comment: "I've just landed back home, with the aid of an ambulance, for I may as well lie up here as in a nursing home. But the first week was pretty grim. When I came to, I felt as though someone had dug a hole in my middle with a garden spade, and then filled the cavity with hot sand. There had, moreover, been internal haemorrhage on a grand scale. I was possessed, indeed, of a blood-red udder that would have shamed a cow. I'm still mighty swollen, and still bleeding, so they warn me. But one must make *some* sort of movement at some time or other. As if this were not enough, I discovered, some hours later, a complete inability to perform one of Nature's simplest, and yet most vital, functions—shock, I guess. This lasted for just over three days, during which I was milked at necessary intervals. The procedure is doubtless familiar to you, and I'll waste no words describing its horrors. Meanwhile, the nursing sisters set to work on me in earnest, and with a determination that at times approached the comic. They loaded me with drinks—hot drinks, cold drinks, acid drinks . . . all sorts of damn drinks. They gave me lemons to suck. They left taps running, well within earshot, for hours on end (this alleged remedy, it seems, is supposed to be based on a well known psychological fact). And finally, they gave me hypodermic injections, dozens of them, of a substance rejoicing in the name of carbaminoylcholine chloride. Well, as I have said, I resisted (albeit most unwillingly) for three days. And when relief finally came, I could at first hardly believe it. Ah, micturition!"

As any first-year medical student will at once perceive, the procedure described in the above account is now outdated in at least one important aspect. In those unenlightened days, it was *de rigueur* for a hernia patient to remain flat on his back for a period of at least three weeks after the surgeon had done with him—on the grounds, presumably, that undue movement might give rise to a renewed extrusion. As one who has recently undergone this operative procedure for a third time, I am happy to be able to report that the interminable lying-in routine has now been abandoned, for on this last occasion I was hauled out of bed and made to indulge in a painful walkabout within hours of regaining consciousness. Another vast improvement to be observed was in the realm of general anesthesia. Nowadays, a preparatory intravenous injection, in the guise of a prick on the back of the hand with the needle of a hypodermic syringe loaded with barbiturate, suffices pleasantly to produce almost instant loss of consciousness, as opposed to the inceptive use of a face mask exuding suffocative fumes of nitrous oxide, diethyl ether, cyclopropane, and the like—at one time or another in days gone by, I've been asphyxiated and nauseated by them all.

"My own adventure": Alas, failing our long proposed meeting, I never did hear Mencken's account of his experiences with suppressed functions. Doubtless what he had in mind was the occasion of which he makes mention in a letter (CB-1) written to Carl Van Vechten in 1939. In this he refers to "Dr. Howard Smith, of the Johns Hopkins, one of the ornaments of the craft. He spayed me a couple of years ago, and I am now a new man."

May 25, 1945

Dear Mr. Cleator:

My best thanks for that very interesting cutting from the *Liverpool Echo*. It tells me a lot of things that I was completely ignorant of. I am passing it on to my brother, who is an engineer and greatly interested in the subject.

Now that the war is over, the great wizards who ruined the United States seem to have increased rather than ameliorated transportation difficulties. Why this should be I can't tell you, but it is apparently the will of God. I shall not travel the Atlantic until I can do so in complete comfort. There is nothing worse on this earth than a crowded sea voyage, as I can testify by bitter personal experience. Let us be patient.

My best thanks for the additional cuttings. They are valuable indeed, and I am always delighted to have them. I certainly hope that you have recovered completely, and have resumed in full blast a life of sin.

Sincerely yours,
H. L. Mencken

"Let us be patient": Somewhat ominously, Mencken's earlier expressed intention "to leap aboard the first passenger boat that sails for Liverpool" had now been replaced by a desire to make the journey in comfort and at a later date. In the event, it was not destined to be undertaken at all.

June 15, 1945

Dear Mr. Cleator:

I assume that it will not astonish you to hear that now that the war is over and humanity is saved once more, the restrictions on travel are even worse than they were while the show was going on. No one can move off the American coast without a series of papers fit for a papal legate. I have applications in at forty or fifty different offices in Washington, but I am not hopeful of any favorable action until late in 1949. The American jobholder was an irritating fellow even in the days when he was a rarity. Now that he numbers nearly four million head, he becomes an uncrackable nut.

I sure hope that Unwin finds the paper for your two books. Here in America the shortage seems to be worse than ever. My publisher hints that he hopes to get my Supplement I on the press within the next week or two, but I fear that he is only talking to keep up his own courage. There is actually no prospect of getting the book out for months and months.

History will probably record that the death of Roosevelt plunged this great Republic into inconsolable grief, though that will be a considerable exaggeration. As a matter of fact, there was a great deal more relief than despair, at least among the more literate classes. Truman so far has played a cautious game, but Washington seems to be full of hopes that in the long run he will rid it of the Marxian quacks that now infest it. That, of course, may take a couple of years, for a Socialist once in office hangs on like a wood-tick.

I hope you are in reasonably good health and spirits. The weather here at the moment is truly infernal, so I feel pretty brisk. I can always work best when I am sweating like an archbishop.

Sincerely yours,
H. L. Mencken

"Unwin": Allen & Unwin, my London publishers. The dire paper shortage which Mencken reported as existing in the U.S. was more than matched by the situation in England, where the dearth of this essential material was to remain acute for several years. Of the two books of mine referred to, supplies were immediately forthcoming for neither of them.

"Truman": Harry S. Truman, successor at the White House to President Roosevelt, whose sudden death had occurred on April 12.

("The answer is YES!": A slip of paper bearing these printed words had been pasted in the top left-hand corner of Mencken's letter. Since he makes no reference to it in his note, its meaning must forever remain unclear—unless some perceptive student of American affairs can explain its significance).

July 13, 1945

Dear Mr. Cleator:

The best of luck with the book. I only hope that after it is accepted it doesn't encounter the difficulties that now afflict mine. I turned in my manuscript last Autumn and my book was set up before the end of the year, but the lack of paper to print it is still unrelieved. However, I am in hopes that my publisher will find some in the not too distant future.

Why common victuals should be so scarce in this great Christian Republic I simply can't tell you. Explorers in the far West report that the cattle ranges are swarming with cattle. Nevertheless, meat is almost unobtainable along the Atlantic Coast. I have not, in fact, tasted beef for months, and the supplies of pork, veal and lamb have been reduced to mere shadows. I don't care much, for I am really omnivorous and can eat anything short of anthracite coal, but the situation is a tremendous affliction to housekeepers.

I have decided to remain on this side of the ocean until travel is really comfortable again. I am now too old for hardships and, moreover, I object to them on philosophical grounds.

Let me hear about the book as soon as you have any news. I am very eager to see it. The censorship is still so strict in this country that it is simply impossible for me to do any writing on public events. Before I had got to the end of the first page I'd be on my way to jail. Jail life used to appeal to me as romantic, but that was long, long ago.

God help every honest man, if any.

Yours,
H. L. Mencken

The book above referred to was *Sidelights on the Slaughter,* my irreverent history of the fray just ended, the MS of which I had once more taken to London in a vain search (as I later reported) for "an interested publisher with paper to spare—a seemingly impossible combination."

"I have decided": This further delay in his making the proposed crossing of the Atlantic may well have been brought about by my reply to Mencken's earlier note on the subject: "There is certainly no reason for rushing to These Isles before you can travel in comfort, and my guess is that the trip won't be desirable before 1945 has run into 1946. By then, perhaps, you'll be able to get something to eat when you arrive here."

August 7, 1945

Dear Mr. Cleator:

A copy of Supplement I to "The American Language" is on its way to you. If it doesn't reach you within a reasonable time, let me know and I'll complain to the League of Nations. The book, after long and vexatious delays, came out rather unexpectedly. My publisher looked for serious trouble in the bindery, but it did not develop.

I surely hope that those abdominal pains are passing off. Patients always underestimate the kick of surgery. When they get out of hospital they assume that they are restored to normalcy. This, unhappily, is a false view. I have been told by good surgeons that it takes on the average of a full year to get rid of the damage done by the knife.

I am choking with hay-fever vaccines, but they don't give me much hope. In a couple of weeks I'll probably be badgered, as usual. The physical discomfort is not very great, but I am always alarmed by the effects upon my psyche. Not to put too fine a point upon it. I curse and swear like an archbishop. Thus I always emerge from hay fever full of an uneasy feeling that my soul has been imperilled. Moreover, all of the clergy of my acquaintance agree that this is probably the case.

The result of the English elections surprised everyone in this great free Republic. We all thought that Churchill had the situation well in hand. I assume that Laski is boss of the country and that efforts will be made at once to drive the United States into the Marxian orbit. Whether they succeed or fail I don't care a damn. One government, it seems to me, is just as bad as the other. That is certainly true over here.

God help all honest men, say I.

Sincerely yours,
H. L. Mencken

"Those abdominal pains": I had been experiencing considerable discomfort in the region of the incision, and the torment, far from showing signs of abating, grew steadily worse until it became almost unendurable. At this, I dragged myself off to the surgeon who had undertaken the blood-letting, "to enquire what the so-and-so he'd done. It appears that I'm suppurating internally at the site of the incision, thanks to the use of silk suture instead of gut. His theory is that, given time, it'll clear itself. My theory is that it'd better hurry up!"

"The English elections": In the voting which had taken place the month before, Winston Churchill had unexpectedly been defeated by Clement Attlee, leader of the Labour party.

"Laski": Harold Joseph Laski, a prominent English political scientist and socialist.

August 21, 1945

Dear Mr. Cleator:

I certainly hope that those horrible pains have passed off. An infection in an incision is a really hellish thing. The silk sutures were really probably not to blame, for the same unpleasantness often follows the use of gut. I hope that by the time these lines reach you you'll be comfortable again. My chaplain is on his knees in your interest, and I encourage him ever and anon by giving him a smart tap on the head with a walking-cane.

Supplement I to "The American Language" was dispatched to you on August 5th. If it has not reached you, let me know and I'll file a protest with the League of Nations. The mails have been improving of late, but are still very far from perfect. Here in the United States those between New York and Baltimore seem to be carried by ox-cart. It sometimes takes three days to get a letter, and more than a week to get a parcel. All these inconveniences are to be ascribed to the hellish wickedness of the infidel Japs.

Sincerely yours,
H. L. Mencken

Although it would have been churlish to suppose that Mencken's ecclesiastical assistant was giving other than of his best, I was unable to announce any apparent response to his impassioned supplications: "I regret to report that the efforts of your chaplain on my behalf have so far been in vain. The surgeon seems loath to resort to the scalpel again, and has expressed the hope that the infected suture will ultimately find its way to the surface, and so lend itself to a gentle pulling out. All I pray is that it happens soon. At the time of this fevered writing, I'm nursing a lump the size of a governmental hen egg, and it's giving me Hell. I know your prayers will continue. . . ."

September 15, 1945

Dear Mr. Cleator:

I am sorry indeed to hear that my book has not reached you. A copy dispatched by the same post seems to have been delivered to H. W. Seaman in Norwich very promptly. It may be that you are under suspicion as an infidel, and that your copy is being examined page by page by the censors. If so, I hope they find profit and illumination in it.

Let me hear of the result of that surgery. I am distressed indeed to see you still in the hands of the bloodletters, and only hope that they have made a good job of it at least. My hay-fever this year has been extraordinarily virulent, and at the moment I am somewhat depleted, and indeed almost despairing. Despite enormous doses of the vaccines, I got no relief whatever.

I certainly hope the book reaches you in time to spiritualize your convalescence.

Sincerely yours,
H. L. Mencken

Prior to receiving this note, I had been able to announce that the protest to the League of Nations, earlier contemplated, need not now be made: "By a happy coincidence, your letter of August 21st and the copy of *Supplement I* came in together. I've had time as yet to do no more than glance at the book but it promises to keep me intellectually alive throughout the coming Winter. I hope to let you have my comments later. You are very kind in your remarks about the few contributions I was able to make. The monumental nature of the work, and the tremendous amount of labour it must have involved, appals me. The task of collating so much material would take me a hundred years, not including the Index."

October 2, 1945

Dear Mr. Cleator:

I hope that infected suture clears up and, meanwhile, I hope you don't take it too seriously. Such things are always badgering the surgical brethren, and they have learned by long and bitter experience to let them alone as much as possible. My late wife suffered from one for months, but in the end it disappeared completely. It is really amazing that they are so few. Certainly a suture can't be quite aseptic; nevertheless, it is only seldom that one of them cuts loose.

I needn't tell you that I'll be delighted to have your notes on Supplement I. It is full of minor errors, and also shows a few major ones. The third edition is now on the press.

My very best thanks for the cuttings. As always, they are amusing and valuable. I hope to discuss war terminology at length in my second Supplement. Unless angels visit me in my dreams and bring me a divine mandate to begin at once, I shall postpone tackling it until next Spring. In the meantime, I am hard at work on various other things, most of them useless.

           Yours,
           H. L. Mencken

I had in the meantime imparted the news that although the contaminated suture had at last emerged, the suppuration nevertheless continued: "If you got the postcard which I sent chasing after my last letter [of September 18th], you'll know that I blew a stitch the day after my writing. But it would seem that I whooped too soon. At all events, the scene of the infection still rises and falls with the tides, and I'm beginning to wonder just how many sutures are infected. I hope, meanwhile, that you'll get that Rev. of yours to work again. I've great faith in his powers of persuasion over the Almighty."

To this request, I now found it necessary to plead for an abatement: "Your letter of October 2nd arrived about two weeks ago, but until today, alas, I've been too ill to tackle it. The old trouble—complicated, according to the diagnosis of my medical friend, hastily summoned last Sunday, by a nine-tenths intestinal blockade. At the moment, two methods of persuasion are being tried—constant fomentations and aperients by the gallon. Were I by birth a Red Indian, my nickname would undoubtedly be Running Water. In my last letter I remarked upon the success of your chaplain. Since then, three more sutures emerged in quick succession. I am persuaded that it is now time that he be prevailed upon to request the Lord to moderate His bounty. If I drop any more stitches, the odds are I'll fall apart. . . ."

           October 22, 1945

Dear Mr. Cleator:

I predict formally that by the time you receive these lines that stitch abscess will be gone forever. Such things hang on in an exasperating way, but soon or late they depart. I have added a third chaplain to my staff, and am plying him with corn liquor from the wilds of the Great Smoky Mountains. It contains 80 per cent methylated spirits, which appears to have a powerful effect upon the rev. clergy.

My best thanks for those incredible directives from the Postal and Telegraph censors. Here in the United States there was apparently nothing of the sort—mainly, I suppose, because all sorts of correspondence was prohibited. The American authorities proceeded on the assumption that every third citizen of the Republic was in the pay of the Japs. To the best of my knowledge and belief, this was an exaggeration.

I am hard at work upon a revision of my old book, "Treatise on the Gods." The first four sections can stand almost unchanged, but the fifth needs rewriting. I am trying to get into it some indication of my spiritual progress since the great war to save humanity began.

I am certainly glad that I am not in Wallasey at this minute. It is not that I fear murder, but that I fear the charge of it. I only hope that the criminal is taken at once, and that it turns out that he is a faithful Presbyterian.

Sincerely yours,
H. L. Mencken

"I predict formally": This was a prognostication which proved to have some substance, as (on November 20) I was now able to disclose: "Since writing my letter of November 2nd I've contrived to pick up somewhat, and have even ventured to dismiss the hearse from the door. But I'm still not too well, and my guess is that I'll be booked for some more surgery in the months ahead. Your three chaplains, I know, will be set to petitioning the Lord from now on, and I share your faith in their influence upon Him. If at the same time they could contrive to get me a few extra clothing coupons. . . ."

"I am hard at work": As I placed on record at the time, I was highly delighted to receive the news of the impending revision of *Treatise on the Gods:* "I've very fond memories of it indeed, for it was the first of your books I happened upon, and I well remember the incredulous delight with which I turned page after page. It seemed to me then—as it seems to me now—as though my very thoughts about such high matters had somehow been extracted from my mind, and set down with a knowledge and ability I could wistfully envy, but never hope to approach."

In the event, a copy of the revised version of the work was dispatched almost exactly a year later—on October 3, 1946—duly inscribed "This is my best book, though I'll probably have to go to Hell for it." It reached me at the end of the month, in a parcel which also contained another Mencken classic, sent "With Christian greetings"

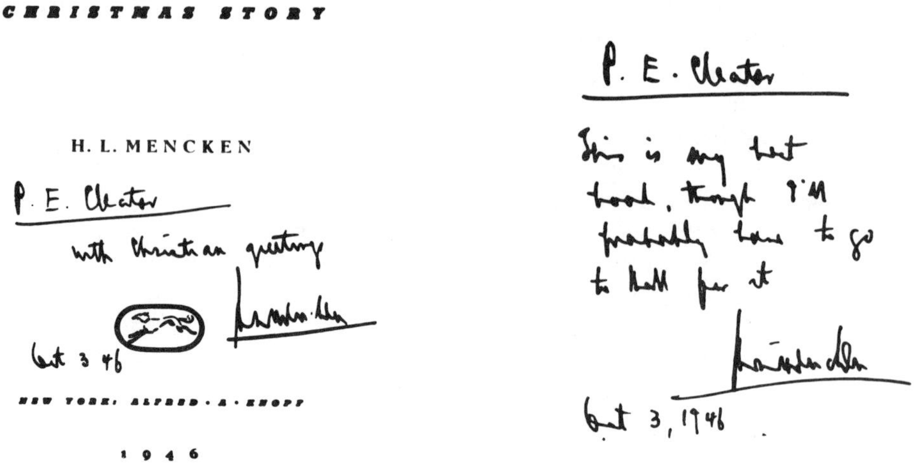

PLATE 11. The Mencken epigraphs—3. An inscribed copy of the revised edition of *Treatise on the Gods (right)* was duly dispatched in October 1946, accompanied by a slim volume which recounted "a Christmas story to surpass, transcend and put an end to all other Christmas stories" *(left)*.

and bearing the title *Christmas Story*. My perusal of this "Christmas story to surpass, transcend and put an end to all other Christmas stories," as I reported on November 1, "all but burst every suture in my body, and there were times when I suffered real agony whilst reading it." Consisting of a mere thirty-two pages, it was liberally illustrated by Bill Crawford, whose drawings were as superb as the prose.

"I am certainly glad": I had earlier announced that a maniac was on the loose in Wallasey, roaming the streets at night in emulation of the Düsseldorf murderer who appeared in the wake of the ending of World War I: "Instead of shooting, he slashes—lone women for preference. You can imagine the uproar. . . ."

November 29, 1945

Dear Mr. Cleator:

God knows I am sorry to hear that the chiropractors have grabbed you again. I have shot my chaplain and buried his carcass at a lonely crossroads. I only hope that you have been disentangled this time, and that you'll have a reasonable amount of comfort hereafter. My own health report must remain cautious. I am still alive, but further than that I don't care to go.

The use of *to script* by the B.B.C. does not surprise me in the slightest. Radio men are always up-and-coming fellows, and those of England may be trusted to make use of all of the magnificent new words invented in this great free Republic.

A certain amount of disillusionment begins to show itself. The evidence turned up by the Pearl Harbor investigation shows only too plainly that the American people were taken for a dizzy ride.

Sincerely yours,
H. L. Mencken

"The use of *to script*": I had reported the use of the phrase "scripted by" among the credits at the end of a play broadcast by the BBC.

(Prior to his note of November 29, Mencken's letter paper had resumed its virgin whiteness, but it now assumed a pale yellow tint.)

December 13, 1945

Dear Mr. Cleator:

I surely hope that the hearse will be wrecked on its way back to the garage and that you'll never see or hear of it again. After all, it is reasonable to look for better luck in 1946, for it is impossible to imagine any year being worse than 1945.

Once, during the war, I made a rash promise to replace all the destroyed copies of my own books. Unhappily, I now find myself confronted with the fact that all of them are out of print, and that the copies appearing in the second-hand shops are mainly dog's-eared. I am still, however, in hopes of turning up some presentable ones. I'll send you a copy of the revised "Treatise on the Gods" the instant it comes out. When that will be I don't know precisely—maybe in April.

My very best thanks for the cuttings. When I look at the pile of them that you have sent during the past half dozen years, I am really staggered by your generosity. I hope to make good use of them in the second supplement to "The American Language."

There is no news here. The more alert and progressive minority of Americans are beginning to suspect that the conquest of Hitler and the Japs did not quite solve all the problems of humanity. They are still, however, buoyed up by hope. We shall see.

Sincerely yours,
H. L. Mencken

"I made a rash promise": This notification from Mencken that his earlier undertaking to replace the lost copies of his works had encountered difficulties came as no surprise, for even in prewar days I had been put to considerable trouble in obtaining some of the early titles myself. Accordingly, I hastened to give assurance of my understanding of the problem: "You are most certainly not to worry about those out of print volumes of yours. One of these days, perhaps, there'll be a reprinting on a grand scale, in which event my name will go down instanter for the lot."

(Epistolary note: The primrose hue exhibited by Mencken's previous letter had now become a bilious yellow color, painful to the unaccustomed eye.)

Dear Cleator,
Dear Mencken
(1946–1948)

January 28, 1946

Dear Mr. Cleator:

It is good news that you are feeling better. I suspect that the worst is now over, though you may occasionally loose a seam. My own carcass gives way frequently, and in a great variety of places. Since January 1st each and every one of my joints have developed twinges. Fortunately, no more than four or five are ever in eruption together. This, at least, is a mercy, and I don't fail to give my humble thanks to our Heavenly Father.

Please don't mourn my chaplain. He was, at best, a raffish fellow, and I am glad to be rid of him. I hear confidentially that he is now a gambler. It is a suitable promotion.

Latrineograms is a new one to me and, I think, to the American Army. *Latrine rumour,* of course, has been in use for a long while. The extension in the meaning of *casualty* is also new to me. I shall inquire whether or not it is in use by the heroes of the Republic.

I am plugging away at Supplement Two to "The American Language," and making fair progress. The job, however, is extraordinarily tedious, and I'll be at it for a long while. I hope that you finish your sequel to "Rockets Through Space" in short order. The book should sell magnificently in these days. Here in the Republic the radar boys are shooting at the moon every night. I hear confidentially that they lately received some disconcerting replies.

H. L. Mencken

"Please don't mourn": The alert and attentive reader will have noted the return from the dead of the luckless chaplain earlier reported (November 29, 1945) to have been shot for failing in his precatory duty. His resurrection, I like to believe, was prompted by my protesting at the harshness of the treatment meted out to him when I replied to Mencken's letter containing the news of the culprit's summary execution: "I'm sorry to hear of your treatment of your chaplain. Couldn't you have demoted him to the level of a Baptist preacher, or something, so letting him off with a caution?"

"The extension in the meaning of *casualty*": My information on this point had come from a British army officer: "If a man is promoted, his name duly appears on a casualty list, apparently on the grounds that he has ceased to function as he used to. In general, any man who suffers a change of status is technically a 'casualty,' and is listed as such."

"I hope that you finish": On a recent trip to London, I had made tentative arrangements with my publishers to produce a sequel to *Rockets through Space*—on the understanding that the still-prevailing paper shortage precluded any prospect of early publication.

January 30, 1946

Dear Mr. Cleator:

I needn't tell you that I am delighted to have those notes on my book. They are full of interesting and valuable material, and I am sorting them out at once and filing them away against a possible revision in a year or two. The book is doing pretty well at the moment, and I am putting in all the time I can spare upon Supplement II, but soon or late Supplement I will need an overhauling. Nearly all of the stuff you send me is quite new to me, and I am glad to have the cuttings. You will be rewarded in Heaven throughout the life to come.

I am making rather poor progress with Supplement II, mainly because I am constantly interrupted by visitors. One of them came in to lunch yesterday, and stayed until 5 o'clock. He was an interesting fellow and had a good deal of material that was useful to me, but losing half a day is a serious thing for a man whose sands are running out. Unhappily, I am informed that there will be no writing or printing in Heaven. The holy saints are unanimously opposed to it.

I hope you are reasonably comfortable, and that the chiropractors soon devise a way to cure you completely. There is nothing more unpleasant on this earth than a continuing discomfort. I hope you have got to work on the revision of your book, and that it is making quick progress.

Sincerely yours,
H. L. Mencken

On completing my reading of *Supplement I* of *The American Language*, I sent Mencken a sheaf of notes containing minor corrections and comments. At the same time, I continued to inundate him with newspaper cuttings and other material for use in *Supplement II*.

February 14, 1946

Dear Mr. Cleator:

I surely hope that the bomb has been removed, and that you are once more free to carry on your work in peace. Over here things begin to be lively. I have lately entered suit for damages against a neighbor for maintaining a barking dog. He removed the dog within twenty-four hours after I filed my bill, but he has still to give an account of himself in court. I hope to recover at least a million dollars, and maybe two. If I succeed I'll lay out part of the money on a new steam yacht and come to England to see you.

I trust that you are more comfortable than you were the last time I heard from you.

Sincerely yours,
H. L. Mencken

I had reported the discovery of an unexploded bomb in a neighbor's garden. Happily, after spending several weeks digging down to it, the disposal squad was able to remove it without incident.

"I have lately entered suit": The owner of the offending dog was one Charles Fortenbaugh, and the story of Mencken's protracted efforts to silence the animal made headline news. Several items of correspondence relating to this long-drawn-out saga will be found in Bode (CB-1). The nuisance was eventually abated when, under the threat of legal action, the canine cause of the disturbance was placed in the care of the Baltimore Humane Society.

So far as I am aware, the anticipated million dollars compensation payment was not forthcoming, and to the best of my knowledge, no steam yacht from Maryland's shores managed to reach and cast anchor in the Mersey River.

March 21, 1946

Dear Mr. Cleator:

My claim to be suffering with the gout was simply a boastful exaggeration. What I really had was a bursitis. The chiropractors at the Johns Hopkins tied it up in a magnificent manner, and after wobbling about for a week or so I was once more able to navigate normally. Save for an occasional mild twinge, it has now disappeared altogether. Without question, our Heavenly Father had His thumb in the business. I had been a little sinful a week or so before the pain seized me. However, we had better not go into such matters. They are always embarrassing to truly Christian people. You say nothing whatever about your own afflictions, so I assume hopefully that they have passed off. I certainly trust that no more surgery will be necessary. Let me hear about this in your next.

The enclosed may be somewhat mysterious to a benighted Englishman, so I explain briefly. The Proclamation of January 1, 1863 was the one which emancipated the slaves, and the Articles of the Constitution mentioned under it were those which gave effect to the emancipation. The aim of the Petition is simply to restore slavery. The older I grow the more I believe in it. It was comfortable to the white people of this great free Republic, and it was very little resented by the blacks—in fact, some of the old ones who survived into my time showed a plain nostalgia for their days of servitude. They were then as well cared for and as free from responsibility as the guests in a first-rate prison. Now their descendants are thrown about from pillar to post, and nine-tenths of them, I believe, are acutely unhappy. I ask your support in this great effort to restore an institution which made for human felicity.

I have been upset by a head infection, and have hence done very little work on my book. Nevertheless, it is moving, if only slowly, and I hope to be near the end of it come Christmas.

My best thanks for the cuttings and other documents. They grow more and more sweller.

Sincerely yours,
H. L. Mencken

Disguised as an attack of gout, an account of Mencken's bursitis was considered of sufficient international importance as a news item to cross the Atlantic and appear in the pages of the ever solicitous London *Daily Express,* where it duly caught my eye.

"The enclosed": This took the form of a petition calling upon the Congress of the United States to repeal those Articles of the Constitution which led to the emancipation of the colored folk, thereby restoring them to their accustomed state of slavery, and hence to a life of comparative happiness and ease. Despite Mencken's call for my support in furthering this deserving cause, I neglected to append my signature to the document when, after due prayer and silent meditation, the unworthy thought occurred to me that it might just conceivably be a hoax.

(Note on the Mencken stationery: For this and his next letter, Mencken's standard half sheets were exchanged for a quarto page, replete with a multicolored heading and border [mainly red and blue]. In the first example, the heading depicted an American eagle perched

A Petition

TO THE CONGRESS OF THE UNITED STATES

Whereas, more than eighty years of unhappy experience have demonstrated that the Proclamation of the President of the United States dated January 1, 1863; Article XIII of the Constitution of the United States, proclaimed by the Secretary of State on December 18, 1865; Article XIV thereof, proclaimed July 28, 1868, and Article XV thereof, proclaimed March 30, 1870, have failed to provide and maintain, as was hoped by their proponents, a reasonable degree of peace, justice and good will between the white and colored peoples of the country; and

Whereas, there is no present evidence that relations between the two races will improve hereafter, but every reason to believe that they will worsen, as they are even now worsening;

Therefore, the undersigned, citizens of and voters in the States listed after their names, do hereby respectfully petition the Congress to clear off the existing misunderstanding and enmity, and open the way for a new and more rational attack upon the problem by repealing and nullifying, by Joint Resolution, the said Proclamation of January 1, 1863, and by submitting to the several States, under Article V of the Constitution, an Amendment repealing the aforesaid Articles XIII, XIV and XV.

As in duty bound, the said Petitioners humbly pray, etc.

NAME   STATE

_____   _____

_____   _____

_____   _____

_____   _____

_____   _____

_____   _____

N? 3244

Maryland State Board of Madstone Examiners

State of Maryland, SS:

  Know all men by these presents that the madstone to which this certificate is attached under seal has been subjected to the laboratory and clinical tests provided by Article 2654, Section 18a, of the Public General Laws of Maryland, and has been passed as authentic and efficacious.

For the Board:

Annapolis, Md., _____ 19__ _____ Inspector

A penalty of $100 fine or 30 days in jail or both is provided for the use of a madstone not lawfully inspected and passed. Half the fine if any may be awarded to the informer.

PLATE 12. Baltimorean buffooneries—2. Reproductions *(top)* of the Mencken petition to the U.S. Congress, calling for the repeal of those articles of the Constitution which led to the emancipation of the Negroes, thereby restoring them to their accustomed state of slavery, and hence to a life of comparative happiness and ease; and *(bottom)* of an authentic label of the famed Maryland Madstone. Among other things, this powerful prophylactic was reputed "to cure headaches, relieve impotence, combat hydrophobia, and pull teeth." Reported its inventor and dispenser: "I always carry mine in an asbestos sack. I have seen one knock a policeman down and set him afire."

```
                    H. L. MENCKEN
                   704 CATHEDRAL ST.
                      BALTIMORE        March 12, 1936.

    Dear Mr. Cleator:
```

```
                         Sun Square
                        Baltimore, Md.

    Editorial Department

                                     March 4, 1938.


          Dear Mr. Cleator:
```

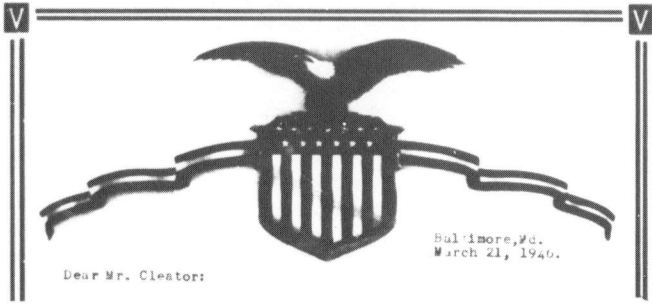
```
                                          Baltimore, Md.
                                          March 21, 1945.
    Dear Mr. Cleator:
```

```
                                          Baltimore, Md.
                                          March 25, 1945.

    Dear Mr. Cleator:
```

PLATE 13. The Mencken notepaper. Soon after the topmost letter was written, Mencken left Cathedral Street to return to the family abode at 1524 Hollins Street. Almost invariably, his notepaper took the form of octavo sheets, usually white though sometimes tinted, with a simple central printed heading bearing his name and address. On two separate occasions, however, he had to resort to quarto writing paper—during March and April 1938, on his assuming the temporary editorship of the Baltimore *Evening Sun,* when he made free use of that publication's departmental stationery; and in March 1945, at a time when World War II was nearing its end. It was then, in a sudden burst of patriotic fervor, that he turned to gaudily colored pictorial headings, two examples of which are shown above.

atop a shield emblazoned with the stars and stripes, while in the second another member of the Falconidae family presided over a display of America's armed might on land, sea, and in the air. A victory "V" sign and the United States motto, *E Pluribus Unum* [Out of many, one] completed the picture.)

March 25, 1946

Dear Mr. Cleator:

Please don't think I have forgotten my promise to restore the Mencken books that you lost in the blitz. Unhappily, two-thirds of them are out of print and getting hold of first editions in many cases turns out to be almost impossible. Would you be content with later editions? If so, I'll be delighted to send you a few from time to time. If you prefer first editions, I can probably turn them up soon or late, but it may take a long time.

I certainly hope that you have been delivered from the chiropractors at last. At the moment, I am in their hands myself, but what ails me is simply an upper nose infection of the sort that always floors me at this season of the year. They examined me very elaborately, and then advise me solemnly to wait until the sun comes out. I am in hopes that this will happen at some time within the next two weeks.

Sincerely yours,
H. L. Mencken

In making reply to this expression of concern about the delay attending the promised replacement of the Mencken books missing from my shelves, I hastened to reassure the would-be donor: "Far be it from me to hold out for first editions of your works. My original collection, indeed, was by no means wholly composed of such. Half of my volumes of *Prejudices* were Capes, and half Knopfs. I remember I contrived to obtain Series I, II, III, V and VI without too much trouble. But for some reason or other, it was months before I managed to grab a copy of No. IV. Recent attempts to secure copies here have proved hopeless—and this applies, indeed, to almost all works of note issued pre-war. Hence I shall welcome with triple delight anything you can locate on my behalf. At the time of this writing, I possess your recently sent *Supplement I* and two of my original collection which happened to be on loan at the time of the blitz—*Americana 1925* and copy No. 1275 of *Heliogabalus*.

"By way of reverse lease-lend, I'm hoping in due course to be able to send you a copy of my new opus on rockets. Unwins have indicated that they hope to publish the work eventually, but they have also made it clear that the queue of books awaiting publication is a long one, and that there is little hope of it appearing this year." (In the event, the book was not destined to emerge under the Allen & Unwin imprint until 1953!)

April 11, 1946

Dear Mr. Cleator:

I certainly hope you come to terms with Unwin. The publishing situation in this great free Republic is really serious. There is now a reasonable supply of paper, but the printing crafts' unions have pushed up the cost of production to such an extent that it becomes almost prohibitive. The strikes in the coal mines and the steel industry have wrecked production, and it is impossible to get ordinary building materials. Lumber is also virtually unobtainable. The kitchen in my house as above needs rebuilding, but my brother, who is an engineer, figures that it will take eighteen months to do the simple job.

That barking dog disappeared within twenty-four hours after I filed my suit. The suit itself is still pending, and I am hoping to see my lawyer about it tomorrow.

You say nothing about your health. I certainly hope that you have recovered completely.

Sincerely yours,
H. L. Mencken

"The kitchen in my house": Mencken's trials and tribulations in the department of reconstruction were more than matched by my own: "Here, if anything, things are worse. On May 3rd, 1945, I instructed an architect to set about rebuilding the family's house, which was totally destroyed. He has been at it ever since, and he still awaits permission for the builder to make a start. The delays occasioned by a dozen or so different Government departments are maddening. As for building materials, they are almost unobtainable. To obtain even a door hinge, or a pot of paint, the requisite Form must now be completed, and signed and counter-signed. In this house-starved land, half the builders are out of work, and the other half spend their time filling up forms. It has actually got to the stage where it is necessary to fill up forms to obtain forms—may heaven help the homeless!"

"You say nothing about your health": At the time, I was in the midst of making arrangements for yet another session upon the operating table, and in response to Mencken's invitation, I obligingly gave news of it: "As regards my own fearful afflictions (to which, with great pleasure, I now turn) I am provisionally booked for some more surgery later in the year—merely another burst seam, and not a matter of immediate urgency. But my surgeon friend is not too happy about it. Last time, apart from the suture infection which developed, it transpired that there was internal haemorrhage on a grand scale, and that I nearly passed out. On the face of it, it seems probable that the same thing will occur next time. No wonder he's somewhat worried. If the responsibility were mine, I'd be frightened half to death!"

May 16, 1946

Dear Mr. Cleator:

After a long and diligent search, I have managed to unearth eight books that you lack, and they are going to you in five packages during the next few days. Unhappily, I have found it impossible so far to find four of the six Prejudices books. They have been out of print for some time, and second-hand copies seem to be rare. However, they do pop up from time to time, and whenever I encounter one I'll send it to you. Some of my earlier books are even harder to discover—for example, A Book of Burlesques and In Defense of Women. But they, too, are not quite unobtainable, and I am full of hopes of finding them soon or late.

I advise you to look through the Days books in the order in which they were published—that is, taking Happy Days first. Making a President belongs to political archaeology rather than to living history. It pleases me to find that all of the predictions that I made in it turned out to be false.

I surely hope that your uneasiness about that surgery is not borne out by the event. Surgeons have a way of alarming their customers. In the long run, in my experience, they do their work very well, but they are greatly given to foreboding. Certainly I hope the operation can be escaped altogether.

I trust that Unwin bestirs himself and brings out your book on rockets promptly. Here in this great free Republic, the publishers are all in a state of demoralization. There is not only a dreadful paper shortage; there is also trouble in the printing crafts. I recall the day when a journeyman printer who got five drinks a day and plenty of chewing tobacco regarded himself a lucky man. Now he demands an automobile, a radio and victuals fit for an archbishop.

My best thanks for the cuttings. That income tax form is almost as imbecile as the one used on this side. Whether or not I'll

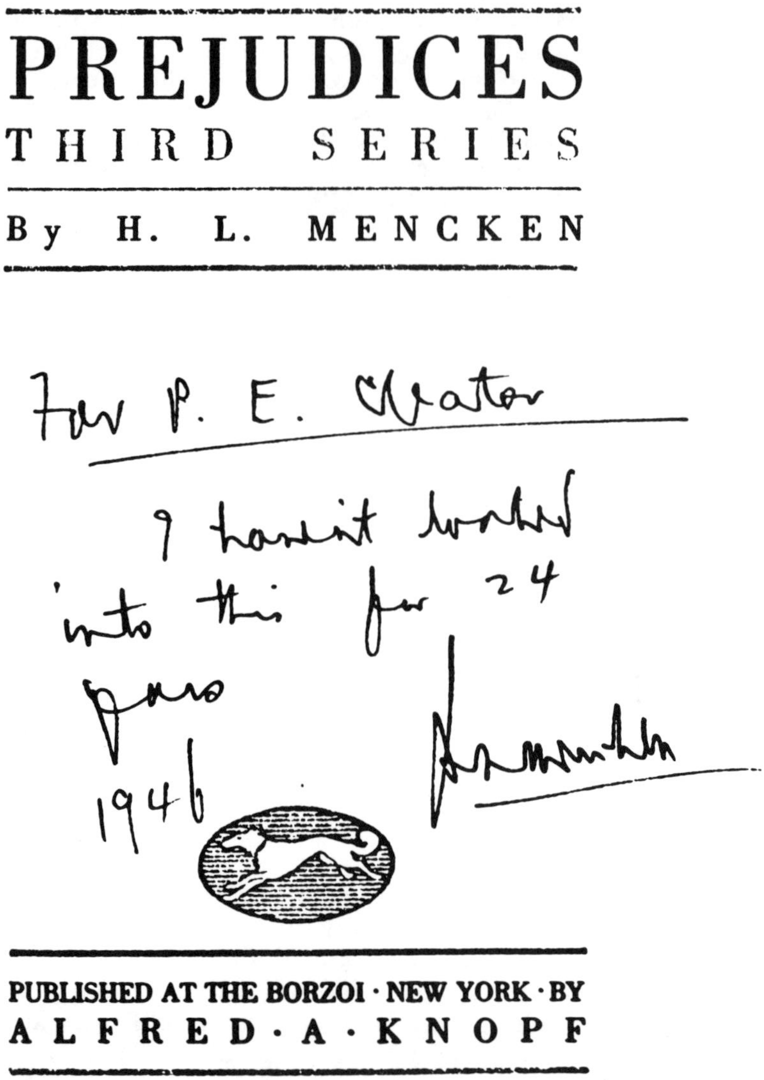

PREJUDICES
THIRD SERIES

By H. L. MENCKEN

For P. E. Cleator

I haven't looked into this for 24 years

1946 — *HLMencken*

PUBLISHED AT THE BORZOI · NEW YORK · BY
ALFRED · A · KNOPF

PLATE 14. The Mencken epigraphs—4. From the seventh printing (1926) of *Prejudices, Third Series*. The work first appeared in 1922.

be able to get to England in the near future remains to be seen. Sometimes I suspect that my travel days are over.

                                    Yours,
                                    H. L. Mencken

The contents of the above letter merited two acknowledgments, dispatched respectively by surface mail and by air: "Your letter of May 16th beat the copy of *Happy Days* (to hand an hour ago) by a short head. Be sure I'll keep a diligent look-out for the remainer of the packages. Meanwhile, the very extent of your generosity appals me, for I shall remain in your debt for evermore."

This first note was quickly followed by a second: "I acknowledged your letter of May 16th by ordinary mail two days ago, and with it the copy of *Happy Days*. Since then, the remainder of the five packages have come safely in. It has, indeed, been raining Mencken books for the past forty-eight hours, to my continuous delight and the postman's despair. I'll attempt no more thanks—but I'd rather have those books on my shelves than the holy crown of England on my head. It's kind of you indeed to promise to continue the search. Over here, I'm searching anew myself, not, perhaps, with any great hopes, but at any rate regardless of expense. At all events, I'm re-advertising in certain trade papers, and you may be sure that I'll keep you informed as to the result."

"I trust that Unwin": Each time I made enquiry in London about the paper situation, the news seemed to grow worse. My publishers, it now transpired, were particularly badly placed, in that a million and a half of their stock copies had been destroyed in the blitz, many of them standard text books whose replacement was a matter of the utmost priority. In the light of this unpromising situation, the possibility of first arranging for publication overseas appeared to offer a solution to the problem: "Just when Unwins will permit me to send you the threatened lease-lend I can't say for the moment. But I believe they will consent to Messrs. Knopf acquiring the American rights of the work, if it interests them. I sent the typescript off some days ago—and discovered, immediately afterwards, that it is *verboten* to send MSS. out of These Isles without a permit! Just how long this nonsense has been in force I can't say, for it's the first I've heard of it. Meanwhile, the MS. has not yet come back, and I'm beginning to hope that it's slipped through the blockade."

"Sometimes I suspect": The prospect of Mencken making his long proposed voyage to the Port of Liverpool seemed to be fading.

                                                      June 15, 1946
Dear Mr. Cleator:
Knopf is really interested in your book, and I am in hopes that he'll take it for America. The state of the publishing business, of

course, is still far from exhilarating. The paper shortage continues, and wages are still going up in the printing crafts. An ordinary printer is now paid more every week than an archbishop used to earn in my boyhood.

You say nothing about that threatened operation. I surely hope that you have avoided it. Let me hear about this.

That plumber's bill is really superb. It could be matched in every detail on this side of the water. My kitchen has been a wreck for a year past, but it is simply impossible to have it rebuilt. Even common flooring is unobtainable.

I am still grinding away at Supplement II. It is moving slowly, but nevertheless it is moving.

Sincerely yours,
H. L. Mencken

The report of Alfred Knopf's interest in the book was encouraging news, and in my reply I was able to impart the information that I had an appointment with him in London early in July.

June 24, 1946

Dear Mr. Cleator:

I am delighted to hear by your air mail letter that the books have all arrived. I am keeping my eye open, and if any others turn up they will follow. Unhappily, many of my early books are completely out of the market, and finding stray copies is a matter of accident. But they'll turn up soon or late, and I'll be on the watch.

You say nothing about that threatened operation. I surely hope that the chiropractors gave it up. As for me, I am enjoying my usual poor health, but nevertheless managing to get in a few licks on my book. If I were not so horribly interrupted by telephone calls and visits from strangers, I'd be making pretty good progress. Even as it is, I hope to complete the manuscript by the Autumn of 1963.

The present state of the world really delights me. The human race is at last showing what it can do when it settles down in earnest.

Sincerely yours,
H. L. Mencken

"You say nothing": Mencken's continued request for information about the impending surgery found me without anything to add to what had already been said, and I chose to avoid further reference to the subject until such time as a firm date for the blood-letting had been arranged.

July 8, 1946

Dear Cleator:

In the name of God the Father, the Son and the Holy Ghost, why should you and I go on mistering each other? My true title is not Mister, nor even Esquire, but Dom. I suggest that we drop all such fripperies hereafter.

I surely hope that Unwin sets up the book in the very near future, and that he and Knopf come to terms. Knopf is really interested. He is in London at the moment, and I assume that he and Unwin will sit down for a palaver. The machinations of publishers, of course, are highly mysterious and sometimes they savor of the sinister, but let us be hopeful.

I continue to hope and pray that you escape that fourth bout with the chiropractors. They are, in private life, very charming fellows, but once they put on their praying robes and spit on their hands they forget altogether that the patient before them is a poor Christian and deserves all the consideration ordained in Holy Writ.

My own afflictions gradually become worse, but I don't repine, for such is God's will. Fortunately, I am still able to get in a reasonable day's work almost every day. My book is going slowly, but nevertheless it is moving.

Those permit forms are almost fabulous. I begin to despair of matching them in the Republic.

Yours,
H. L. Mencken

"In the name of God": The suggestion here made in no way found me averse to the adoption of a more intimate mode of address between the two of us: "By all means let us give up mistering one another, as you suggest. I must confess, indeed, that behind your back I have for years affectionately referred to you by your initials. Hence, to address you as H.L.M. comes to me as easily and as naturally as the rev. clergy take collections and politicians graft."

"I surely hope": At the time Mencken wrote, word was already on its way to him announcing the verdict on the book: "In my last letter, alas, I had to report that your kind efforts to get Knopf interested in the rocket *opus* came to nothing."

July 22, 1946

Dear Cleator:

I was distressed indeed when Knopf told me that he and his advisers have decided against doing your book in this great country. His reasons, so far as I have heard them, are somewhat vague. I hope to see him in New York in the near future and to cross-examine him at length. In such matters, of course, it is useless to argue with a publisher. He operates his business on hunches, and he has to follow his bad ones as well as his good ones. I hope that Unwin will bring the book out in the near future, and that he'll find some other American publisher to do it here.

There is no news from this side. I am plugging away at my infernal book, and making very slow progress. The weather has been humid and uncomfortable, and I begin to realize that at 66 a man lacks a good deal of his energy at 40. There was a time when I was a prancing gazelle, but now I begin to move like a somewhat senile ox.

Yours,
H. L. Mencken

Both the aspirations here expressed about the rejected book were in due course realized—though not in the immediate future.

August 7, 1946

Dear Cleator:

I am distressed indeed that Knopf did not take the book, and I only hope that Unwin gets it a little ahead of his programme. Such delays are now frequent all over the publishing world. There is a genuinely serious shortage of paper, and the extortions of the printing crafts have reached such a stage that costs have been almost prohibitive.

If you cease to write to me I shall consult my lawyer, DeWitt C. Feinberg and sue you in the courts. I am always delighted to hear from you, and am only sorry that we are too far apart for an occasional palaver. I have signed my application for the Defence Medal, and hope to receive it promptly.

Most of my books are out of print, and some of them seem to be scarce in the second-hand book shops. I have had orders in for at least six of them for a year past, without result. I am continuing the search for those that are missing from your collection, and they will be forwarded to you the instant they turn up.

           Sincerely yours,
           H. L. Mencken

"If you cease to write": In his note of June 24, Mencken's complaint about interruptions to his work brought with it an awareness of the fact that my postal bombardment over the years must also have contributed to a marked slowing down of his literary labors: "Your mention of *Supplement II* being held up by telephone calls and visitations brings the guilty realisation that letters from correspondents must also be the cause of a tremendous amount of delay. . . ."

"The Defence Medal": With the cessation of hostilities, practically every man, woman, and child resident within the confines of the British Isles automatically became eligible for this particular decoration. I hastened to pass on to a more deserving recipient the application form relating to it which came my way.

"DeWitt C. Feinberg": Undoubtedly a close drinking companion of Mencken's imaginary Uncle Julius.

           August 12, 1946

Dear Cleator:

I object to being addressed as H.L.M. on the ground that the use of initials is almost universal among the slaves of the American Babbitts. The head of a factory is always so-called. To be sure, I own and operate a factory, but I have no slaves. The colored people here in Maryland commonly call me Mr. Meekins. My own name, being unfamiliar to them, baffles them, so they translate it into the closest familiar name. I have been carrying on for many years a war against the mistering disease which afflicts so many Americans. Nine-tenths of them proceed directly from Mr. Jones to Charley. There seems to be no half way station.

I am glad you have sent your manuscript to Simon and Schuster. It is a good firm, though a large interest in it has been acquired by Marshall Field, the Chicago traitor to the unearned increment. If Simon and Schuster fails to take it, there are plenty of others.

I haven't seen a copy of my "Treatise on the Gods" for four or five years. It seems to be completely non est in this great country. Knopf tells me that the new edition should be out in October.

My book is lagging once more. I have been hard beset by legal business of the Baltimore *Sun,* and have lately spent the better part of a week listening to lawyers. It is a dreadful experience.

Sincerely yours,
H. L. Mencken

"I object": In the face of this expression of amicable dissent, I tendered a hasty retraction, at once replacing the offending initials with the cognominal Mencken as a more acceptable form of greeting: "Your letter of August 12th came in on the tail of your previous note of the 7th—in time, that is, to prevent a repetition of the H.L.M. salutation, for which my profuse and profound apologies. Such a mode of address is somewhat rare in These Isles, and generally reserved for those divine or otherwise above the level of ordinary men, *e.g.,* J.C. and G.R.I. In view of your objection, I have, of course, withdrawn the offending initials instanter, and you'll encounter them no more in the future. Meekins I refuse to countenance. As for proceeding directly from Mr. Jones to Charley, my addressing you as Henry seems to me an unwarrantable impertinence, though I'm prepared to concede that given time and perhaps a little encouragement, I might get round to it."

Curiously enough, Mencken does not seem to have been averse to signing many of his letters with his initials. While it is true that he at no time did so when writing to me, his correspondence published by Bode (CB-1) abounds with examples, more than half a hundred in all.

"I own and operate": A reference to the family business of Aug. Mencken & Bro., cigar manufacturers.

"American Babbitts": Emulators of George Babbitt, the credulous central character of a novel by Sinclair Lewis, published in 1922.

"Mr. Meekins": In the early days of his journalistic career, Mencken's superior on the staff of the Baltimore *Herald* was Lynn Meekins, and the two names were often confused, the one with the other, by the uninformed.

"Marshall Field": Presumably a reference to the late Marshall Field III (1893–1958), the then proprietor of the Chicago *Sun* and grandson of the multimillionaire department-store owner whose name he bore.

"Simon and Schuster": The American publishers of my first book on the subject of space travel. It in due course emerged that they were not disposed to repeat the experience.

"I haven't seen a copy": On July 24 I had been able to report: "My Mencken scouts brought great news on Monday last—the discovery of a well preserved copy of *Treatise On The Gods,* which I secured at the published price of 10/6d (52½p)—great going in these days of inflation. The inside cover bears the label: Des Forges Books De Luxe, Milwaukee."

(After a long lull, Mencken's half sheets once again exhibited a chromatic aberration, on this occasion appearing a light blue in color.)

September 26, 1946

Dear Cleator:

I certainly hope that by the time these lines reach you you'll be home from hospital and feeling sound and lively. As I approach my hundredth birthday I begin to believe more and more that the most dreadful thing in life is illness. It takes all the vigor and ambition out of a man, and leaves him a mere shell. I certainly trust that the chiropractors do a good job this year, and turn out a masterpiece. My ten days at the Johns Hopkins Hospital did me no good, but it also did no harm. Two days ago I was in a taxicab collision and shed a few drops of blood. Fortunately, there seems to be no serious damage, and I am able to navigate as usual.

You were lucky indeed to find that copy of "In Defense of Women." Here in this great free Republic it seems to be almost unobtainable. I have had scouts out looking for it for months past, but have never encountered a presentable copy. Inasmuch as 100,000 copies were printed first and last, I marvel that it should have disappeared so completely. Most of my other early books are popping up now and then, but no "In Defense of Women." If I ever encounter a first edition I'll send it to you instantly.

My best thanks for those elegant and instructive clippings. They are really very valuable, and my obligation to you mounts up to astronomical lengths. I shall give you full credit in my Supplement II, and mention incidentally that you are a baptized man and a hero of many wars.

The rule in America is that save among Rotarians Christian names are evaded politely until the high contracting parties have succumbed to alcohol together. I surely hope that you and I will be doing that before long. It is an elevating and exhilarating experience. More and more I am beginning to believe that ethyl alcohol is the most valuable gift our Heavenly Father has ever bestowed upon His poor creatures.

I am making very slow progress with Supplement II, but it is nevertheless moving. The amount of material in hand is so enormous that picking and choosing keeps me puzzled.

Yours,
H. L. Mencken

On September 6, I had at last been able to announce the date proposed for my impending vivisection: "My execution has been provisionally arranged for the 30th of this month. Your prayers, I know, will accompany me to high heaven. I'll drop you a line from the morgue in due course."

On October 1, however, I had to report a last-minute postponement: "I write in some haste. My execution was to have taken place yesterday. Then it was delayed. And now I have just learned that it is to be tomorrow, and that I'm required in dry dock to-night. The rush has been terrific, and half the things I should have done, including half an hour's prayer in thanks for what I'm about to endure, have had to be abandoned."

"Two days ago": The news of Mencken's misadventure on the highway was received with due concern: "I read with alarm of your taxi accident, and trust that all is now well. I hope you will sue all concerned. As between friends, I'm prepared to take half of whatever you get—be it 10 years or 10 thousand dollars."

"You were lucky": I had sent details of another success in my never-ending search for missing Mencken works—the acquisition of a slim, leather-bound volume—Knopf's tenth printing—whose contents dealt with such esoteric topics as the feminine mind and the war between the sexes.

"The rule in America": To this elaboration of the niceties of trans-Atlantic etiquette in the matter of ceremonious forms of address, I responded as follows: "I'm glad the salutation question is now comfortably settled between us. From now on, I shall look forward to that alcoholic session. You may be sure that by the time I've so far forgotten myself as to address you by your Christian name, I shall be permanently under the table, and no caring whether you address me as the Devil or Jehovah."

October 17, 1946

Dear Cleator:

I certainly hope that the chiropractors have turned you out by the time this reaches you, and that you are fast returning to normalcy. There is nothing more disagreeable and discouraging in this lovely world than illness. At the moment, I am in the hands of the Johns Hopkins brethren once more. A bursitis on my left elbow developed enormously, and had to be opened yesterday. I am now outfitted by a bandage so tight that my fingers are numb. Can it be that sin is responsible? I am not conscious of having done anything deserving such afflictions. Let me hear from you as soon as you feel like it.

Knopf's objections to your book, it turns out, were grounded

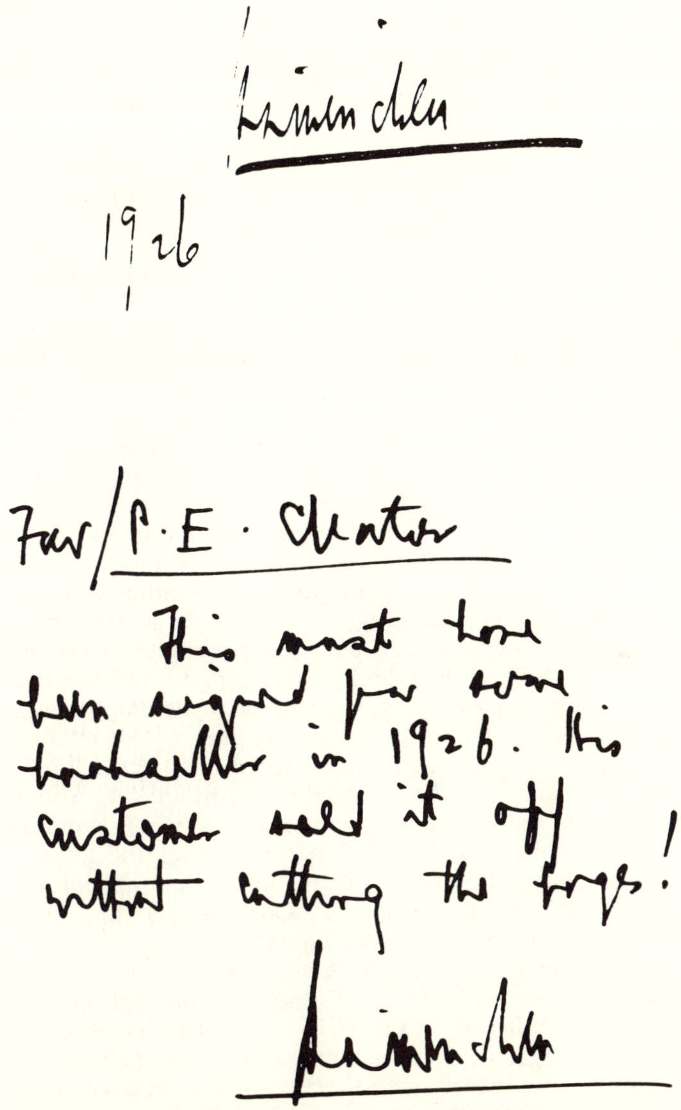

Mencken

1926

For / P. E. Cleator

This must have been signed for some bookseller in 1926. His customer sold it off without cutting the pages!

Mencken

PLATE 15. The Mencken epigraphs—5. *Americana, 1926*. As the inscription records, when Mencken acquired this copy on the recipient's behalf, it was to find that the original purchaser, for whom it had been signed by the author, had not even bothered to cut the pages!

simply on the theory that it wouldn't sell. Whether or not this was sound I can't tell you. In such matters it is quite useless to argue with a publisher. He does business by hunches, and the advice of a witch doctor sounds much more plausible to him than that of a literary critic.

Sincerely yours,
H. L. Mencken

"At the moment": From the periodic accounts he gave, Mencken's bodily ailments appeared to be as interminable as my own. In making response to this latest installment, I sounded a suitably commiserative note: "Your left elbow, I trust, is no longer afflicted with the Holy Ghost and the shades of Allah. Probably you are right in your assumption that sin is at the bottom of the matter, and all I can console you with is the thought that even archbishops sometimes break their legs, and suffer from boils and sacerdotal belly-aches, not to mention defective kidneys, and other such afflictions visited upon them by God. In short, we are all of us damned from the start, no matter what we do."

"Knopf's objections": A writer cannot argue with such a conclusion. Clearly, those who produce books for sale need to concern themselves with what, in their judgment, is likely to prove to be a profitable enterprise. And although the world of authorship abounds with pleasing accounts of best-selling works which, after being turned down by one hundred and forty-five publishers, then made a fortune for entrepreneur number one hundred and forty-six, this present tale is not one of them. On the other hand, neither is it a record of abject failure. When the paper situation allowed, the rejected MS, entitled *Into Space,* was in due course issued by Allen & Unwin in London, where it quickly ran into a second edition, and then into a third under the aegis of the Scientific Book Club. Elsewhere, meanwhile, it had appeared in the U.S. under the imprint of Thomas Y. Crowell, and had also been translated into German, Spanish, and Japanese.

As a matter of speculative interest, a possible sidelight on the Knopf rejection has since been provided by a sight of the Baltimore correspondence made public by Bode (CB-1). It appears that in 1927, Mencken, who during his career as a magazine editor, gave encouragement to a number of convicts with literary aspirations, was favorably impressed by an account of penitentiary life written by a San Quentin inmate by the name of Robert Tasker. At Mencken's instigation, a copy of the MS found its way for consideration to 730 Fifth Avenue, New York City. Thereafter, as the sponsor wrote to his writer friend Jim Tully, who was acquainted with the would-be author:

"Tasker's manuscript is now in the hands of Knopf's reader. I am keeping hands off because experience has taught me when I show too much interest in a book, opposition to it is raised in the Knopf office."

It was perhaps as a result of this forbearance that Tasker's *Grimhaven* came to be added to the Alfred Knopf list of titles.

October 24, 1946

Dear Cleator:

Your postcard is really alarming, and I only hope that your state is now better. Let me have a bulletin when you feel like it.

There is no news here, save the usual burglaries of banks and the usual massacres in the South.

Yours,
H. L. Mencken

The card I dispatched on regaining consciousness must have been more horrific than I intended, or indeed than the circumstances warranted, as I hastened to explain in a subsequent note.

October 31, 1946

Dear Cleator:

I rejoice that you have escaped the chiropractors, and only hope that you are making rapid progress toward complete recovery. The ladies of the hospital, now that they have read the subversive book, will never be the same again. No more will they be in awe in the presence of eminent bone-setters and distinguished lookers at tongues. This, I hope, will be put to my credit when I face the divine court of King's Bench.

My own troubles seem to be passing off. The war wounds I acquired in that automobile accident are reduced to a few scabs. On the heels of it, I acquired a bursitis on my left elbow. It is still there, but I am in hopes that it will be gone before the time comes to stuff me for posterity. My book is still going very slowly. It is an extraordinarily tedious job. My very best thanks for the additional clippings. They are always amusing, and always useful.

The Fortean Society is a one-man outfit run by a foolish fellow named Thayer. He insists upon treating me with respect, though I can't recall every mentioning Fort without denouncing him.

Yours,
H. L. Mencken

To while away the recuperative hours, I had entered the nursing home loaded with literature of all kinds, including a representative share of the Mencken classics: "I took my newly acquired copy of *In*

Defence of Women to hospital, with a view to improving my education by a timely re-reading of it. But alas, first one of the night nurses got hold of it, and then another. Eventually, it went the entire rounds, from the porter to the sister-in-chief. Finally, my surgeon friend grabbed it, and at the time of this writing, I'm without it still."

"Fort": The late Charles Fort (1874–1932), an eccentric American journalist and author. His published works, bearing such titles as *The Book of the Damned* (1919) and *New Lands* (1932), dealt with the occult and allied phenomena, not to mention lost planets and unidentified flying objects. This interest in the paranormal was accompanied by a prolonged and unrelenting attack on the findings of traditional science, for which disservice Fort has since been hailed as the "Prophet of the Unexplained."

"Thayer": Tiffany Ellsworth Thayer, a native of Freeport, Illinois, where he was born in 1902. His career took in acting, advertising, and novel writing, by which time (ca. 1930) he had become an ardent disciple and associate of Charles Fort.

"The Fortean Society": Founded by Tiffany Thayer in 1931, it was an association dedicated to promoting the reading of the master's works and to promulgating his zany ideas. Among those present at the inaugural gathering of the organization were several notables with Menckenian associations, in the persons of Theodore Dreiser, Ben Hecht, and Burton Rascoe.

"The Fortean Magazine": A publication founded by Thayer in 1937. Its title was changed to *DOUBT* in 1944, under which heading it continued to appear until production ceased with the death of its instigator in 1959.

Concerning this periodical, I had written to Mencken: "Some infidel has recently sent me a copy of *DOUBT* (No. 15), published, I gather, by the Fortean Society. I note on page 222 thereof that you have been elected a Named Fellow for the year 4 F.S. If you happen to be unaware of this elevation, and are interested, let me know, and I'll mail the journal to you." I added that among others suggested for Named Fellows (in the guise of Posthumous Forteans) were Ambrose Bierce, Samuel Coleridge Taylor, Edward Gibbon, James Joyce, Rudyard Kipling, and Thorstein Veblen, the last-named the *Doctor obscurus* about whose polysyllabic literary outpourings Mencken had published a scathing condemnation in the first of his *Prejudices* books.

November 18, 1946

Dear Cleator:

I am delighted to hear that the chiropractors have at last liberated you from their animal house. If you can now crawl around the block, maybe you'll be able to take an easy trot by next week. I surely hope that there is no pain left, and that your spirits are good.

That book on the Australian language is a really excellent piece of work. The author, Baker, seems to be a man of enormous diligence. At all events, he has got together more material single-handed than the whole faculty of the University of Chicago was able to amass for the Dictionary of American English.

I hope you have acquired a sufficiency of ethyl alcohol against Christmas. I am planning to spend the day, as usual, in a state of semi-consciousness.

Yours,
H. L. Mencken

"That book": *The Australian Language,* by Sidney J. Baker. Originally published in 1945, it was reissued in 1966.

December 2, 1946

Dear Cleator:

It is good news that you are once more ambulant, and I certainly hope that there is no surviving pain. The after-effects of ether are really appalling, and I marvel that the chiropractors still use it. There are various substitutes that seem to be superior. To be sure, they are sometimes dangerous, but what is danger compared to discomfort? I'd much prefer to fight Joe Lewis [*sic*] than spend five days with a pebble in one of my shoes. This explains why I keep away from divine service. The spectacle of the rector in his robes gives me such acute discomfort that I can't fix my mind upon the great truths of Holy Writ.

I am still plugging away at my infernal book. It is moving so slowly that I begin to suspect that I'll never finish it. God's will, not ours, be done.

Yours,
H. L. Mencken

"Joe Lewis": Joe Louis, a precursor of Muhammad Ali, and the world champion heavyweight boxer of his day (1937–49) who retired undefeated.

December 16, 1946

Dear Cleator:

I enclose two pieces of instructive Americana. The American government is actually paying for the training of poor soldiers as chiropractors. What is more, it is employing other chiropractors in scientific capacities in Washington. Try to imagine this in the realm of Britain if you can.

I seize the opportunity to hope that you get through Christmas without material damage, and that luck pursues you in 1947.

Yours,
H. L. Mencken

The pieces of instructive Americana above referred to concerned the high and lofty art of the chiropractor—i.e., of a person expert in the removal of nerve interference by manual adjustment. Of the two memorabilia, one was a cutting from the Washington *Star* for December, 1946, recording the accidental death from asphyxiation of Dr. Eugene Davis Owen, an elder of the First Church of the Nazarene, who combined his manipulations of the human spinal column with his teaching activities at Union Bible College in Westfield. The other was a copy of a duplicated bulletin from the president of the Reaver School of Chiropractic, addressed primarily to service veterans who, it was announced, were entitled to free enrollment as students under the G.I. Bill of Rights. Although an enrolment fee of $25 was demanded on application, this sum was returnable as soon as reimbursement from the U.S. government was forthcoming.

January 9, 1947

Dear Cleator:

The followers of Charles Fort have a national organization called the Fortean Society, and it includes many dignitaries. The late Theodore Dreiser, the novelist, was a leading member. These idiots devote themselves on the one hand to sneering at all reputable science, and on the other to whooping up Fort's nonsense. Farmsworth [*sic*] is a new one to me, but your account of him does not surprise me.

The report that all the whiskey in England has been sent to the United States is false. Sound Scotch is extremely scarce here, and almost ruinously expensive. Somewhere along the line someone unidentified is making a fortune. I can only hope that he will suffer in Hell. I lately made a contract with a Canadian movie company whereby it agreed to send me a case of sound ale once a month for the rest of my natural life. This is in return for permission to use an uncopyrighted newspaper article printed in 1917. How the company proposes to turn it into a movie I simply can't make out. Meanwhile, the ale is coming in and my brother and I are finding it very salubrious. It comes from the Lablatt's [sic] brewery, the best in Canada. Nothing so good is made in the United States.

I am still plugging away at my infernal book. It is moving very slowly.

Yours,
H. L. Mencken

"Farmsworth": This was R. L. Farnsworth of Glen Ellyn, Illinois, the leader of a local group of rocket enthusiasts. He had published a pamphlet about man's forthcoming occupation of the moon, concerning the overexuberant contents of which I ventured to offer some adverse criticism in an issue of the *Bulletin* of the British Interplanetary Society (vol. 2, no. 1, January 1947). Although I can find no reference to the matter in my correspondence, I had evidently sent a copy of the review to Baltimore, wherein its mention of Farnsworth as a self-confessed admirer of Charles Fort seemingly prompted Mencken's further diatribe against this gentleman and his followers.

"Lablatt's": This should read Labatt's.

"My infernal book": *Supplement II* of the *American Language*. It eventually came out in the following year, bearing the inevitable Knopf imprint.

February 3, 1947

Dear Cleator:

I am distressed to hear that you are having so many difficulties. The food supply here in the Republic seems to be increasing, but it is still almost impossible to find really good stuff. The situation with respect to clothing is worse. My tailor tells me that he hasn't seen a decent bolt of cloth for five years, and that there is no sign of any coming upon the market. I don't care much, for the Summers here are warm, and if the worst comes to the worst I'll go naked for six months of the year. I have long since passed the age when my appearance in public would cause riots among women.

What a beautiful mess the statesmen of the world have made of it! Some day I hope and pray that the intelligent minority of human beings will raise [sic] up against them and hang them unanimously. We'd be much better off if our governors were chosen as juries are chosen.

Yours,
H. L. Mencken

Complaints I voiced about the quality and the quantity of the provender we were being called upon to ingest were not without justification. I had reported: "The food, indeed, is truly dreadful, and the only compensation is that as it gets worse, it also gets less. We're now down to two ounces of bacon a week—may God help us all!"

"My tailor tells me": Mencken's reference to his arrayment problems caused me some mirthless merriment: "Your clothing difficulties? I give a hollow laugh! Without a fib, I haven't a shirt to my back with a collar to match, or that isn't in threads and patched inside out. As for suits, not only is the available cloth inferior Utility material, but it calls for nearly a year's supply of clothing coupons. Disregarding my lack of shirts, shoes, underpants *et al* I recklessly ordered a suit a month ago—and learn today that nothing can be done because the electricity is cut off, and the machines are dead. Would it be too much to suggest that any useless, worn out, good-for-nothing cast-off clothing you may have . . ."

Here, of course, I was merely jesting, if in a somewhat lugubrious vein. But Mencken's reaction, to my subsequent embarrassment, was to treat the problem of scarecrow raiment seriously.

(The Mencken notepaper now exhibited a pale yellow color.)

February 17, 1947

Dear Cleator:

The newspapers here are full of miserable cablegrams about the troubles of England. All this, I believe, gives the indigenous morons a certain Christian satisfaction. They are always delighted to hear of the difficulties of other people. I certainly hope that the horrible cold has passed off, and that you are once more reasonably comfortable. We have had a hard Winter also, but the threatened coal shortage was prevented by Truman's heroic defiance of the labor leaders. It took him a long while to get up his courage, but after the November votes had been counted he began to see the light.

I have no news. I am plugging away slave-like at my infernal book. It is extraordinarily complicated and tedious. Fortunately, I seem to be making some progress, and if all goes well a copy should be in your hands by the early days of 1949.

Yours,
H. L. Mencken

The cablegrams reaching the States from England did not exaggerate the miseries of the populace, thanks to an untimely return of the Ice Age: "At the time of this writing (January 28th) we're in the midst of the worst Winter for years—without coal, with electricity invariably cut off when it's most wanted, and with cooking gas at a pressure so low that it can't decide which way to run in the pipes. Right now, I'm preparing to burn the garden fence, the furniture, the floor boards, and the bulk of my library—in that order. Rest assured that when I'm discovered frozen to death, it will be with an unburned Mencken volume in my hand."

I was able to conclude however, on a more warming note: "I have to report a letter from the Fatherland came in yesterday—the first for eight years or so. What memories it revives!"

March 24, 1947

Dear Cleator:

All sorts of linens continue to be scarce here, but we have not yet reached the stage that seems to prevail in England. I'd certainly like to send you some underwear, if you will let me. Call it a belated Christmas present, as one Christian to another. If you will send me your shirt, undershirt and underpants measurements, I'll see what I can find. White shirts are almost unobtainable, but those in color with collars attached seem to be coming back. What colors do you prefer? Also, what of socks? Do you wear thick woollen ones or thin silk or rayon ones? Let me know. I assume that such things can be got through the English customs without paying duty—that is, if they are a gift.

God knows I wish you were coming this way. All sorts of clothing is still scarce and of bad quality, but there is no longer any shortage of food. Even alcoholic beverages are obtainable in almost unlimited quantities. The prices thereof continue very high, but the native boozers are quite willing to pay them.

Yours,
H. L. Mencken

This was Mencken's generous and well-intentioned response to my ill-considered jest about castoff clothing. I replied in a lighthearted vein, in the hope that I'd hear no more of it: "The kind promise of all your underwear heartens me greatly, as the bits and pieces I have about my person at the time of this writing will most certainly not hold together until next Winter. I am, indeed, planning to put on an undercoat of varnish—if I can get the varnish. I am informed that, if carefully mixed with a solution of yellow phosphorus in carbon bi-sulphide, such a coat of varnish can be quite warming."

April 8, 1947

Dear Cleator:

God knows that I am delighted to hear that the Winter is passing in England. Here in God's chosen playground we have

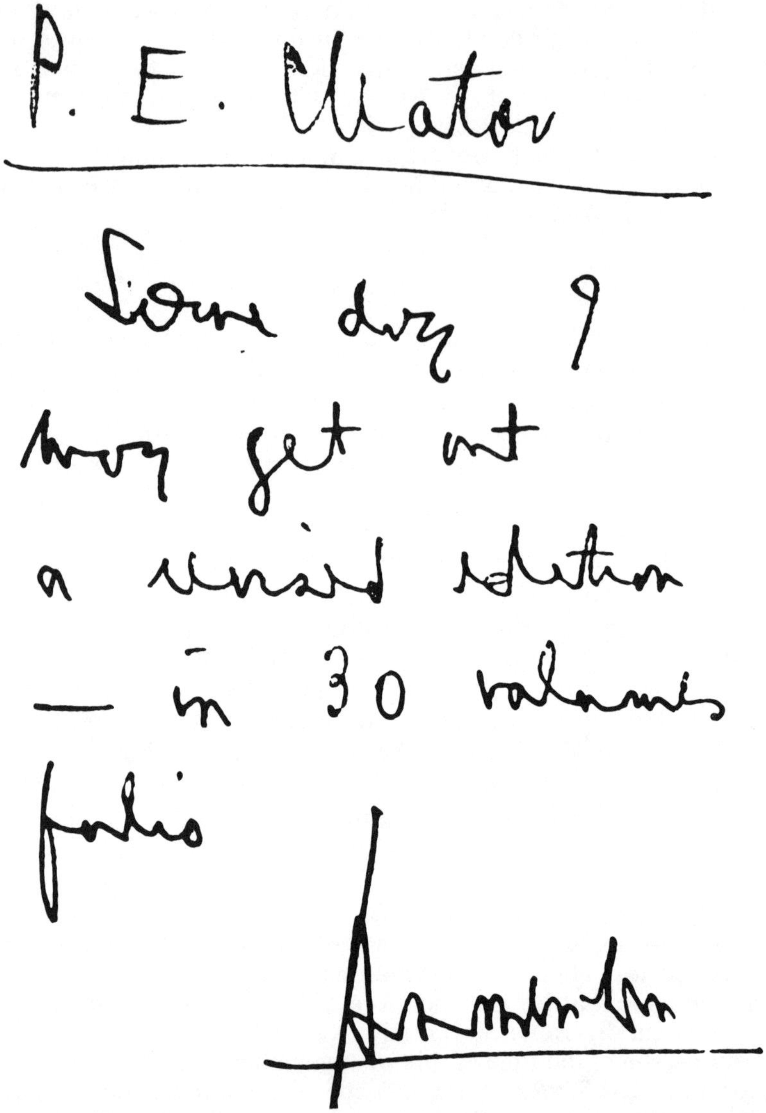

P. E. Cleator

Some day I may get out a revised edition — in 30 volumes folio

H. L. Mencken

PLATE 16. The Mencken epigraphs—6. *Menckeniana*, published in 1928. The proposed revised edition, in thirty volumes, was not, alas, destined to appear.

already had one day with a temperature of 85 degrees. I should add that the mercury dropped the very next day to 38. That is the sort of weather a really heroic people have been bred to endure.

I wrote to you a week or so ago about underwear and such things. I'd surely like to have the privilege of sending you some from this side. Will you let me know what your sizes are? You had better mention them in inches, for sizes apparently differ somewhat in England and America. What sort of stockings do you wear? Such things are now obtainable here, and it would be a great pleasure to send you a little package. I only wish I could add two or three hundred bottles of Maryland rye whiskey. It has a strange taste to a Briton, but I have never encountered a Briton who did not get used to it within three hours.

Yours,
H. L. Mencken

"I wrote to you a week or so ago": In the light of my failure to end the discussion about the proposed garmenture lend-lease, the time had evidently come squarely to face the issue. This I did on May 4: "Since my reply of April 20th to your letter of March 24th, your further letter of April 8th has come in—and with it the realisation on my part that you are really in earnest about helping to cover up my Gothic nakedness. God knows I'm more than enough in your debt already, and your latest offer is not one that I'll easily forget. The temptation, indeed, is strong to make out a formidable list. But fortunately for your pocket and for my self respect, the British Board of Trade has decreed gifts from abroad *verboten*. Strictly, even a toothbrush requires an import licence—which will in no circumstances be issued. But although official permission to import cannot be obtained, I believe an odd, small and generally insignificant parcel is usually permitted to pass—once Customs have received their 20% of value in cash, plus Purchase Tax (a further ⅙th, again in cash).

"Under separate cover I'm sending you a shirt, or, more exactly, what remains of what was once a shirt. I send it just as it came in from the laundry, and I offer it as a typical example of all my shirts—between 6 and 10 years old; the fabric rotten with age; torn, patched, darned, bits from the tail grafted onto the neck, and the cuffs gone completely to Hell. When I say, without a fib, that it was a toss up whether I sent the thing to you, or put it on as usual, you'll understand that I'm about ready to sell half my hypothetical soul for a single, in-one-piece honest-to-God shirt. So—and illegal though it may be—I offer to barter any books published in These Isles for which you may have need, in exchange for a shirt, with or without collar attached, preferably blue in colour, or brown this failing. As to size, allow somewhat larger than the sample aforementioned: it's been washed for so many years that it's shrunk to Hell."

May 8, 1947

Dear Cleator:

Thanks very much for that elegant copy of *Science and Health*. I have already read it seven times, and begin to find my infidelity weakening. I shall devote the rest of the Summer to hard study of it, and by the time the hot weather is over I may be ready for baptism.

That *Fortean Magazine* is operated single-handed and alone by a strange fellow named Tiffany Thayer. He has shown an almost incredible mixture of intelligence and imbecility. As the war was coming on he wrote about it with great realism and complete plausibility, but nevertheless he insists that Fort was a great scientific reformer and that all other scientists are frauds and scoundrels. I am glad that he noted that fact that I am not a member of his organization.

I still mourn when I think of you running out of underclothes. Why not send me the measurements of your undershirts, drawers and stockings, and let me ship you some as a small gift from one Christian to another? I am not sure what such things are called in England, but you know what I mean. It is also possible to get shirts, though they are inferior to the pre-war varieties. Please do this, and it will give me great pleasure to send you a few specimens.

I do not advise coming to the United States. The war boom is beginning to subside, and in a little while there will be a desperate struggle for jobs and money. If a war with Russia develops the situation of the Republic will be really precarious. I thus look forward with pleasanter and pleasanter anticipations to my probable early translation to bliss eternal.

Don't forget those measurements. I have no idea of your bulk, beam and tonnage.

Sincerely yours,
H. L. Mencken

"*Science and Health*": An opus penned in 1875 by Mary Baker Eddy, famed for her advocacy of divine healing. In mischievously sending Mencken a copy of the book, I was well aware that in matters spiritual and occult, La Eddy ranked as his No. 1 *bête noire*.

"I still mourn": Determinedly intent upon replenishing my entire wardrobe, Mencken had not yet received my reply of May 4 to his letters of March 24 and April 8.

"I do not advise": In view of the situation which prevailed in England, I had mentioned that we were considering emigrating with the idea of seeking a land overflowing with the Anglo-Saxon equivalent of milk and honey. As a possible destination, the U.S., though a likely haven in this respect, presented currency transference problems which at the time appeared to be insuperable.

"Don't forget those measurements": The words "I have no idea of your bulk, beam or tonnage" were added in longhand.

May 22, 1947

Dear Cleator:

The fossil shirt and your note of May 4th arrived together this morning. I'll certainly make an effort, and at once, to get some replenishments to you. Perhaps the best plan will be to send the shirts one by one. I'll mark them "gifts," for I am informed that that device sometimes induces the customs brethren to waive the duty. The pioneer will be despatched tomorrow, and another will follow in a week or two. Let me hear at once when the first reaches you, so that I can prepare for future operations. I note that English shirts have long tails. This is now unheard of in this great free Republic. The tails were shortened steadily during the war, and the shirtmakers have never restored the old length. Thus you will probably find them somewhat strange, but I can assure you that it is easy to get used to them. Plenty of shirts are now obtainable here, but the materials are almost uniformly bad. My shirtmaker told me only the other day that madras and other such fabrics had been out of the market for three or four years, and that he saw no probability of ever getting them again. In New York last week I managed to get a suit of clothes, my first in almost six years. The material was inferior, but the price had been doubled. I ascribe all these evils to the wickedness of the infidels.

Just a week ago I finished the last word of the first draft of my book, and feel as relieved as a woman delivered of a 30-pound baby. To be sure, the revision remains, and also the two long indexes, but I hope to knock them off by July 4th, the anniversary of the Declaration of Independence.

Let me hear of it if the first shirt reaches you safely, and without too much expense for duty. I'll then follow with the others.

Sincerely yours,
H. L. Mencken

"The fossil shirt": I had modestly suggested a single replacement. Now, it appeared, there were to be several.

May 26, 1947

Dear Cleator:

Shirt No. 1 is on its way to you. I was advised by the highest authority to rumple it a bit before shipping it, and to mark it "used" on the package. This does not indicate that I wore it to church on Sunday, but simply because I was trying to change its status and thus save you some possible duty. Let me hear of it if it arrives safely, and tell me if it is your size. If not, send me more accurate specifications and the others will follow. When your dilapidated garment arrived in Baltimore it made a sensation. No one here had seen such good material in a shirt for six or seven years. We are all forced to submit to sleazy fabrics and third-rate workmanship. My own shirtmaker, who has made shirts for me for years, says flatly that he despairs of ever getting good shirting again.

I have finished the first text of my infernal book, and am engaged upon the revision. It is a dreadful job, and I'll appreciate the prayers of Christian people.

What of underwear? If you need any, send me your measurements and I'll dispatch some at once. You will have a chance to repay me after I reach an internment camp. I enclose a circular explaining how the shirt is operated.

Yours,
H. L. Mencken

Mencken's letter containing the news that shirt No. 1 was on its way arrived by the same post as his two previous communications, as I mentioned in my reply, in which I once again raised the question of books for barter: "By divine whim, your three letters of May 8th, 22nd, and 26th have landed in a bunch, and my problem is where to begin answering what. The shirt you have so kindly sent has not yet reached me, but be sure that I'll let you have a full report the moment it comes in. Meanwhile, there's the little matter of our bargain. What can I offer you from my shelves—Roget's *Thesaurus?* Toller's *No More Peace? The Electronic Theory of Valency?* Whitaker's *Almanack?* Please let me have a full list with your next letter.

"Please cease to mourn my lack of underclothes forthwith. The problem of undershirts (vests?) I got over in the early days of the war by discarding them altogether. As for underpants, I am, for an Englishman, relatively well off in this department. Some little time ago every pair I possessed fell to bits within a week, and thus something desperate had to be done. By dint of sacrificing a new suit, I was able to produce enough clothing coupons to purchase 4 pairs—sufficient to last me until the day of my demise (I hope). Socks? These, I confess, are a headache, and just as soon as I hear from you about those books, I'll send you a sample pair which will find a place of honour in the Baltimore Museum forthwith. They were first worn, I believe, by John the Baptist, and thereafter by a long line of Popes. None of the original sock now, of course, remains—the wonder is, indeed, that anything remains."

July 3, 1947

Dear Cleator:

I surely hope that the shirt reaches you before the end of the present Christian era. Send that sample sock, by all means. Such things are now plentiful here, and I'll be glad to forward some. I refuse to take books until this cruel peace is over. The index of my second supplement to "The American Language" will show how heavy my debt to you is. You have supplied me with some of the best stuff in the book.

The news that you have four pairs of what we call drawers is really astonishing. Very few Americans under the rank of plutocrats make so good a showing. As soon as I hear from you I'll send you some more shirts. They are very inferior in quality, but they will at least cover your nakedness. Like you, I long ago gave up the garments that you call vests and we call undershirts.

I have finished my second supplement at last, and the manuscript is in the hands of the printer. It will take him months to set it, and it will take me more months to make the two indexes, and read the proofs. Thus I fear I'll be stuck here in Baltimore until the end of the year. Despite the occasional infernal heat, the town is not uncomfortable. The malt liquor supply diminishes steadily, but it still remains sufficient for an aged man whose thoughts turn constantly to Heaven.

Yours,
H. L. Mencken

"I refuse to take books": Mencken's rejection of the proposed bargain left me with no option but to cease trading forthwith. As a result, the worn-out socks continued to be worn.

July 10, 1947

Dear Cleator:

I have turned your No. 2 shirt over to the National Museum at Washington. It turns out to be almost identical with the one that

Andrew Jackson wore at his inaugural in 1865, just after the Japs murdered Abraham Lincoln. So far I have got no word that you have received the shirt I sent to you about six weeks ago. If it turns out to be a reasonable fit, let me know and I'll send some more. The cut of the collar is certainly not to my taste, but it is what fashion now ordains in this great commonwealth of more or less free States.

Now that my Supplement II to "The American Language" is off my hands, I feel somewhat exhausted and have done no work whatever for ten days. This fatigue, of course, will pass, and by the end of July I hope to be hard at some fresh and worse insanity.

Sincerely yours,
H. L. Mencken

The day before Mencken dispatched the above letter, I had written to him to announce the arrival of the awaited garment No. 1. I added that : "A week or so ago, in hopeful anticipation of the shirt's arrival, I rashly discarded yet another of my remnants. It should have reached you by now, in not more, I trust, than half a dozen pieces. I bequeath it to you free of any restriction or direction: you have my full permission to do just what the Hell you like with it!"

"It turns out": Attentive students of American history may feel it incumbent upon them to make the point that after the assassination of President Lincoln in 1865, his successor was not Andrew Jackson (who had attained this high office as early as 1829), but Andrew Johnson. Was Mencken, then, here guilty of a solecism inexcusable in a college freshman? Or did his secretary, perhaps, make an understandable slip which went unnoticed when the letter came to be signed? With respect, my inclination is to accept neither of these explanations. Whereas I, the unsuspecting recipient, might possibly have been expected to raise a quizzical eyebrow at the unlikelihood of Nipponese involvement in the death of Lincoln, for me to distinguish between Andrew Jackson and Andrew Johnson might well have been considered a feat of scholarship well beyond the range of a benighted Englander. In short, I predicate a jest within a jest, perpetrated in the immemorial Mencken manner.

July 28, 1947

Dear Cleator:

I am delighted to hear that the shirt is a reasonable fit. Today I am sending you two more, again with apologies for their quality. It seems to be simply impossible in this great country to find shirts of good material and plausible cut. What we call customs shirtmakers, of course, still make them, but the customs shirtmaker will not undertake a commission without seeing his client. More shirts will follow as I find them. I enclose a little ticket which shows how those I am sending should be handled in the laundry.

I am looking forward with horror to reading the proofs and making the two long indexes to my book. The printer has had the manuscript a month, but not a word has come out of him. I suppose that all of his workmen are busy with golf tournaments. American printers now work but seven hours a day, five days a week, and are already agitating for a thirty-hour week. Worse, their rate of production is scarcely more than half what it was before the war. Such are the benefits we are deriving from the great crusade to save humanity.

Sincerely yours,
H. L. Mencken

My acknowledgment of the safe arrival of the shirt read as follows: "I hasten to pass on the glad tidings that the shirt has arrived safely and in one piece. There were times when I feared that the Customs must have seized it, or that some Post Office official had taken an illicit fancy to it. But no such Act of God befell—indeed, so blind was His all-seeing eye in the matter that neither Duty nor Purchase Tax was demanded.

"The garment fits perfectly, and with it snugly tucked into my pantaloons, I'm possibly the best dressed Englishman in this island prison, not even excluding my Lord Woolton, who has recently made public confession that one of her Ladyship's prime duties is the grafting of the tails of his shirts onto the necks thereof."

August 18, 1947

Dear Cleator:

Thanks very much for that copy of the *Literary Guide* containing the review of my book. I say thanks, but I am really horrified that anything of mine should be praised in so atheistic a publication. I'll be careful not to let my pastor see the review.

One thing at least you miss in England, and that is the horrible heat that we have been having in the Republic this Summer. For more than two weeks past the temperature in Baltimore has been over 90 degrees every day, and along with it there has been 80 or 90 degrees of humidity. This combination is sufficient to make life almost insupportable even to a native. I have been tempted more than once to curse God and die. Fortunately, there seems to be some relief in sight, and in another couple of weeks the land will be restored to normalcy. Meanwhile, the heat has been accompanied by a plague of Japanese beetles, so that half the trees are stripped of their foliage. Yet more, there has been a dreadful epidemic of fleas, and more than once I have seen a bishop on his throne jump and scratch.

My book is now in the hands of the printer, and the proofs are beginning to run. I look forward with horror to the two long indexes, but I'll probably be able to get through them safely. The thing will run to more than 800 pages. It will probably bring in some money when it is out at last, but meanwhile it will almost kill me.

Yours,
H. L. Mencken

"The *Literary Guide*": The inoffensively entitled organ of the Rationalist Society, of which I was a member. The review concerned the second edition (1946) of *Treatise on the Gods*.

September 11, 1947

Dear Cleator:

The news that those shirts have not reached you is really astonishing. The parcels post service between the United States and England seems to be far slower than that between the United States and the Continent. I ascribe this to the activities of the jobholders. They are probably searching the shirts for secret communications.

I hope that the news about your book is good. There is nothing worse on this earth than seeing an enterprise drag.

I am beginning to get the proofs of Supplement II, but it will probably be the end of the year before I finish with it.

The weather here for six weeks past has been really infernal. I can recall no such bath of heat and moisture in sixty years past. The humidity is so high that rain squeezes out of the air every hour or two. The temperature oscillates around 90, and there is seldom as much as a breath of wind. I ascribe all these horrors and calamities to the evil operations of the Holy Spirit. The United States has sinned, and now it is paying for it.

Yours,
H. L. Mencken

"The news about your book": With paper still in short supply at home, my agents had sent the MS of *Into Space* to their New York office, from where they had recently received word of an expression of interest, cautiously described as "tentative."

September 18, 1947

Dear Cleator:

I rejoice that the shirts have reached you at last, and can only deplore the fact that the customs charged you duty. From such things there seems to be no escape. We are in the hands of jobholders, and our liberties are fast disappearing. In the United States the doctrine is now openly preached that a man's income does not belong to him at all. The state has first call on it, and not until the state is satisfied is he entitled to the meagre remainder. This idea is not spread by idiots, but by Truman himself, and in plain terms.

I hope you are having a reasonably placid time of it on your holiday.

Sincerely yours,
H. L. Mencken

In acknowledging the arrival of, and expressing thanks for, a parcel containing two more shirts, I added that on this occasion their delivery had been accompanied by a demand for import duty and purchase tax. The combined levy amounted to a modest eleven shillings and sixpence—the equivalent of 57½p.

October 13, 1947

Dear Cleator:

Please don't forget that I still have the manuscripts of your "Dictionary for the Damned" and "My Kingdom for a Hearse." Do you want me to return them? If so, let me know and I'll dispatch them at once. The mails now seem to be perfectly free.

I have no news to offer. Strikes and lock-outs have paralyzed transport between New York and Baltimore, and as a result three large packages of my proofs are lost. One of them has been missing for nearly three weeks. Soon or late, I suppose, they'll be recovered, but meanwhile I am seriously incommoded.

I surely hope that you had a pleasant time of it on your holiday.

Yours,
H. L. Mencken

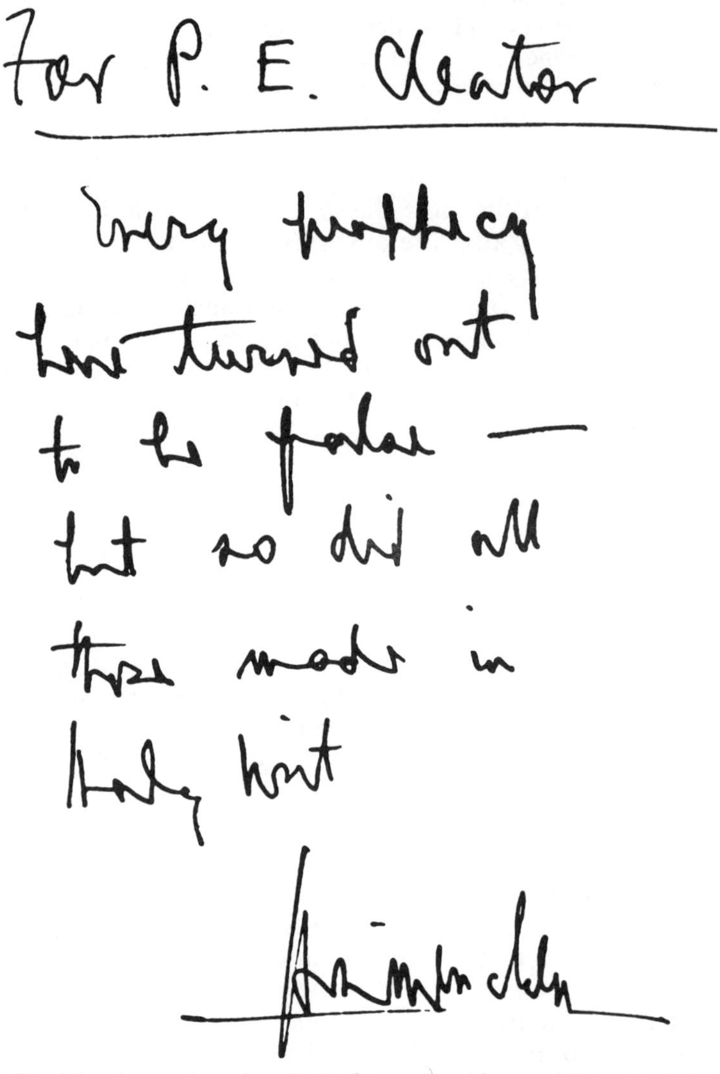

> For P. E. Cleator
>
> Every prophecy
> has turned out
> to be false —
> but so did all
> those made in
> Holy Writ
>
> H. L. Mencken

PLATE 17. The Mencken epigraphs—7. *Making a President*, published in 1932.

As I had emerged from the recent conflict with copies of the two MSS intact, I suggested that those retained in Baltimore should be consigned to the nearest wastepaper receptacle.

October 16, 1947

Dear Cleator:

I am delighted to hear that the shirts have reached you safely. I'll now suspend sending them, and give you a chance to wear them out. I suppose you have already discovered that their quality is anything but superior. Americans are now wearing and using imitations in nearly all departments.

I surely hope that you have come to terms with Sloane. As I wrote to you a few days ago, two of your manuscripts are still in my office. If you want me to return them, let me know.

Supplement II is now being set up. I have had a dreadful time with lost proofs. There was an express drivers strike in New York for three weeks, and it threw an extra burden on the parcels post. As a result, the parcels post blew up, and some of my proofs were lost for twenty days. They have come in at last, and I am now blazing away at the two long indexes to the book. It is a very severe labor, and I am sustained in it only by patriotic passion.

Yours,
H. L. Mencken

I had earlier reported the arrival of a fourth shirt, and at this considered it time to call a halt: "To my thanks for this further garment, I add a plea: your great generosity has indeed gone far enough in the matter of clothing Europe. I alone, in the entire kingdom, I dare say, possess four, spanking new shirts. And quite frankly, I feel a bit uneasy about it. Somehow, it doesn't seem quite right. . . .

"As for my debt to you, it is now piled mountain high. Can I persuade you to descend upon These Stricken Isles, and half starve for a while at my expense? It seems a very happy solution, and I hope you'll decide to risk it."

"Sloane": William Sloane Associates, of New York, had in the meantime been identified as the U.S. publishers who had expressed a tentative interest in *Into Space*.

November 17, 1947

Dear Cleator:

I surely hope that Mrs. Cleator is making a good recovery, despite the shortage of hospital supplies. It must be truly maddening to face such a situation. The idiots who run the world seem to be getting their wish. They have made it almost intolerably uncomfortable for every decent person. This is true not only in Europe, but also in this great free Republic, the envy and despair of all lesser nations. The cost of living has gone up to dizzy heights, and the constant demand from labor for more money only accentuates the process. What the end will be only our Heavenly Father knows. A bust of some sort seems to be inevitable. I am more and more convinced that bringing those Asiatic barbarians into Western Europe was the master imbecility of the times.

The state of affairs in Germany, as I hear it from friends there, is genuinely appalling. The people are not only desperately short of food and clothing; they are also forbidden to pursue their ordinary avocations. I know of plenty of educated men, quite free from the Nazi taint, who are working as day laborers, and trying to live on the equivalent of the Chinaman's eight cents a day.

My best thanks for the clippings. I am always delighted to have them.

I am now in the final stages of my two long indexes—a really infernal job. Altogether, I believe that there will be nearly 25,000 entries. My secretary takes over a large part of the burden, but plenty remains for the Old Man.

Sincerely yours,
H. L. Mencken

My wife had recently undergone some abdominal surgery, and her recovery, though proceeding well enough, was not greatly assisted by the prevailing diet: "Doctors, of course, live in another world. 'The patient,' runs the edict, 'shall have plenty of milk' (we get half a pint a day), 'fresh eggs' (unknown and illegal), 'chicken' (ditto), 'and anything else that is fancied' (may God help us all!)"

"The state of affairs in Germany": The contents of Mencken's report confirmed all that I had heard from various sources: "Your news from Germany agrees with all that I have heard. A friend of mine, living in Wallasey, has recently been to Berlin to visit her people there, and some of the tales she has to tell almost surpass belief. I am driven to seek consolation in the thought that all this suffering is in strict accord with divine whim."

"I am now": The welcome news that *Supplement II* was in its final stages reached me at a time when I was busily engaged in a terminal task of my own: "I've just been clearing out my files of an accumulation of dead matter, and sorting out the rest. And the extent of our correspondence has amazed me. The copy of this letter will start a fifth file bearing your holy name. I hesitate to guess how many thousands of words are involved. But it grieves me somewhat to reflect that, one way and another, I've probably denied the world at least a couple of new Mencken works."

December 26, 1947

Dear Cleator:

The *Journal of the British Interplanetary Society* reached me safely this morning, and I shall go through it with the greatest pleasure. Your own article awakens plenty of memories in the so-called breast of a journalist. All of the lunatics on earth make their first calls at newspaper offices. It is only after they have been thrown out there that they ever begin to pester better men.

I am sorry to hear of Sloane's decision. I only hope that you don't let it induce you to scrap the book. There are plenty of other publishers.

Your two manuscripts are being turned over to the Mencken collection in the public library here. They will be investigated and whooped up by the scholars of posterity.

I am in the last stages of my proofs, and hope to finish them by the end of the year. I should take a holiday at that time, but another big job already impends.

My very best thanks for the clippings, and the best of luck in 1948.

Yours,
H. L. Mencken

"Your own article": This was an offering entitled "Messages in Morse from Mars" (JBIS-4), which dealt with a choice extract from my lunatic post-bag. I append the opening sentence:

> While I do not here presume to question the mental well-being of those (including myself) who profess an intelligent interest in space travel and its possibilities, it nevertheless remains a curious and no doubt significant fact that the interplanetary idea has a seemingly irresistible fascination for the somewhat crack-brained, the near demented, and the hopelessly insane. . . .

"I am sorry to hear": William Sloane's reader vetoed *Into Space* on the grounds that by the time the book appeared in print, it would be out of date. In the event, it was to be another two decades or so before American space voyagers actually set foot on the moon.

"Your two manuscripts": The scholars of tomorrow will search for them in vain, for in the confusion which followed the onset of Mencken's long illness, the MSS were neither scrapped (as I had suggested) nor turned over to the Enoch Pratt Library of Baltimore (as I assume Mencken intended from his reference to "the public library here"). Instead, after his death, they found their way back to me, though not before they narrowly escaped being deposited in the Manuscripts and Archives Division of the NYPL, in company with much of the correspondence Mencken had with the literati. The reason for this change of plan is discussed later.

"Another big job already impends": This was the task of editing and annotating a selection of his out-of-print writings, which appeared as *A Mencken Chrestomathy* in 1949.

January 29, 1948

Dear Cleator:

I am delighted to hear that Mrs. Cleator is making good progress. The news that you bagged a turkey for Christmas really surprises me. They were very scarce and very expensive in this great free Republic. Luckily for me, a customer in the Christian State of Kansas sent me one weighing at least twenty pounds. My brother and I gnawed at it for nearly a month. Between us we probably put on ten pounds of weight. Now it is gone, and we begin to feel hollow again.

It is astonishing that in a country so rich so many foodstuffs should be scarce. The theory that this is a curse laid on by our Heavenly Father hardly stands up under examination. Why should He afflict the one country in the whole world that is without sin? All the decayed principalities of Europe have engaged in wholesale malpractices, but here is one land where the government and the people are alike chemically pure. Yet, as Americans say, we get it in the neck—worse, we get it in the gluteus maximus.

My horrible book is off my hands at last. I hope to get a copy to you by April. It is a really formidable tome.

Yours,
H. L. Mencken

I had reported: "I was lucky enough to bag a turkey, and for once we fed to our heart's content. My outraged stomach is still recovering from the shock. . ."

Actually, luck had little to do with the acquisition of this prize. With a postoperative invalid in the house, an empty larder, and Christmas fast approaching, I devoted a whole day to scouring the surrounding countryside, armed with a pocket full of pound notes and a determination to visit every farm within a radius of fifty miles, if need be.

March 10, 1948

Dear Cleator:

My infernal book is off the press at last, and a copy is already on its way to you. If you try to read it I'll have a commission appointed to inquire into your sanity. My own began to shake before the job was done, and toward the end of February I resolved to take a little holiday—my first in eight years. My brother and I went to St. Petersburg in Florida, and returned pretty well rested. The weather here all Winter was horrible, but in Florida the sun was shining and the temperature was above 70. St. Petersburg is a town that would delight you. It is full of old people, retired from the struggle for existence. The average age of the Winter inhabitants is probably no less than 70. Some of them are so feeble that they can barely navigate. It is a fact that at all of the street intersections there are ramps at the curbings, so that the customers will not have to undertake to step up. There are also ramps in the churches, to enable the saved to get in without losing breath.

I surely hope that Sloane takes the manuscript. It is precisely the sort of thing that should do well in this emergency. Things in this free Republic are going rapidly from bad to worse. Truman is under heavy fire, and there is talk of scaring him out of the contest. I am, however, not too optimistic. He has a war scare in his pocket, and that always makes effective ammunition. If things grow really alarming, he will probably discover that the Huns are once more on us.

I feel somewhat empty now that my horrible book is finished. My publisher wants me to put together a volume of extracts from those of my books as are out of print, and I incline to do it.

I surely hope the Spring is dawning pleasantly, if not cheerfully, in England. My best thanks for the clippings.

Yours,
H. L. Mencken

"I surely hope": A personal correspondence had developed between William Sloane and myself, in which he expressed a wish to see more of my work. At the time I had nothing to offer, apart from my record of the recent conflict. As this was limited to events within the confines of the British Isles, I considered it unlikely to be of interest to an American audience. However, I sent it along as a sample of my wares, and at the same time began extending the MS of the play.

"Truman is under heavy fire": The fusillade came from the supporters of Thomas E. Dewey, the Republican contender for the presidency.

"My publisher wants": The aforementioned omnibus edition of extracts from Mencken's early writings.

March 26, 1948

Dear Cleator:

My Supplement II to "The American Language" went forward to you on March 10th. I surely hope that it has been safely delivered. It is a dreadful tome indeed, and reading it seriatim would be a sheer impossibility. I recommend it for occasional dipping into on despondent days.

I enclose a circular that tells some bitter truths about this great free Republic. The Population Reference Bureau is a highly respectable outfit, and its publications are always worth reading. I gather from the enclosed that the Republic is on its way to Hell. I am sorry to have to add that I don't care.

I surely hope that you come to terms with Sloane, and that Unwin digs up some paper. The paper shortage over here has begun to lessen, mainly because the printers are on strike everywhere. They are being misled by New Deal leaders, and are fast going broke. Those that remain at work are already paying a great proportion of their wages to their strike fund. Some of the largest papers in the country, including all those in Chicago, are being printed without printers. Their columns are set up on a new machine called the Veritype, which can be operated by any high-school kid.

Substitutes for the common foodstuffs are as common here as in England. The Pure Food laws seem to be suspended. There is no telling what one gets when one sends an order to a grocer. I am training myself to eat hay. It seems to be beneficial to horses, and I see no reason why it shouldn't nourish man.

God help us all.

Sincerely yours,
H. L. Mencken

"I enclose a circular": This was a leaflet entitled *Population Bulletin*, and its somewhat pessimistic contents began with the announcement:

> During its short history the United States has lost one-third of its topsoil—four-fifths of its standing timber—and many of its mineral and wildlife resources are nearing depletion.

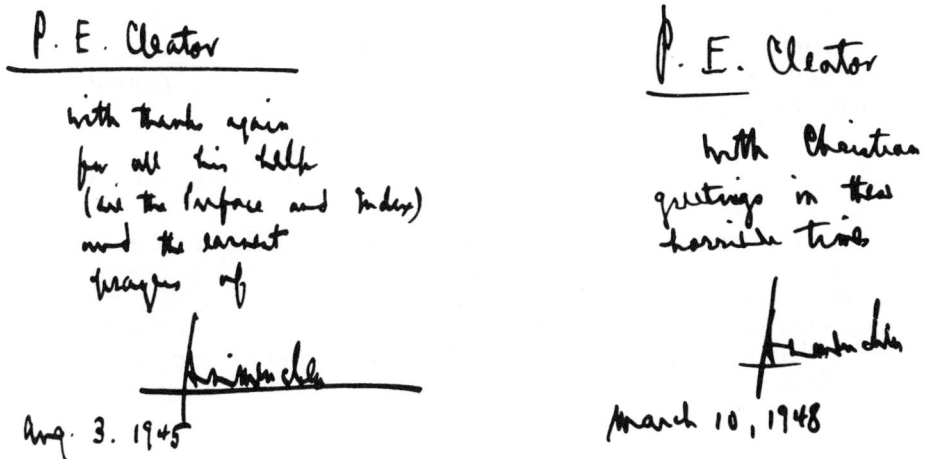

PLATE 18. The Mencken epigraphs—8. From *The American Language*, Supplements I *(left)*, published in 1945; and II *(right)*, which appeared in 1948.

"Substitutes for the common foodstuffs": I was astonished to learn of the dearth of eatables in the U.S., and intent upon offering assistance in the emergency, I drew upon our wartime experience: "Your mention of a foodstuffs shortage astounds me, and if a lack of cooking fats is one of your difficulties, you may care to instruct your cook to follow our example, and use medicinal liquid paraffin. We ourselves use it as a fat substitute for almost everything, including frying fish and making cakes. The shops, indeed, go a stage further, and lubricate their pastry with vaseline, *alias* petroleum jelly. I don't know why, but the effect is not nearly as good as that achieved with the paraffin."

April 30, 1948

Dear Cleator:

I am delighted to hear that the book has reached you at last. Please don't undertake to read it. It is the sort of thing that resists continuous reading, but I am in hopes that you may dip into it now and then and find it more or less edifying. If you encounter any errors, please let me hear of them.

I am certainly glad to hear that Sloane is interested in "My Kingdom for a Hearse." His troubles with paper and printers might be easily duplicated here on God's favorite footstool. I turned in my manuscript July 1st last and did not see a bound copy of the book until March 25 of this year.

The Presidential campaign promises to be really superb. All the worst frauds in the Republic have thrown themselves into it, and we'll presently see a combat not matched since Apostolic times. I believe that, as usual, the worst man will win.

Yours,
H. L. Mencken

"I am certainly glad": In giving news of the safe arrival of, and expressing thanks for, the copy of *Supplement II,* I was able to provide some further information about my own endeavors: "Wm. Sloane professes to like very much my thesis on the recent conflict. But this is not to say that he intends to publish it, for even publishers, it appears, must eat. However, he's asking for more, and I've been sweating blood for the past 28 days revising, extending and bringing up to date *My Kingdom For A Hearse*. I finished it yesterday, and have now fallen back exhausted. If it fails to fetch him, I give up!"

May 5, 1948

Dear Cleator:

If you tackle Supplement II serially I shall apply to the proper authorities for your incarceration in what is known in this great country as the booby-hatch. The thing needs to be taken in very small doses, and at long intervals.

Most of my earlier books have been out of print since the great plate-melting rage that went on during the war. I am hoping to reprint the essential parts of them in a sort of omnibus, planned for next year. Meanwhile, they are hard to come by and some are downright unobtainable. I ascribe this to the fact that most Christian people, after reading them, burnt them on sacrificial fires.

If a poll were taken in the United States at least 80% of the people would vote for clearing out. Life is gradually becoming unendurable all over the so-called civilized world. I wish I had enough confidence in man to predict a revolution. Unhappily, I haven't. I have been advocating hanging 100,000 job-holders a month, but so far there has not been a second.

Sincerely yours,
H. L. Mencken

In response to Mencken's earlier call for me to let him have a note of any errors my reading of *Supplement II* might reveal, I had announced that a start had been made: "As I mentioned in my previous note, *Supplement II* landed safely, albeit with a bump which rocked these premises for a full minute and a half. What is more, I've actually begun reading it, though I hasten to confess that I've not yet got very far. I note on an early page that a *Supplement III* is highly improbable, and God knows, you cannot be blamed for declining to produce another such monument. As things are, give me a couple of years or so, and I'll have ready a collection of comments and notes."

"Most of my earlier books": I had applauded the idea of an omnibus reprinting as one which I had long been demanding: "Your publisher's suggestion about producing a volume of extracts from earlier works is an excellent idea, and I certainly hope you do it. If I remember aright, I agitated for just such a volume years ago, and I cheerfully renew that agitation now. My acute dismay at finding half your works out of print must have been shared by many others in recent years. For that matter, why not an omnibus edition, in 500 volumes, of *all* your works?"

"If a poll were taken": As regards emigration from the British Isles, a recent Gallup poll had indicated that no less than 42 percent of the resident population wished to abscond from our socialistic heaven, news of which I dutifully relayed to Baltimore. As regards emigration from the democratic paradise of the U.S., Mencken, in making reply, managed to go one better.

June 10, 1948

Dear Cleator:

I think you are giving up too soon. The reminiscences of the literati are full of stories of manuscripts that were rejected ten, fifteen, and even forty times, and yet got into print at last and staggered humanity. I hope you go on, despite the failure of Sloane and Unwin.

A copy of Plain Words has already reached me. It is a swell book, and I have been enjoying it very much. If the copy you have ordered has not yet come in, please cancel your order, I am grateful nonetheless for your thought of me. Also, for the excellent clippings.

The three national conventions begin their unearthly progress next week. All are to be held in Philadelphia, which is only an hour and a half from Baltimore. I am planning to attend them and may do some writing about them, though I am not sure. At my age daily journalism begins to be a dreadful chore. I am, however, eager to see them for, by 1952, I'll undoubtedly be too old for the job. My guess is that Truman, if he is bold, can be reëlected. He has a war scare in his pocket, and that is worth millions of votes. All he has to do is to sound the alarm and all the patriots will leap up to support him. I begin to despair of the Republic.

Yours,
H. L. Mencken

PLATE 19. Baltimorean buffooneries—3. Recipients of Mencken books sent to them by the author were apt to find between their pages a selection of printed treatises and tracts, calling upon the godless to see the light, upon drink addicts to sign the pledge, and upon the starving to break their fast. The items shown above afford a representative sample of these pious and gratuitous exhortations.

In suggesting that I was giving up too soon, Mencken was here responding to the mournful tidings that both William Sloane and Allen & Unwin had shied at *My Kingdom for a Hearse,* and to the accompanying intimation that, at any rate for the present, I proposed to peddle the play no more. The frustrating fact was that while both parties professed to hold this example of my prose in the highest esteem (Allen & Unwin even went to the length of preparing a printing estimate—I have their cost sheet before me as I write), neither could bring themselves to regard the work as a commercial proposition. And this realistic assessment was afterward unanimously confirmed by later attempts to find a sponsor for it. In the meantime, however, that this twofold rejection was not intended as a reflection upon my capabilities as an author was demonstrated by the fact that both these publishing houses subsequently issued specimens of my literary wares. On the one hand, Allen & Unwin in due course not only found paper for my *Into Space,* but they afterward offered contracts for several other titles, while on the other hand, in 1957 William Sloane Associates bestowed their imprint upon the U.S. edition of a collective work (whose subject was space travel!) to which I had been invited to contribute a chapter.

"Plain Words": This was a publication issued by the British government for the benefit of members of the Civil Service and other dispensers of edicts couched in incomprehensible gobbledegook.

"My guess is that": This conjecture reestablished Mencken's reputation as a political prophet. Contrary to the predictions of most other pundits, both at home and abroad, Harry S. Truman was reelected president by the comfortable margin of 303 electoral votes to 189.

June 26, 1948

Dear Cleator:

"Plain Words" has reached me safely. As I wrote to you last week, a copy of it had already come in, but yours will certainly not go to waste, for I know an eminent American statesman who will devour it with delight. May the Holy Spirit reward you.

I went to the Republican National Convention in Philadelphia for the Baltimore *Sun.* I am too old for such exercises, but I simply can't resist. Four days after arriving in town I came down with tracheitis and had to come home. I should add that this was probably not caused by the effluvium from the delegates, but by an air-cooling machine in the bedroom I had to sleep in. I am now almost completely recovered, and hope to return for the Democratic orgies two weeks hence.

The Democrats always give a better show than the Republicans. They are a good deal less elegant, and there are many wild men among them. Even when they are unanimous, they commonly quarrel, and once they begin to quarrel they carry on all night. Very few of them hold their liquor in a civilized manner. It is not uncommon to see United States Senators and even higher dignataries so far gone that they have to be assisted to bed. I enjoy such obscenities, and thus hope to get to this one.

Dewey, the Republican nominee, is a smart fellow, but not to be trusted. He seems to be convinced that he can't be elected without the Jewish and Negro votes, so he will probably make elaborate efforts to woo both gangs. If they fail him and he is elected nevertheless, he will throw both of them over without compunction. I know him quite well, and have a somewhat low opinion of him, but I should add that he is a competent administrator and will probably start off, if elected, with an enormous massacre of Federal jobholders. Whether or not he can be elected remains to be seen. Truman still has that war scare in his pocket, and war scares are always potent with American numskulls.

              Yours,
              H. L. Mencken

"I went to": When assessing the outcome of the impending presidential election, a wary Mencken was now hedging his bets.

                  July 20, 1948

Dear Cleator:

I have read your Autopsia with the greatest interest, but I should add at once that it hasn't surprised me in the slightest. American officialdom was equally idiotic. It was not, indeed, until the war was over that the brass hats began to take rocket motors seriously.

I have just completed terms of servitude at the Republican and Democratic National Conventions. Both were inconceivably idiotic. At one of them I met an Englishwoman who sat with her mouth open for days on end. She simply couldn't fathom the obscenities going on. Now comes the Henry Wallace Convention. Wallace is one of the most preposterous mountebanks ever produced, even in America. Yet he has accumulated a large following, and his pow-wow will probably be a grand show. I am going to Philadelphia to see it tomorrow.

My very best thanks for the clippings. I am always delighted to have them.

Yours,
H. L. Mencken

Autopsia was the title of a postwar essay (JBIS-5) in which I somewhat caustically reviewed the nondevelopment of rocket propulsion in the British Isles from the early 1930s onwards, with particular reference to the profound and obstructive indifference of successive governments. The article subsequently reached a wider audience when it was accorded a place, in company with more than a score of other items of astronautical import, in Arthur C. Clarke's *The Coming of the Space Age* (London and New York, 1967).

"American officialdom": An instance of Mencken's charge of similar official lack of interest in the U.S. is provided by an experience which befell Robert H. Goddard, the world-famous American pioneer of rocket research. When the Japanese assault on Pearl Harbor took place, Goddard hastened to offer his services to the Army Air Corps, only to be politely informed that it was not considered the rocket was destined to play a part in the impending hostilities. Rather, it was suggested, was the war going to be fought with trench mortars!

"Wallace": At the Democratic National Convention held at Chicago in 1940, Henry A. Wallace had earlier been nominated as candidate for vice-president under Franklin D. Roosevelt.

August 3, 1948

Dear Cleator:

The Baltimore *Sun* prints a dispatch from Berlin today saying that the military there believe that the Russians will evade war, at least for the present. My guess is that they are afraid to tackle the Western Powers. They know very well that the United States has accumulated an enormous armament of atomic bombs, and they fear if they declare war there will be an immediate bombardment of Moscow. I confess shamelessly that I hope that this show starts in the not too distant future. I'd like very much to see it before I am snatched up to Heaven.

The discovery that the Germans have merits and deserve to be helped toward recovery has been made in this country as well as in yours. I needn't add that that makes me larf. In a little while, after all the surviving Japanese generals have been hanged, it will be discovered that the Japs are virtuous. I begin to believe seriously that the whole human race is insane.

I covered the three national conventions for my old paper, the Baltimore *Sun*. It was my first appearance in its columns for seven years. I quit in disgust when it began to support Roosevelt's war schemes. But now it is disillusioned, and I can go back with something resembling a smirk.

The Wallace show was really incredible. I have never seen a more appalling exhibition of human imbecility. Wallace and his friends let the Communists seize their party, and as a result it is in a bedraggled and forlorn state today. Whether or not it will poll any votes in November remains to be seen. I incline to think that it will get relatively few, but maybe it will get enough to defeat Truman. Under fire, he turns out to be an appalling jackass. I sat less than twenty feet from him when he made his speech of acceptance in Philadelphia. It was the snarling and defiant harangue of a badly scarred man. The more he whooped and hollered the more manifest it was that he was fighting with his back to the wall.

Sincerely yours,
H. L. Mencken

This was Mencken's considered response to my report, heightened by the somber circumstances of the Soviet attempt to blockade Berlin, that the conviction was growing in England that, sooner or later, war with Russia was inevitable: "There is nothing, however in the nature of a scare—merely resignation. There are so many other troubles and difficulties of more immediate importance—such as the eternal problem of locating and consuming something fit to eat—that the threat of yet another war seems relatively unimportant and remote. Nevertheless, subtle preparations for the conflict are already afoot. In a widely reported speech by none other than Churchill, we have just been called upon not to hate, but to love, the Germans, *i.e.*, the human butchers of yesterday and the day before. And tomorrow, you may be sure, there'll be a clarion call, as a prime Christian duty, to extirpate the godless hordes of the U.S.S.R.

"To unpatriotic outlaws such as myself, all this is very amusing. But it is also very depressing. Is *Homo* the *Sap* about to destroy himself? Then let it be soon, O Lord—and above all, let it be thorough!"

"Wallace and his friends": In 1946, while serving as secretary of commerce under the Truman administration, Henry Wallace was asked to resign, following his criticism of the government's stiffening attitude toward Russia.

August 26, 1948

Dear Cleator:

I have so many doubts about the immediate future of the United States that I hesitate to advise you to come here. Unless the defeat of Truman is really overwhelming, Dewey will face an enormous number of difficulties, chiefly resident in the Democratic opposition. He is not the sort of man to deal with such things effectively. He is far too timorous for that, and his own principles are too fluid. Business is already showing a sharp decline, and the authorities that I respect tell me that it is bound to go further in a little while. I therefore suggest that you put off deciding until towards the end of the year. By that time it will be easier to weigh your opportunity.

Incidentally, what do you propose to do here? If I knew that precisely, perhaps I could advise you better. Certainly you do not want to go to Australia or South Africa. The United States at its worst would probably be better than either. But the United States at its worst can be very bad indeed. Maybe in a year or two the restrictions on sterling will be lifted.

Let me hear more particularly what your plans are. I'd be delighted to see you here myself, but I do not want to lead you into a morass.

Sincerely yours,
H. L. Mencken

We were still thinking in terms of seeking to make a new life elsewhere, but where to go was proving to be a problem. Although for various reasons the U.S. beckoned, a move in that direction promised to involve severe financial restraints, as the amount of so-called hard currency that could be exported from dollar-starved Britain was strictly limited. On the other hand, English-speaking countries within the sterling area, such as Australia or South Africa, which presented no such difficulty, rightly or wrongly appeared to offer many of the attributes of an intellectual desert.

September 7, 1948

Dear Cleator:

I am still convinced that it would be imprudent to come to the United States at any time in the very near future. The state of affairs here is by no means reassuring. The cost of living is still spiraling, and there seems to be no way out. Truman, who is an almost incredible ass, proposes to reduce it without cutting down wages. That, of course, would be quite impossible, but he sticks to his programme [*sic*]. My belief is that he will be knocked off in November, and that his successor, Dewey, will show a great deal more sense. But there is never any trusting a politician. The best of them are unmitigated scoundrels.

I have been hard at work on a sort of omnibus of my earlier writings, now all out of print. It has been a lot of fun putting the book together, but I begin to wonder who will ever buy it. When my publisher sees the manuscript he will faint. It now runs beyond three hundred thousand words.

Yours,
H. L. Mencken

Mencken's well-intentioned advice did little toward solving the problem of our emigratory destination. Tentative enquiries had revealed that whereas passage to America could be secured after a wait of only two months, a journey to Australia or South Africa promised to entail a delay of as long as two years.

September 23, 1948

Dear Cleator:

My best thanks for the clippings, which are amusing and edifying, as usual.

Your plan to come to the United States by way of Australia certainly has some merit. If you can get your money to Australia, or any considerable part of it, it should be easy to bring it all the way. The politicos of Australia, I gather, are amenable to persuasion.

Unhappily, if you come here and are expecting to live on manuscripts you'll probably be on the dole in short order. There was never a time in human history when the publishing business was so bad. Even best-sellers are losing money. The reason for that, of course, is that the costs of production have become fabulous. The printers, going crazy, are demanding the pay of fashionable surgeons, paper increases in price every few months, and all other expenses keep pace.

I have some doubt that the present horrible state of affairs in England will last. Such things have a way of curing themselves. Unfortunately, the cure sometimes lasts longer than the normal lifetime.

I have just finished putting together a sort of omnibus of my out-of-print stuff. I propose to call it "A Mencken Chrestomathy." My publisher protests that this title will ruin us, but I think I'll stick to it.

Yours,
H. L. Mencken

"Your plan": This (very tentative) proposal involved reaching the U.S. by a somewhat circuitous route: "I have toyed with the idea of heading for the States *via* Australia. This scheme has the advantage that my blocked sterling would be left beyond the immediate reach of both the Russians in Siberia and the Russians in Westminster. The great difficulty is to reach Australia before old age sets in."

"If you are expecting": I was under no illusions about the uncertainties of living by my pen, and Mencken's account of the low state of publishing in the U.S. left us more undecided than ever.

"I have just finished": My applause on hearing that Mencken had completed the omnibus version of his early works was muted somewhat on learning of its proposed title: "That you've finished putting together the omnibus of your early works is the best news I've heard in years. But when it comes to calling it *A Mencken Chrestomathy* I'm on the side of Alfred Knopf and the angels. Holy mackerel—what a title! For one thing, it's an affront to the human eye, not to mention the average human brain. For another, it's not strictly accurate. And for a third, *A Mencken Miscellany* is ten thousand times better. I send it on in haste, and pray that the Lord will make you see the light in time."

October 18, 1948

Dear Cleator:

If I could only speak English I think I'd come to England. By all accounts, the state of affairs there is considerably better than in the United States. The cost of living here has gone so high that it is really preposterous. The railroad fare to New York from Baltimore is actually almost what it used to be from Baltimore to Chicago. I have been lucky in late years in getting money, but it disappears as fast as it arrives at my exchequer. I expect to die bankrupt, and probably in a debtor's prison.

I had a lot of fun putting the new book together. When it will be published God alone knows—probably not until the Autumn of next year. Printers now demand more than $100 for a 35-hour week. Moreover, they do less than half as much work as they used to do. I well recall a time when it cost $1.50 to set up an ordinary column of newspaper type. It now costs more than $5, and on some papers nearly $10. This may sound incredible, but I call your attention to the fact that the wonders of God are past finding out.

Yours,
H. L. Mencken

In response to Mencken's continued dehortations concerning our proposed journeying to America, I suggested that he might care to consider seeking sanctuary with us instead: "God only knows where we shall finally end up. At the time of this writing, there's not a vestige of a plan, much less a decision. My present inclination is to wait awhile, and see what happens. Your dire and continued warnings about the state of things in the U.S. have meanwhile been noted. You almost persuade us, indeed, that it is our bounden duty to insist upon your joining us here immediately, that you may spend the rest of your days in relative ease. We hasten to add that you won't be able to afford to drink or smoke (assuming, most unwarrantably, that you will be able to obtain supplies), and that good eating, like sane government, has gone forever. The state of *our* inflation you may gather from the cry of a Liverpool street vendor: Penny balloons—a shilling each!"

"I expect to die bankrupt": According to Charles Fecher (*Mencken: A Study of His Thought,* New York, 1978), the would-be bankrupt left an estate valued at more than a quarter of a million dollars!

November 3, 1948

Dear Cleator:

You are reinforced in your objection to chrestomathy by an enormous gang of Americans, including two United States Senators, an archbishop and five wife-beaters. I am taking your caveat into prayer[ful] consideration. Unfortunately, I have had a long battle with my publisher on the subject, and I hate to yield. Once I did so he'd have me at his mercy for all eternity.

Australia sounds anything but inviting. I have lately entertained some Australian pilgrims here in Baltimore. Their dialect of English really alarmed me.

My best thanks for the clippings.

Sincerely yours,
H. L. Mencken

In the face of the argument here advanced, I at once withdrew my previously expressed objections to the proposed omnibus title: "I say no more about chrestomathy, for I perceive you have a real problem on your hands, and far be it from me to urge capitulation in the matter after so gallant a stand. On the other hand . . ."

When the book was published, it contained a preface in which Mencken began by stoutly defending his choice of title, in part on philological grounds, but also for the reason that he considered the available alternatives, such as treasury, omnibus, and miscellany, to be overworked.

December 15, 1948

Dear Mr. Cleator:

Unfortunately, your letter comes in while Mr. Mencken is ill in hospital. He is making a good recovery, but I fear that he will be forced to remain there for a couple of weeks. His doctor has suggested that his mail be held up here until he is feeling somewhat better. I shall hand him your note at the first chance. I need not tell you that he will be delighted to have it.

Sincerely yours,
Rosalind C. Lohrfinck
Secretary to
Mr. Mencken

The letter above referred to was my reply to Mencken's note of October 18, and the news that he was in hospital, but that he was making a good recovery, made no mention of what was amiss. In an acknowledgment wishing him well, I appended a postscript: "I take this opportunity to announce an impending change of address. The indications are that we shall be departing These Isles in 5–6 months. Until further notice, please address all correspondence. . . ."

December 22, 1948

Dear Mr. Cleator:

Your letter of December 1st comes in today. Mr. Mencken is still in hospital, but I am glad to be able to tell you that he is very much better and is full of plans for a trip to Florida sometime in February. Meanwhile, I am still holding his mail here. He has been working entirely too hard, and his doctor insists upon complete rest for another two weeks. I shall give him your letter and the clippings at the first chance.

Sincerely yours,
Rosalind C. Lohrfinck
Secretary to
Mr. Mencken

This note was in acknowledgment of the last letter I addressed to Mencken personally—henceforth, all my communications to him were to be by way of Mrs. Lohrfinck, to whom I now sent the following reply: "Your letter of December 22nd brings more reassuring news, and I'm glad to have it. I hope the improvement continues, and that the proposed trip to Florida completes the cure. On no account bother Mr. Mencken with my trite communications until all is well. Meanwhile, I trust you'll have the time and energy to spare to send an occasional report on progress."

At this time, I was still unaware of the nature or of the extent of Mencken's illness, and having regard for his many more or less routine visits to hospital in past, I had no reason to suppose that anything really serious was amiss. But in fact, as I was soon to learn, on November 23 Mencken had suffered a massive stroke which, catastrophically, was effectively to put an end to his outstanding and controversial career.

The letters from his secretary which follow, reporting on the ups and downs of his long illness, speak for themselves, and call for no comment from me.

Last Days (1948–1956)

January 11, 1949

Dear Mr. Cleator:

Mr. Mencken is now home and seems to be making excellent progress. His eyes are giving him some difficulty, and he has asked me to write to you saying that he is always delighted to hear from you, and that he hopes that you'll be able to leave England in a few months.

I note your new address, and I surely trust that Mr. Mencken will be writing to you soon. I am holding the clippings until he is fully restored.

                        Sincerely yours,
                        Rosalind C. Lohrfinck
                        Secretary to
                        Mr. Mencken

February 11, 1949

Dear Mr. Cleator:

My best thanks for your letter of January 21st. Mr. Mencken is improving rapidly, and I am hoping that he will be completely restored on his return from Florida. He enjoys being in the hot sunshine, so I am confident that a few weeks in the South will enable him to regain his usual good health. He is in good spirits and is looking forward to his holiday with great pleasure.

                        Sincerely yours,
                        Rosalind C. Lohrfinck
                        Secretary to
                        Mr. Mencken

February 21, 1949

Dear Mr. Cleator:

Thanks very much for your letter of February 4th. It is still impossible for Mr. Mencken to write to you, but he is going to Florida at the end of the week and is hoping that he will be able to do so on his return to Baltimore. If you can stop off in Baltimore on your way to Australia, Mr. Mencken will certainly be delighted to see you. By that time I surely hope he will be fully recovered.

Sincerely yours,
Rosalind C. Lohrfinck
Secretary to
Mr. Mencken

March 25, 1949

Dear Mr. Cleator:

Thanks for your letter and the clippings for Mr. Mencken. He is delighted to hear that your plan for going to Africa will probably materialize. He continues to make progress, but he is still unable to write to you. How long this condition will continue remains to be determined, but I fear that it will be several months. He is still in the hands of the Johns Hopkins doctors, most of them old friends of his, and he is hoping to be ultimately restored to his former good health.

He is sorry indeed to hear of your leaving England, though he certainly doesn't blame you for doing so. I surely hope that my next report of his condition is much more optimistic.

Sincerely yours,
Rosalind C. Lohrfinck
Secretary to
Mr. Mencken

April 22, 1949

Dear Mr. Cleator:

Thanks for your letter. It goes without saying that Mr. Mencken is extremely sorry to hear that you are going to South Africa. It seems highly unlikely that he'll ever be able to meet you there. Unfortunately, it is still impossible for him to write to you. He can understand, of course, what is read to him, and it makes him very sad to think of you so far away.

The best of the doctors at the Johns Hopkins are hard at work trying to find some one to help him, and they believe that he will be cured soon or late. His general health is very good—in fact, he eats regularly and sleeps very well, and devotes himself in the evening to sampling the various alcoholic drinks. He certainly hopes that you will find life pleasant in South Africa. He is delighted to have the clippings for his files, and he hopes that you'll continue to write to him as often as possible.

Sincerely yours,
Rosalind C. Lohrfinck
Secretary to
Mr. Mencken

May 16, 1949

Dear Mr. Cleator:

I read your letter to Mr. Mencken, and he was naturally glad to have word from you, but he certainly regrets that you are going so far away. He is hoping that you'll be able to get to the United States soon or late and, meanwhile, he hopes that your move to Africa will turn out to be beneficial.

Mr. Mencken's general health is very much improved, but his difficulty in reading and writing continues. The doctors are confident that he will ultimately recover, but they fear that it will probably take a long time. His greatest distress is his inability to write to his friends. He sends the best of luck to you in your new venture, and hopes that he will some day meet you in Baltimore.

Sincerely yours,
Rosalind C. Lohrfinck
Secretary to
Mr. Mencken

August 15, 1949

Dear Mr. Cleator:

Mr. Mencken is delighted to hear that you have arrived at Capetown. Unfortunately, it is still impossible for him to write to you. However, he is in the hands of the medical men, and there is every reason for believing that he will be all right by the end of the year. His inability to read and write naturally greatly distresses him, but he is hopeful that the doctors will get rid of his difficulties soon or late. He will write to you at the first opportunity and, meanwhile, he sends his best wishes.

Sincerely yours,
Rosalind C. Lohrfinck
Secretary to
Mr. Mencken

September 24, 1949

Dear Mr. Cleator:

Thank you very much for your letter of September 13th. Unfortunately, Mr. Mencken's condition is unchanged. He has been taking treatments three times a week at the Johns Hopkins Hospital, but so far they have failed to help him, although the doctors there are hopeful that he will be cured eventually, but they fear it may take another year. His general health seems to be fairly good, but he is still unable to read or write. I only hope that I'll be able to write you a more hopeful letter in a few more months.

                                      Sincerely yours,
                                      Rosalind C. Lohrfinck
                                      Secretary to
                                      Mr. Mencken

February 16, 1950

Dear Mr. Cleator:

Thanks very much for your letter. Mr. Mencken has made some progress, but it is still quite impossible for him to write to you. His general health is good; he eats and sleeps well and takes a fair amount of liquor. He has been devoting himself to getting his office in order, and he is hopeful that he may be able to do some writing within the next six months. He certainly hopes that you'll be able to come to New York. If so, he will be glad to see you in Baltimore if his condition permits, but at this time he is seeing practically no one. He sends his best wishes, and the hope that you are quite well yourself.

                                      Sincerely yours,
                                      Rosalind C. Lohrfinck
                                      Secretary to
                                      Mr. Mencken

June 26, 1950

Dear Mr. Cleator:

Thanks for your letter. Unfortunately, Mr. Mencken is still ill and it is impossible for him to write to you. However, his general condition is pretty good and he is hopeful that he will ultimately recover. He was very glad to hear of your letter and certainly trusts that you will be able to come to the United States sometime during the year. He sends you his very best wishes, and is looking forward to seeing you here in Baltimore.

Sincerely yours,
Rosalind C. Lohrfinck
Secretary to
Mr. Mencken

July 24, 1950

Dear Mr. Cleator:

Mr. Mencken, of course, would be delighted to see you in Baltimore, but I should add at once that talking to him would be extremely difficult. However, if you manage to get to this country, he surely hopes that he will be sufficiently recovered, by that time, to have a session with you. Meanwhile, he sends his best thanks for your thought of him. He surely hopes that some American publisher will be interested in your MSS. at some time in the near future.

Sincerely yours,
Rosalind C. Lohrfinck
Secretary to
Mr. Mencken

August 31, 1950

Dear Mr. Cleator:

As you say, Mr. Mencken's condition is distressing indeed. He is definitely better than he was a year ago, but nevertheless he is still unable to read anything and, of course, he can't write. He hopes that he'll see you soon or late. Unfortunately, you must remember that talking with him will be very difficult, but I feel sure that you will be able to understand him. His illness has been very severe, but it is possible that he may improve immeasurably during the next year. I surely hope that you will be able to get to Baltimore. Mr. Mencken will certainly be delighted to see you.

Sincerely yours,
Rosalind C. Lohrfinck
Secretary to
Mr. Mencken

October 17, 1950

Dear Mr. Cleator:

Your pamphlet, "The Periodic Problem," has come in. Unfortunately, Mr. Mencken is quite ill at the moment and so I am unable to show him the article. I am holding it for him and hope he will be better in a couple of weeks than he is at the moment. My very best thanks for your thought of him.

Sincerely yours,
Rosalind C. Lohrfinck
Secretary to
Mr. Mencken

November 1, 1950

Dear Mr. Cleator:

Mr. Mencken is now making steady progress, and it is hoped that he will be able to leave hospital in several weeks. As you well know, his condition has been serious for a couple of years past, but his last attack was alarming indeed and I am greatly relieved that he seems to be getting along so well.

I only hope that you'll manage somehow to get to the United States. Mr. Mencken will be delighted to see you.

Sincerely yours,
Rosalind C. Lohrfinck
Secretary to
Mr. Mencken

December 8, 1950

Dear Mr. Cleator:

Thanks for your letter of November 16th. Mr. Mencken is still in hospital, but he is getting stronger every day and the doctors believe that he will be well enough to return to his home by Christmas. I surely hope that you will soon be comfortably situated yourself, and that you have good luck in 1951.

Sincerely yours,
Rosalind C. Lohrfinck
Secretary to
Mr. Mencken

December 30, 1950

Dear Mr. Cleator:

Thanks very much for your charming Christmas card for Mr. Mencken. He is still in hospital, but he is feeling very much better and is hopeful of being well enough to return to his home

in a couple of weeks. It was kind of you to think of him, and I offer my best thanks again. And a very Happy New Year to you!
Sincerely yours,
Rosalind C. Lohrfinck
Secretary to
Mr. Mencken

April 7, 1951

Dear Mr. Cleator:

Mr. Mencken is back home again, after five months in hospital. He has made some progress, but it is still impossible for him to read anything at all. Whether he will be able to do so later on remains to be determined. He has been extremely ill during the past six months, but he is now slowly improving.

I am delighted to hear that you have found a home at last, and I hope that the weather is now warm and pleasant.
Sincerely yours,
Rosalind C. Lohrfinck
Secretary to
Mr. Mencken

June 18, 1951

Dear Mr. Cleator:

Mr. Mencken is certainly glad to have the clippings from the Johannesburg Transvaal, and sends his very best thanks for your kindness. They will be put into the clipping book at once.

Mr. Mencken is delighted to hear that you are at last comfortably situated. His own condition is virtually unchanged, but he is still hopeful that he will continue to improve.
Sincerely yours,
Rosalind C. Lohrfinck
Secretary to
Mr. Mencken

October 2, 1951

Dear Mr. Cleator:

Thanks very much for your letter. Mr. Mencken's general health is considerably improved, but he still can't read anything at all. He may improve within the next year, but of course it is not at all certain that he will. The doctors are making every effort to help him, but so far they have been unsuccessful. He surely hopes that you are in good health yourself. He greatly appreciates your thought of him and he sends you his very best wishes.

Sincerely yours,
Rosalind C. Lohrfinck
Secretary to
Mr. Mencken

December 27, 1951

Dear Mr. Cleator:

Thanks very much for your letter of December 13th. Mr. Mencken's condition is still far from good. He can't read anything at all, and I now fear that the written page is closed to him forever. His situation grieves everyone close to him, but after three years we have learned to endure it. He is most unhappy, particularly in Winter when he can't get put in the garden and he finds it difficult to keep himself occupied. I told him of your letter and he has asked me to offer his best thanks for your thought of him. He surely hopes that you and your wife are perfectly well and that you are lucky in the New Year. I certainly join him in that hope.

Sincerely yours,
Rosalind C. Lohrfinck
Secretary to
Mr. Mencken

April 21, 1952

Dear Mr. Cleator:

Mr. Mencken's condition is virtually unchanged, and it is still impossible for him to read or write anything at all. Otherwise, he seems to be in pretty good condition. Whether or not he will improve later on remains to be seen. Meanwhile, he enjoys working in his garden and spends many hours every day in it. He asks me to give you his best regards, and he is sorry indeed that it is not possible for him to write to you.

Sincerely yours,
Rosalind C. Lohrfinck
Secretary to
Mr. Mencken

August 29, 1952

Dear Mr. Cleator:

Mr. Mencken is really delighted to hear that your book will be published early in the New Year, and he surely hopes that it makes a big success. It goes without saying that he will be glad to have a copy, though he is still unable to read.

His general condition remains fairly good, but at the moment is somewhat disabled by hay-fever. The new drugs are a great help and so he complains very little. He sends his best wishes and good luck.

                          Sincerely yours,
                          Rosalind C. Lohrfinck
                          Secretary to
                          Mr. Mencken

                          December 15, 1952

Dear Mr. Cleator:

Thanks for your note. Mr. Mencken is delighted to hear that your book has made such good progress, and he is sorry indeed that he will be unable to read it. He surely hopes that it will make a big success.

                          Sincerely yours,
                          Rosalind C. Lohrfinck
                          Secretary to
                          Mr. Mencken

                          August 21, 1953

Dear Mr. Cleator:

Mr. Mencken was very glad to have your message. He is still unable to read anything but his brother often reads to him when the patient is interested. Mr. Mencken is certainly delighted to hear that your book is at last to be published and he surely hopes that it has a good sale. Although he can't read it himself, he will naturally be glad to have it for his files. And he will be especially interested in the illustrations. The book sounds interesting indeed.

It is pleasant news that another book is on the way. By the time it is ready perhaps the condition of the publishing business will be improved and you will escape the long and vexatious delays.

                          Sincerely yours,
                          Rosalind C. Lohrfinck
                          Secretary to
                          Mr. Mencken

October 26, 1953

Dear Mr. Cleator:

Thanks for your letter. I can't suggest that you write a regular letter to Mr. Mencken. His condition is such that he can't concentrate on anything for any length of time and I edit all letters before reading them to him to save him any undue stress.

Your Into Space came in today and Mr. Mencken has handed the copy to his brother, who is greatly interested in the subject and who will read it at once and with great pleasure. He will probably write to you directly when he has gone through the book. I surely hope that it has a large sale and that you will soon be able to come to the United States for your long-delayed visit.

Sincerely yours,
Rosalind C. Lohrfinck
Secretary to
Mr. Mencken

October 29, 1953

Dear Mr. Cleator:

My brother turned your book, "Into Space," over to me and it delighted me indeed. We have our fair share of "experts" here who bombard us constantly with their half baked ideas and it was a great pleasure to get the story from someone who knows his subject. Many thanks.

My brother, unhappily, cannot read but he is greatly interested in your work and I gave him an outline of your book as best I could. He asked me to send you his kindest regards.

Yours sincerely,
August Mencken

May 10, 1954

Dear Mr. Cleator:

Mr. Mencken is glad indeed to hear that your Into Space will be published by Crowell sometime this year. He surely hopes that it has a good sale and that you'll be able to get to the United States for your long-delayed visit.

Mr. Mencken's own condition is not too good. He feels fairly well on warm, sunny days but cold weather seems to affect him adversely and so he is depressed and unhappy. Unfortunately, the weather here at the moment is very cold for this time of the year and the low temperatures have hurt the flowers and fruit.

Thanks very much for your thought of Mr. Mencken. He hopes that you and Mrs. Cleator are in the best of health.

Sincerely yours,
Rosalind C. Lohrfinck
Secretary to
Mr. Mencken

December 3, 1954

Dear Mr. Cleator:

I have read your letter to Mr. Mencken and he is certainly delighted to hear that your book is finished at last and he only hopes that it has a good sale. He was greatly interested to hear that Into Space is being translated into German and he hopes that you have good luck with that also.

Last week Mr. Mencken was very far from good, but now he seems to be feeling much better and he was almost jovial today. It is wonderful to see him in a cheerful mood after all his difficulties. He is glad to hear that you and Mrs. Cleator are reasonably comfortable. He trusts that if you manage to get to the United States you will drop in to see him. It won't be very pleasant but it will be at least a good thing for him.

Sincerely yours,
Rosalind C. Lohrfinck
Secretary to
Mr. Mencken

December 26, 1954

Dear Mr. Cleator:

Mr. Mencken sends his best thanks for your charming Christmas greetings. He surely hopes that you and your wife are in perfect health and that you'll be lucky in 1955. His own condition is not too good, but nevertheless he is able to potter around in his garden when the weather permits. I join him in wishing you a bright New Year.

Sincerely yours,
Rosalind C. Lohrfinck
Secretary to
Mr. Mencken

February 3, 1955

Dear Mr. Cleator:

Mr. Mencken is enormously upset by the death of his old

friend H. W. Seaman. He had known him for many years and he had a great admiration for him. He had worked with him at different times and he regarded him as a very important journalist. He is naturally glad to have the clipping and offers his best thanks for your thought of him. Your letter was the first news he had of it.

Mr. Mencken surely hopes that you and your wife will be able to make the trip to America while he is still alive. He asks me to tell you that you had better hurry. Nothing would give him more pleasure than seeing you here in Baltimore.

Sincerely yours,
Rosalind C. Lohrfinck
Secretary to
Mr. Mencken

February 23, 1955

Dear Mr. Cleator:

Mr. Mencken spends a great deal of time getting his files in order and he discovers that he does not have the date of your birth. He would be greatly obliged if you will let him know precisely when you were born so that he may bring his files up to date. He has an immense collection of letters, which are to be presented to the New York Public Library, with the provision that they will not be open to anyone until twenty-five years after his death.*

He sends his best wishes and the hope that you are in good health and spirits.

Sincerely yours,
Rosalind C. Lohrfinck
Secretary to
Mr. Mencken

March 19, 1955

Dear Mr. Cleator:

Mr. Mencken sends his very best thanks for your answer to his inquiry. He will record the date of your birth in his letter file which is to be presented to the New York Public Library at his death, for the edification of posterity.

He surely hopes that you'll be able to come to this country in

---

*Subsequently reduced to a period of fifteen years.

the not too distant future. He wishes to remind you that he will be seventy-five years old on September 12th, and so there is no time to be wasted.

Yours,
Rosalind C. Lohrfinck
Secretary to
Mr. Mencken

May 20, 1955

Dear Mr. Cleator:

Mr. Mencken is delighted to hear that you have finished "The Robot Era." He is confident that Unwin has done a good job with the book and he trusts that it will be a big success.

He surely hopes that soon or late you'll be able to get to America and so drop down to Baltimore to see him. His condition is very far from good and it would give him great pleasure to see you here in Hollins street. The very best of luck!

Sincerely yours,
Rosalind C. Lohrfinck
Secretary to
Mr. Mencken

July 29, 1955

Dear Mr. Cleator:

Mr. Mencken is amazed and delighted to hear that you are hard at work on a new book and he is only sorry that he'll never be able to read it. He hopes that you are making good progress with it, for it sounds interesting indeed. He hopes also that The Robot Era will sell sufficient copies to enable you and your wife to make the trip to the United States.

We have had one of the worst Summers for more than fifty years, with temperatures above ninety for twenty-two consecutive days, with several days of ninety-seven and a couple of one hundred. Thus you can well imagine that Mr. Mencken has been very far from comfortable. Fortunately, the temperature today has dropped to eighty and we are promised several days of comfort.

Sincerely yours,
Rosalind C. Lohrfinck
Secretary to
Mr. Mencken

October 7, 1955

Dear Mr. Cleator:

Mr. Mencken is delighted to hear that you have finished The Robot Era and he laments the fact that he will not be able to read it. But sometimes he is in the mood and I shall read it to him from time to time. He greatly appreciates your thought of him and he only wishes that his report might be more encouraging. He wants me to wish you the best of luck.

Sincerely yours,
Rosalind C. Lohrfinck
Secretary to
Mr. Mencken

October 8, 1955

Dear Mr. Cleator:

Your book came in safely this morning and Mr. Mencken sends his best thanks for sending it. He is sorry indeed that he can't read it, but his brother is greatly interested in it and he is looking forward to reading it at once. He'll certainly tell Mr. Mencken all about it. It looks interesting indeed.

Sincerely yours,
Rosalind C. Lohrfinck
Secretary to
Mr. Mencken

December 18, 1955

Dear Mr. Cleator:

Mr. Mencken is delighted to hear that a German edition of Into Space has been printed and that a Spanish version is on its way and he surely hopes that the book does very well. His brother is greatly interested in The Robot Era and has been going through it with the greatest pleasure. Mr. Mencken is particularly pleased to have your picture in the leaflet. He surely hopes that you have a very happy holiday and that you'll be lucky in the New Year.

Sincerely yours,
Rosalind C. Lohrfinck
Secretary to
Mr. Mencken

December 29, 1955

Dear Mr. Cleator:

Mr. Mencken was delighted to have your Christmas greetings. He was feeling fairly well during the holidays and he enjoyed having dinner with his sister and brother. His condition, of course, is far from good but nevertheless he is still able to work around in his garden and to enjoy a few guests who may drop in. He surely hopes that you had a pleasant holiday and that you are lucky in the New Year, in which I certainly join him.

                                        Sincerely yours,
                                        Rosalind C. Lohrfinck
                                        Secretary to
                                        Mr. Mencken

AFTERMATH

Henry Mencken's long-drawn-out incapacitation came mercifully to an end in the early hours of January 29, 1956, and word of his decease brought a flood of respectful editorial and other tributes from places near and far emanating from appreciative and reluctant admirers alike. My own sense of deep personal loss, in no way diminished by the circumstance that for the past seven years my contact with him had been maintained through the medium of his secretary, is reflected in the note I received from her at the time. It was typed, as always in the past, on one of the standard Mencken half-sheets:

February 3, 1956

Dear Mr. Cleator:

    Thank you very much for your letter. I had been Mr. Mencken's secretary for twenty-seven years and it is difficult indeed to realize that he is now gone. His death, of course, was a happy release, but I am sorry indeed that he did not live long enough to see his new book published. He had been looking forward to it with great eagerness.

    It is too bad that you did not get to America and so have the meeting that the two of you were hoping for. Mr. Mencken had a very high opinion of your work and he was hoping for the opportunity to meet you.

Sincerely yours,
Rosalind C. Lohrfinck

    The new book above referred to was Mencken's last, his aptly entitled *Minority Report,* brought out posthumously by Alfred

Knopf later in the year. In the meantime, as Mrs. Lohrfinck announced when writing again on March 5, she found herself busily engaged filling the Mencken clipping books with the hundreds of obituary notices which were still pouring into Hollins street ("At the moment I am completely swamped"). Thereafter, she added, she would be "occupied for a month or two putting everything in order here."

This melancholy undertaking ("getting his affairs into order is a dreadful task for me") was actually the culmination of years of preparation (begun at the instigation of Mencken himself) in anticipation of the inevitable outcome of his crippling seizure. With its onset, the somewhat surprising fact had come to light that the writer of those one hundred thousand or more letters, except in a few instances, had not bothered to retain carbon copies of his postal outpourings, an omission the importance of which was brought home to him soon after the disabling event of 1948. Fortunately, much of this correspondence (from 1932 onwards) was recorded in shorthand in Mrs. Lohrfinck's notebooks, and in 1949 she was called upon to make a start on the mammoth task of transcribing these jottings. In the event, this was a labor which, interspersed with her other duties. she did not manage to complete until about the time of the death of the narrator. In the process of their recovery, some fifty thousand items, considered of sufficient importance to be retained, were divided into two groups. Of these, one consisted of Mencken's correspondence with Maryland residents, and was allocated to the local Enoch Pratt Library. The other collection was made up of letters from fellow authors, and these, together with the transcriptions of Mencken's replies, were deposited with the New York Public Library, with the stipulation, earlier mentioned, that they remain unseen and unread until fifteen years after the death of the donor.*

---

*This correspondence was duly made public by the NYPL in 1971. Since then a second collection of time-sealed Mencken material has become available to scholars. It was contained in twelve wooden boxes, deposited with the Enoch Pratt Free Library, labeled "Not to be opened until 1981." With due ceremony and in the presence of a distinguished gathering, this instruction was properly observed on January 29 of the appointed year. In the boxes were found four volumes of "Letters and Documents Relating to the *Baltimore Sunpapers* 1892–1941," five volumes of diaries covering the years 1930 through 1948, and three volumes of "Additions and Corrections" to his three *Days* books.

As elsewhere noted, yet another release of sealed Mencken records is due to take place in 1991—of his two unpublished manuscripts entitled "Thirty-five Years of Newspaper Work" and "My Life as Author and Editor."

That the condition attending the bequest could possibly be of concern to me, quite apart from the fact that my own correspondence was involved, was made evident by Mrs. Lohrfinck in her aforementioned letter of March 5:

> Mr. Mencken has been holding two manuscripts of yours—"A Dictionary For the Damned," with an Introduction by him, and "My Kingdom For A Hearse." His brother has asked me to write to you and find out what you want him to do with the manuscripts. As you probably know, all of his letters and various other documents are going to the New York Public Library but it occurs to him that you may not want the manuscripts to be included in the package for the Library. I am therefore holding the envelope, awaiting your instructions.

As I had made clear at the end of the war, I had emerged from the conflict possessed of surviving copies of the two MSS, and so I was not concerned about the fate of the duplicates I had earlier sent to Baltimore for safekeeping. But a statement contained in Mrs. Lohrfinck's letter sufficed to change my attitude of indifference to one of interest and concern—the words "with an Introduction by him." As noted in my comment on Mencken's letter of September 25, 1940, after the war the MS of the *Dictionary* lay forgotten in my files, and there was no further discussion between Mencken and me about the writing of his proposed introduction to it. The news that he nevertheless appeared to have undertaken the task thus came as a complete—and pleasantly exhilarating—surprise, and I accordingly requested the return of the manuscripts.

Here, let me anticipate any natural curiosity and expectation on the part of the reader, at that time more than matched by my own, by stating that various complications promptly arose, to be followed by eventual disappointment. The first suggestion of a possible holdup, or rather, a whole host of holdups, came in a letter from August Mencken:

March 19, 1956

Dear Mr. Cleator:

Mrs. Lohrfinck referred me to the portion of your letter to her pertaining to your manuscripts here and the Introduction to your book, "A Dictionary For The Damned."

I am sure there will be no serious difficulty about the return of your manuscripts as you did not give them to my brother but only sent them to him for safe-keeping. However, like everything else in his possession at the time of his death they are now in the hands of the Mercantile–Safe Deposit and Trust Company, Baltimore, his executors, and I am lately informed that I must get permission from that Company to return them to you. But I do not think there will be much delay in getting it.

The matter of the Introduction is not quite so simple. We must first know if my brother wrote the Introduction and if it now exists. It is not attached to your manuscripts and we have been unable to find it among his papers, nor have we been able to find any record of it.

It would be very helpful to me in getting permission for you to use the Introduction if you would let me know if you have it, and if so, the approximate date on which you received it. If you have it the executors require that you send me a copy, either typewritten or a photostat. A photostat of a letter from my brother mentioning the Introduction in some way would also be helpful in establishing your right to use it.

I greatly regret that I must put you to so much trouble but under the circumstances I cannot avoid it. Knowing the high regard my brother had for you, you may be sure that I shall do everything possible to save you further trouble.

I should like to take this opportunity to tell you how greatly I enjoyed your book, "The Robot Era." It was very timely and informative indeed.

Sincerely yours,
August Mencken

When making reply to this letter, I had to confess that I was unable to comply with any of the requirements needed to establish my right to make use of his brother's alleged contribution. Not only was the introduction not in my possession, but until a fortnight or so ago I had been unaware of its supposed existence. So it came about that when the manuscripts were eventually returned, they were minus any Mencken addition. And in a covering note, Mrs. Lohrfinck provided confirmation of an unwelcome conviction that was steadily forming in my mind—that "the Introduction apparently was not written by H.L., for it is not in the files here in the office." Her letter, dated June 8, the last I was to receive from her on the Mencken notepaper, also contained the information that on July 15 she was to take up new duties at the Enoch Pratt Library. Here, she had been assigned the task of cataloguing the collection of Mencken "books, papers, and other documents."

No doubt in anticipation of this move, she had earlier furnished me with her private address, and if the correspondence between us now continued, it was at my volition and with an added purpose. For it seemed to me then, as it seems to me still, that of all those closely associated with Henry Mencken, his secretary of nearly thirty years would be in a unique position to know every aspect of his working procedure—how his ideas for a new book arose, what inspired him in his choice of a title, the manner in which he set about compiling his notes, the number of words he managed to write on an average day, the extent to which attending to his voluminous exchange of letters hindered his more productive activities, and his attitude toward this and other interruptive chores, not to mention a thousand and one other details concerned, directly and indirectly, with his *modus operandi* as an author.

With all this in mind, I took an early opportunity to suggest to Mrs. Lohrfinck that she should seriously consider setting down an account of her secretarial experiences for the benefit of posterity, an account which might fittingly be called "Mencken in My Life." At the time (March 1956) she was in the throes of putting Mencken's affairs in order, and understandably pleaded that this was a duty which demanded all her attention. But her reaction to the proposal was not entirely negative:

> How I wish I could undertake it! But I feel very incompetent of such a task but maybe time will change my mind.

With this possibility in prospect, I continued to send reminders, usually in the guise of seasonal greetings at each year's end. These salutations invariably brought an acknowledgment from the recipient, and although several of her replies bear no date, it has been possible to arrange them in what is probably their correct sequence by a process of elimination, in conjunction with internal evidence provided by their contents. The quoted extracts which follow are restricted to references to the proposed book:

I am ashamed to confess that "Mencken In My Life" is still in embryo and I fear that it will be still-born if I don't hasten the delivery. I am hopeful that after my duties become more or less routine and easy I'll be able to devote some time to my own recollections of Mr. Mencken. I have all the data for several books, but I feel incompetent to do a good job. But it is very pleasant to know of your interest and it encourages me to make the attempt.

Another of her undated replies was somewhat less promising:

I am still a State slave and so IT has been delayed—probably for ever. . . . My leisure time is nil—But maybe the luck of the Irish may give me the opportunity I seek to reduce HLM to paper!

On January 4, 1959, the response was much the same:

"Mencken In My Life," alas, is still in embryo, but I do hope some day to put on paper my years with a wonderful man.

In the following December, I decided that the time had arrived to enlist some outside help. To this end, I wrote to Alfred Knopf, explaining what I was about and seeking his support for the enterprise. Two replies from him arrived in quick succession:

January 19, 1960

Dear Mr. Cleator:
Many thanks for your letter of December 28th. I have turned this over to Mr. August Mencken, who will check with Mrs. Lohrfinck. With thanks for your interest, I am,
Yours faithfully,
Alfred A. Knopf

And less than a week later:

January 25, 1960

Dear Mr. Cleator:
Mr. Mencken has now talked with Mrs. Lohrfinck and finds

that while she was greatly flattered by your suggestion, she has no intention of writing either a book or an article about H.L.M.
Yours faithfully,
Alfred A. Knopf

This unwelcome and unlooked for result was hardly what I had intended, and was certainly not in accord with the messages that had been coming out of Baltimore during the past three years. It seemed to me, rightly or wrongly, that far from providing motivation, my latest move might well have led to dissuasion. I accordingly wrote to Mrs. Lohrfinck, offering due apologies for my continued interference in her private affairs, but also expressing my disappointment and bewilderment at the unexpected outcome of my latest obtrusion. However, her reply, written on February 2, threw a somewhat different light on the situation:

> I surely hope that Mr. Knopf did not give you the impression that I objected to your suggestion that I try to get my reminiscences of HLM on paper. I have never had a line from A. K. since Mr. Mencken's death and so he has no idea of what is in mind. He wrote to August Mencken, not to me, and Mr. Mencken wrote to me. I called Mr. Mencken and told him that I found myself completely inadequate to do a book on a man of such stature as HLM, as I have told you in the past. But I am toying with the idea of retiring if I can find my way to pay the rent and enjoy a steak occasionally, but the prices of everything seem to leap with every month and so I fear to make the final step. Whether or not, at that remote time, I'd be able to do anything about the book I don't know. I feel I'd make a bad book and so I have hesitated. I have certainly not had any encouragement from anyone else and so my own timidity added to that fact has made me hesitate. . . .
> I have a wealth of material and much more in my memory and it is sad to be inarticulate. If I could write an account of his dreadful illness—in duration seven long years—I'd be satisfied. Under such circumstances one really gets to know the patient. As you have guessed, I always admired and respected HLM but his last seven years taught me how a real man takes the vicissitudes of this life.

The contents of this revealing letter left me in no doubt that a promising opportunity had been thrown away; what better inducement toward a contemplated retirement, delayed for financial reasons, than a display of interest in the shape of a publisher's contract, an advance payment, and the promise of royalties to come? And in an effort to keep the project alive despite the recent setback, I offered to assist with the writing, and in any other way that I could. After a considerable interval, this pledge brought the following response. It was dated February 22, 1961:

> My apologies for delaying a reply to your nice letter. It is kind of you indeed to offer to help me with the Mencken book when, as and if I get started on it. If anything ever comes of it I shall certainly need a lot of help for I have had no experience whatsoever in the art of writing and the thought of doing a book on HLM really gives me to pause. But if the muse ever beckons I shall certainly try. I agree with [you that] the material should get on paper, but frankly I doubt that I can do it.

I was by now more than ever convinced that what the situation called for was something more than mere words of encouragement from afar, such as I had sought to offer. What was needed was the active intervention of an interested and persuasive publisher near at hand, and as luck would have it, it was at this juncture that I encountered exactly the right person in Richard J. Walsh (now retired) of the John Day Company (since incorporated, by way of Thomas Y. Crowell, with the prestigious house of Harper and Row). The letter I prevailed upon him to address to Mrs. Lohrfinck is self-explanatory:

March 8, 1961

Dear Mrs. Lohrfinck:

Mr. P. E. Cleator, whose book *Lost Languages* we are going to publish later this season, has done me the great favor of telling me of the possibility of your writing a book about your long association with H. L. Mencken. He says that what is chiefly needed to persuade you to undertake such a work is encouragement, with of course a contract before you were to proceed too far so that you would be able to spare the time.

I certainly agree with Mr. Cleator, from what he tells me, that this story ought to be told and I should like very much to pursue its possibilities with you. I wonder if you won't write to me, at whatever length you find the time for, giving me more information about what you believe might be in such a book. Of course it would be still better if you were to prepare an outline and a sample chapter, but if you don't feel like undertaking as much as that to begin with, a letter would serve very well.

I do hope to hear from you.

Sincerely yours,
Richard J. Walsh Jr.

Mrs. Lohrfinck's response to this kindly and encouraging invitation was written on March 22 and was addressed to me—from a sickbed:

> I heard from your publisher and agree with him that a few chapters would be the proper procedure. Unfortunately I am in hospital, suffering from sheer exhaustion and an enlarged heart. I have been here two weeks and fear I must stay two more. This explains my not answering Mr. Walsh's letter. (It is at home, so please explain to him.) My doctor reports that I am progressing satisfactorilly, so I am hopeful to be back to normalcy in a few weeks.
>
> Maybe some day the Mencken book will get itself written.

In the circumstances, there was nothing more to be said or done, at any rate for the time being. And a letter of enquiry I sent in the following year, expressing the hope that the patient was well on the way to a complete recovery, brought an acknowledgment (dispatched on June 10, 1962) which merely stated that she was feeling much better, that she was still working for the state, and hating it more every day.

Her next (and last) letter to me, though undated, was evidently written during the year 1963, since its main purpose was to express thanks for a copy I had sent to her of a recently published book of mine. It also contained a passing reference to the abortive Mencken project:

> I am retiring at the end of this year and maybe my health will permit me to get something in writing about the man I so greatly admire. I fear, though, that I am incompetent for the task. But perhaps a few personal reminiscences would suffice.

Thereafter, my customary seasonal greetings went unanswered, until one day there came a letter from Arnold M.

Lohrfinck, conveying the tidings that his sister-in-law Rosalind had collapsed and died in August 1964.

With Henry Mencken gone, and with his loyal and devoted secretary now also departed, suddenly the world seemed a sadder and a lonelier place.

REFERENCES

CB—Carl Bode
1. *The New Mencken Letters*. New York: The Dial Press, 1977.
2. *Mencken*. Carbondale and Edwardsville, Ill.: 1969.

CJ—*Chambers's Journal* (articles by P. E. Cleator)
1. "Water," March 1931.
2. "The Possibilities of Interplanetary Travel," January 1933.
3. "On Giving Up Shaving." March 1936.
4. "Operation." January 1938.

HLM—H. L. Mencken
1. *Menckeniana*. New York: Alfred A. Knopf, 1926.
2. *Treatise on the Gods*. New York: Alfred A. Knopf, 1930.
3. *Prejudices, Fifth Series*. New York: Alfred A. Knopf, 1926.

JBIS—*Journal* of the British Interplanetary Society (articles about and by P. E. Cleator)
1. "Know Your Council." September 1949.
2. "Appleton's Inferno." June 1936.
3. "Weisberger Moon," February 1936.
4. "Messages in Morse from Mars." December 1947.
5. "Autopsia," May 1948.

PEC—P. E. Cleator
1. *Into Space*. London: George Allen & Unwin, 1953.
2. *Weapons of War*. London: Robert Hale, 1967.

INDEX

Acts of God, 85, 103, 215
"Additions and Corrections" (H. L. Mencken), 257
Adolf. *See* Hitler, Adolf
Afro-American, The, 74–75
Agatha of Catania, 136–37
Agnosticism, 11, 25, 30
Air raids, 100, 106, *110,* 113, 126, *132,* 144, 183
Air raid shelters, 105–6, 108, 133, 144
Ali, Muhammad, 203
Allah, 30, 200
Allen & Unwin, 37, 152, 154, 169, 182, 185–86, 189, 191, 193–94, 200, 224, 227, 229
Almanac, the Hagerstown, 64
Almanack (J. Whitaker), 212
Almighty, the. *See* Yahweh
America. *See* United States
Americana annuals (H. L. Mencken, ed.), *41,* 77, 92, 113, 187, *199*
American Language, The (H. L. Mencken), 12, 37, 50–52, 59, 76, 99, 106, 132, 136, 139, 142–43, 146–48, 150–54, 161, 167, 171–72, 181–82, 205, 213–14, 224–25; *Supplement I,* 51, 59, 99, 106, 132, 136, 139, 142–43, 146–47, 150–52, 156, 159–61, 167, 169–70, 171–73, 182, 185, 205, *225; Supplement II,* 12, 154, 159, 164, 167, 174, 177, 181–82, 184, 192–93, 195–97, 201, 203, 205–6, 211–13, 215–16, 219–21, 224, *225,* 226–27; *Supplement III,* 227
American Mercury, The, 39, *41,* 59, 68, 137
American Speech, 141
"Anaesthetics" (P. E. Cleator), 27
Anesthesia, 168, 203
Anti-Semitism, 52, 70, 73
Apostolic times, 47
Appleton Layer, 42

Appleton, Professor E. V., 40, 42
"Appleton's Inferno" (P. E. Cleator), 42, 45–46, 54–55
Archbishop of Canterbury, 57, 75, 82
Armed conflict: as a permanent state of man, 92, 94; causes of, 26, 94; futility and stupidity of, 26, 90–91, 94, 111, 132
Associated Press, 122, 155
Astrology, 91
Astronaut, The, 70, *71,* 73, 78
Atom bomb, 26, 137, 231
Attlee, Clement, 172
Auschwitz, 151
Australia: as proposed emigratory destination, 242; as prospective intellectual desert, 233; Australian language, 203
Australian Language, The (S. J. Baker), 203
Austria: Innsbruck, 62; Vienna, 150–51
"Autopsia" (P. E. Cleator), 230–31

Babbitt (S. Lewis), 195–96
Babylonian folklore, 30
"Bacteria" (P. E. Cleator), 27
Baker, Sidney J., 203; *The Australian Language,* 203
Baltic Sea, 89
Baltimore: *Afro-American, The,* 74–75; air-raid precautions in, 105, 146, 162; as the Pompeii of America, 88; Cathedral Street, 38, *186;* Enoch Pratt Library, 37, 82, 115, 221, 257, 260; *Evening Sun, 186; Herald,* 196; Hollins Street, 38, 82, 98, 127, 163, *186,* 253, 257; Humane Society of, 183; Independence Day celebrations in, 62; Johns Hopkins Hospital, 82, 127 passim, 148, 168, 183, 197–98, 242,

267

244, 246; medical men of, 56; Mercantile-Safe Deposit and Trust Co. of, 17, 259; Museum, 213; PEC visit to, proposed and eventual, 14, 23, 54, 85, 87–89, 245, 253; philanthropic citizens of, 82; pretended royal descent upon, 85–86; Saturday Night Club, 18, 86, 116; spiritualism in, 60; *Sun*, 44, 62, 73, 122, 137, 196, 229, 231–32; *Sunday Sun*, 111; Sunpapers, 111, 257; threat of IRA activity in, 101; travel to and from, 131, 172, 217, 235; visitors to, 159, 236; wartime liquor supplies in, 130; weather reports from, 62, 64, 76, 80, 84–88, 112, 114, 131, 142, 145, 156–59, 169, 194, 205, 209, 213, 215–16, 223, 253; women of, 56
Baltimorean buffooneries, *41*, 44, 50, 54–55, 76, 114, 118–19, 157, 184, *185*, 194, 213–14, *228*
Baptists: indignity of baptism, 29; preacher, 182; Stygian settlement of, 61; textual labours of, 89
Barabbas, 103
Basic English, 147–48
BBC. *See* British Broadcasting Corporation
Beautiful Spring (P. Lincke), 115–16
Beelzebub. *See* Satan
Beethoven, Ludwig van, 90
Begone Satan, 44
Belgium, Ostend, 62
Benn, Major William Chester, 87
Bermuda, 117
Bible Handbook, The (G. W. Foote), 73–74
Bierce, Ambrose Gwinnett, 202
Bloom, Marion, 30
Bode, Professor Carl, 17, 22, 30, 47–48, 52, 54, 57, 67, 83, 86, 120, 145, *153*, 165, 168, 185, 196, 200; Mencken, 54, 83, 145; *The New Mencken Letters*, 22, 30, 47–48, 52, 54, 57, 67, 86, 165, 168
Book of Burlesques, A (H. L. Mencken), 82, 189
Book of the Damned, The (C. Fort), 202
Bootle Times, 87
Borromeo, Charles, 136–37
Britain, 22, 79, 140, 142, 152, 157, 160, 171, 195–96, 209, 219, 223, 227, 237. *See also* British
British: adjective, 51; army, 182; Board of Trade, 163, 209; Broadcasting Corporation, 18, 64, 74, 142–43, 177; Civil Service, 229; Defence Medal, 194–95; emigration from, 227; Empire, 84; Explosives Act of 1875, the, 51; general election, 172; General Staff, 98; government, 160; Home Office, 51; Hun, 62; immigration laws, 152; Interplanetary Society, 11, 29, 43, 68, 154; Labour Party, 172; Ministry of Food, 92, 130, 166; national anthem, 49; national imbecilities, 39, 55, 77–78, 90–92, 124, 137, 188; National Secular Society, 55; Post Office, 55, 59, 215; public, 49; restaurants, *141*; War Damage Bill, 92
Broadmoor Asylum, 68
Broedel, Max, 116–17
Buchholz, Heinrich, 86, 117
Bulletin of the British Interplanetary Society, 205
"Bulletin on 'Hon'" (H. L. Mencken), *141*
Bulletin, the Philadelphia, 93–94, 122
Bureaucracy: in Britain, 11, 13–14, 55, 90–92, 136–37, 140–41, 143–46, 156, 175, 188, 193, 230–31, 235; in the United States, 11, 55, 136–37, 140, 143, 145–46, 154, 156, 165, 188, 230

Canada. *See* Canadian
Canadian: climate, 85; dignitaries, 159; movie company, 204; paper mills, 128, 131
"Canker, The" (P. E. Cleator), 39–40
Cape, Jonathan, 101, 185
Carey, Henry: "God Save the King," 49
Carlton, Harry (with J. A. Tunbridge): "Mademoiselle from Armentières," 50
Castles and Kings (P. E. Cleator), 264
Chambers, R. S., 28
Chambers's Journal, 27–28, 40, 42, 44, 68–69
Chambers, W. & R., 18
Charlatanry of the Learned, The (J. B. Mencken), 58–59, 66
Cheshire, 26, 42. *See also* Merseyside
Cheslock, Dr. Louis, 18, 52, 117, 120; *H. L. Mencken on Music*, 117
China, geographic location of, 143
Chinese: civil war, 149; living on eight cents a day, 220
Children's Hour, The (L. Gamlin), 73–74
Chiropractors, 60, 166, 176, 182–83,

187, 192–93, 197–98, 201–3
Christendom, 26, 47
Christian: churches, 26, 75; friend, 55; idealism, 104; literature, 79–80; matrimonial mathematics, 77; morals, 89; names, 197–98; people, 40; satisfaction, 206; Science, 61; spirit, 121
Christianity, 63, 75, 103; Apostolic times, 47; archbishopric of Canterbury (Anglican), 57, 75, 82; archbishop of Liverpool (Roman Catholic), 45; archbishop of Milan (Roman Catholic), 137; Atonement, 29; blessed dead, 137; crucifixion, 45, 74; Heaven, 58, 64, 81, 114, 183, 213, 231; Hell, 23, 40, 42, 44, 46, 54, 58, 60–61, 65–66, 114, 119, 137, 145, 173, 175, 204, 209–10, 214, 224; Holy Writ, 30, 48, 55, 58, 75, 83, 193, 203; hopeful air of, 73; Pentecost, 49; Resurrection Morn, 21; Satan, 44, 122, 198; Sixth Commandment, 26; Trinity, 12, 29; truth of, 74; twelve apostles, 64–65; Virgin Birth, 29; witches and demons, 43–44; YMCA, 64–65
Christmas Story (H. L. Mencken), *176*
Churchill, Winston S., 147–48, 171–72, 232
Church of England, 75
Clarke, Arthur C., 154, 231; *The Coming of the Space Age,* 231
Cleator, Alfred (PEC's uncle), 26
Cleator, Catherine (PEC's mother), 13, 26, 81, 109, 116, 118, 133
Cleator, Madelon Bermingham (PEC's wife), 13, 70, *72,* 73, 97, 99, 99, 108–9, 111, 114, 118, 219–20, 222, 248, 251–52
Cleator, Philip Ellaby: alias Running Water, 174; as advocate of space travel, 11, 28, 37; as agnostic, 11, 25, 30; as amateur pathologist, 130; as anti-establishmentarian, 49; as baptised man, 29, 197; as benighted Englander, 184, 214; as compulsive letter answerer, 14, 22; as disillusioned idealist, 25; as handsome fellow, 70, *71;* as humanist, 25; as infidel, 97, 173; as jellyfish, 26; as pacifist, 25; as patriot, 87; as radio broadcaster, 63–64, 143; as skeptic, 25, 39; as seeker after truth, 45; as supposed atheist, 29; as true Christian, 104; as unpatriotic outlaw, 232; as victim of food poisoning, 112; Baltimore visit, 14, 23; baptism, 29, 197; birth, 26; Celtic forebears, 26, 66; childhood of, 27; contemplated literary enterprises, 39–40, 55ff., 66–67, 122, 125, 128; contempt of "God Save the King," 49–50; educational shortcomings, 11, 27; emigration plans, 114, 210–11, 227, 233–36, 242–43; excursions abroad, 14, 62–63; expectation of jail, 11, 136–38; 155; general health, 27, 155; lunatic post-bag, 221; marriage, 97–98; opposition to war, 11, 25, 155; proposed meetings with HLM in the U.S., 23, 73, 77, 84–85, 89, 114, 242–46, 250–53, 256; proposed meeting with HLM in Britain, 22–23, 98–99, 102, 105, 161, 166, 168, 171, 183, 191, 219; proposed meeting with HLM in the subterrestrial Hell of the Christians, 23, 60; scientific interests, 11, 56, 135, 139; suggested collaboration with HLM, 38–39; surgical experiences, 38–44, 56–57, 59–61, 69, 165–68. Unpublished manuscripts: "Canker, The," 39–40; "A Dictionary for the Damned," 82, 84–89, 99–100, 102, 104–5, 169–70, 217, 219, 221–22, 258–59; "My Kingdom for a Hearse," 118, 120, 122–23, 125–26, 128, 131, 217, 219, 221–22, 224–26, 229, 258–59; "Sidelights on the Slaughter," 90–91, 97, 150, 154, 169–71, 223–24, 226. Works: "Anaesthetics," 27; "Appleton's Inferno," 42, 45–46, 54–55; "Autopsia," 230–31; "Bacteria," 27; *Can Castles and Kings,* 264; "Combustion," 27; "History," 229; "Hymn to Progress," 78; "Interplanetary Parade" (series), 81; *Into Space,* 67, 187–88, 191–92, 199–200, 216–17, 219, 221, 223, 229, 254; *Lost Languages,* 263; "Messages in Morse from Mars," 221; "Moon and Mr. Farnsworth, The," 205; "Moonshine," 67; "On Giving up Shaving," 42, 44, 65; "Operation," 62, 68; *Past in Pieces, The,* 253; "Periodic Problem, The," 135, 139, 245; "Possibilities of Interplanetary Travel, The," 28; *Robot Era, The,* 249, 253–54, 259; *Rockets through Space,* 11, 37–38, 181–82; "Satanic Soliloquy" (series), 67, 75; "Wa-

ter," 27; *Weapons of War,* 94; "We Call It Air," 27; "Weisberger Moon," 151
Cleator, Samuel Ellaby (PEC's father), 13, 26, 109, 118, 133
Cleator, Samuel Maurice (PEC's brother), 133
Cleveland, Ohio, 46–47, 49
Cohen, Chapman, 55
Coleridge, Samuel Taylor, 202
Columbus, Christopher, 161
"Combustion" (P. E. Cleator), 27
Coming of the Space Age, The (A. C. Clarke), 231
Communism: definition of, 89; East-West confrontation, 231–32; fraudulency of, 80; Hitler-Stalin alliance, 94; Marxian orbit, 171
Confusion of tongues, 50–51
Coughlin, the Rev. Charles, 49
Crafts, J. M., 29
Crawford, Bill, 176
Crowell, Thomas Y., 200, 250, 263
Crown of England, 191
Cuba, 108
Czechoslovakia: as a German dependency, 83; Prague, 152

Dartmouth College Library, 115
Daily Express, the London, 48, 144, 184
Daily Mail, the London, 118
Daily Post, the Liverpool, 42
Damn—A Book of Calumny (H. L. Mencken), 68
"Dead March, The" (G. F. Handel), 143
De la terre à la lune (J. Verne), 28
Democracy, 80, 147
Democratic National Convention: (1936), 46–47; (1940), 101, 158–59; (1948), 230–31
Democratic Party, 46, 229, 233
Denvir, Bernard, 105
Devil the. *See* Satan
Dewey, Thomas E., 158–59, 162, 230, 233–34
Dichlorodiethyl sulphide, 51–52
"Dictionary for the Damned, A" (P. E. Cleator), 82, 84–85, 99–100, 102, 104–5, 169–70, 217, 219, 221–22, 258–59
Dictionary of American English (Chicago University), 203
Dictionary of Modern English Usage, A (H. W. Fowler), 113
Diesel, Dr. Rudolf, 91

Divine healing, 210
Divine whim, 212, 220
Divine, Father, 67–68
Dorman, Israel, 52, 117
DOUBT, 202
Downey, the Rev. Dr. Richard, 45–46
Drieser, Theodore, 54, 202, 204
Durrant Press Cutting Agency, 112–13, 158
Dutton, Reginald J. G., 119–20
Dykes, J. G., "Nearer My God to Thee," 143

Echo, the Liverpool, 28, 105, 168
Eddy, Mary Baker, 210; *Science and Health,* 210
Edison, Thomas Alva, 56
Edward I (king of England), 87
Edward VIII (king of England), 49, 56–57
Egypt, 152
E-Layer. *See* Kennelly-Heaviside Layer
Electronic Theory of Valency, The (N. V. Sidgewick), 212
Elizabeth, Queen (wife of King George VI of England), 84–87
England: Cambridge, 70, 87; Cheshire, 26, 42 (*see also* Merseyside); Church of, 75; Crown of, 191; King Edward I, 87; King Edward VIII, 49, 56–57; King George VI, 84–88; Lancashire, 42 (*see also* Merseyside); London, 18, 22, 43, 48, 58, 64, 70, 82, 117–18, 122–23, 126, 144, 150, 169–71, 184, 192; Mersey River, 42, 108, 166, 183; Merseyside, 13, 21, 26, 29, 42, 102–11, 130, 132–33, *134,* 166; Liverpool, 28, 40, 42, 45–46, 80, 85, 89, 105, 108, 148, 166, 169, 191, 236; Wallasey, 13, 21, 26–27, 40–41, 98–99, 102–11, *110,* 127, 132–33, *134,* 141, 144, 149, 163–64, 166, 175–76; Norwich, 173; Yorkshire, 51
Escape to Happiness (film), 120
Esperanto (L. L. Zamenhof), 120
Europe, 61–64, 76, 81, 89, 122, 149, 155–56, 162, 165–66, 216, 219–30, 222
Evening Sun, the Baltimore, 70, 75
Extraterrestrial life, 45

Farnsworth, R. L., 205
Fatherland. *See* Germany
Feinberg, De Witt C., 194–95
Fecher, Charles, 236; *Mencken: A*

270

Study of his Thought, 236
Field III, Marshall, 195–96
Finland, 90–91
Fireguards, 148
First Men in the Moon, The (H. G. Wells), 28
F-Layer. *See* Appleton Layer
Florida, 56, 58, 223, 232–33, 241; St. Petersburg, 223
Food: British Ministry of, 130, 166; inedibility of wartime, 129, 205–6; in the U.S., 114, 126, 128–29, 136, 144, 154, 156–57, 165, 205, 224–25; poisoning, 112; rationing, 126–31, 136, 138, 144, 154; search for, 222–23, 232; shortages, 13, 129, 156–57, 165–66, 220, 225; substitutes, 13, 129, 224
Foote, G. W., 73–74; *The Bible Handbook,* 73–74
Forbidden terms, 139–40, 142–43
Fort, Charles, 202, 204–5; *The Book of the Damned,* 202; *New Lands,* 202
Fortean Society, The, 202, 204; *Magazine (DOUBT),* 202
Fortenbaugh, Charles, 183
Foster, Stephen, "My Old Kentucky Home," 113
Fowler, H. W., 113; *A Dictionary of Modern English Usage,* 113
France: Dieppe, 62; German war preparations against, 78; Normandy, 99; Paris, 62; Versailles, Treaty of, 89; warning to Germany, 89
Frazer, J. G., 29
Freedom of speech, 143
Freethinker, The, 18, 55, 67, 76–77
Friedel, C., 29
Friedel and Crafts reaction, 29

Gagarin, Yuri, 42
Gallup poll, 227
Gamlin, L. (Uncle Lionel), 73–74; *The Children's Hour,* 73–74
gas masks, 79
George VI (king of England), 84–88
German circle, 61
Germany: Adlon Hotel, 73; Auschwitz, 151; Berlin, 83, 98, 154, 220, 231–32; bombing of, 149; Breman, 75; Cologne, 62; Dusseldorf, 176; East Prussia, 89; Frankfurt am Main, 52, 122; Garmisch, 62; Huns, 105, 223; letters and papers from, 106, 207; Mittenwald, 62; Munich Agreement, 79, 89; Munich beer, 61–63; Munich streets, 62; Munich waitresses, 62; Navy, 99; Nazis, 52, 70, 73, 103, 113, 151, 220; newly found merits of, 231–32; postwar conditions in, 220; rocket experimenters, 51; shipping, 98; *Sturmer, the,* 52; Third Reich, 151; *Verein für Raumschiffahrt* (VfR), 28; Vistula River, 89
Gibbon, Edward, 202
Gobbledegook, 55, 92, 137–38, 143–44, 229
Goddard, Dr. Robert H., 231
"God Save the King" (H. Carey), 49
God, the Christian. *See* Yahweh
Goldberg, Isaac, 52
Good and Bad English (Whitten and Whitaker), 70
Goodman, Philip, 52
Grimhaven (R. Tasker), 200–201

Hagerstown "Almanac," 64
Halton Magazine and the Daedalus, The, 56–57
Handel, G. F., "Dead March, The" (from *Saul*), 143
Happy Days (H. L. Mencken), 85, 89–90, *93,* 97–98, 136, 189, 191; "Additions and Corrections," 257
Harding, Warren Gamaliel, 56
Harper & Row, 263
Harrison, Julius, 91
Hazelhurst, Dr. Franklin, 117
Heathen Days (H. L. Mencken), *93,* 128, 131–32, 136–39, 158; "Additions and Corrections," 257
Hecht, Ben, 202
Heffer, W. & Sons, 70
Heliogabalus (H. L. Mencken and G. J. Nathan), 113, 118, 185
Herald, the Baltimore, 196
Herbert, A. P., 61
Herrick, J., 18
Hickey, William, 48, 59–60
High Gods, the: Allah, 30, 200; Mazda, 30; Thor, 30; Wotan, 30; Yahweh, 26, 30, 39, 44–45, 51, 56–57, 60, 62, 67–68, 73, 75, 77, 83–85, 93, 103, 105–6, 115, 118, 123–24, 129, 132–33, 137–38, 140, 142, 145–46, 149–52, 158, 161, 162, 163, 164, 165, 168, 170, 174, 175, 176, 181, 183, 193, 197–198, 200, 203, 206–7, 209, 215–16, 220, 222, 224–25, 232, 235–36; Zeus, 30
"History" (P. E. Cleator), 229

271

Hitler, Adolf, 13, 23, 52, 76, 79–83, 89, 93–94, 98–99, 102, 111, 124, 151, 177
Hitler-Stalin Alliance, 93–94
H. L. Mencken on Music (L. Cheslock), 117
Holy: angels, 126, 235; BBC, 142; cause, 157; Christian Faith, 66; Crown of England, 191; Ghost, 12, 67, 73, 97, 103, 161, 200; mackerel, 235; man, 54; oil, 82; saints, 82, 99, 182; Spirit, 229
Holy Writ: behests of, 58; consideration ordained in, 193; *Genesis*, 75; great truths of, 203; *Minor Prophets, Fifth Book of*, 55; *New Testament*, 75; *Old Testament*, 30; prophecies in, 83; *Revelations, Book of*, 48
Hoover, Herbert Clark, 65, 79–80
Hopkins, Johns, 82
Hull, Cordell, 78–79
Hun: the British, 62; the German, 105, 223
Huxley, Aldous, 65–66
Huxley, T. H., 29
Hyde, Henry, 47
"Hymn to Progress" (P. E. Cleator), 78

Ice Age, return of, 206–7
Idaho, 114
Ido, 120
Ignatius, Saint. *See* Loyola, St. Ignatius de
Illinois, 202; Chicago, 82, 101, 224, 235; Freeport 202; Glen Ellyn 205; Westfield, 204
Illustrated, 60
In Defense of Women (H. L. Mencken), 70, 189, 197–98, 201–2
Inflation, 107, 188–89, 192, 194, 196, 204, 220, 234ff.
Ingersoll, Robert, 29
Intermezzo (H. Provost), 119–20, 123
"Interplanetary Parade" series by P. E. Cleator), 81
Interplanetary Society: the American, 28; the British, 11, 68; the German, 28; the Manchester, 70
Into Space (P. E. Cleator), 67, 187–88, 191–92, 199–200, 216–17, 219, 221, 223, 229, 254
IRA. *See* Ireland: Irish Republican Army
Ireland: ancient Irishism, 106; luck of the Irish, 261; Irish Republican Army (IRA), 101
Isle of Man, 66
Italy: correspondence from, 133; mail by way of, 106; Milan, 137; Romans, days of the, 117

Jackson, Andrew, 214
Japan: Americans in pay of, 175; as alleged assasinators of Abraham Lincoln, 214; as a prospective enemy of the U.S., 80; as the Devil in disguise, 122; Japanese beetles, 216; Japanese activity in the Pacific, 132; as the infidel, 172; virtuousness of, 231
Jehovah. *See* Yahweh
Jesuits, 137
Jews: HLM's attitude towards, 52, 54; members of the Saturday Night Club, 116; movie producer, 63; numbers in the U.S., 51, 79; persecution of, 52, 70, 73, 151–52; votes in the U.S., 230; wartime prophet, 156
Jewish friends: of HLM, 52, 116; of PEC, 150–52
"John Brown's Body" (W. Staffs), 166
John Day Company, The, 263
Johns Hopkins: Hospital, 82, 127 passim, 148, 168, 183, 197–98, 242, 244, 246; University, 116
Johnson, Andrew, 214
John the Baptist, 213
Jonah, son of Amittai, 55
Journal of the British Interplanetary Society, 25, 42–45, 47, 151, 221, 231
Joyce, James, 202

Kansas, 48, 222
Kapsner, O. S. B., the Rev. Celestine, 44
Kennelly-Heaviside Layer, 42
Kermode, A., 87
Kipling, Rudyard, 202
Knopf, Alfred A., 17, 52, 235, 261
Knopf, Alfred A. Inc., 17, *41*, 100–101, 117, 126, 152, 156–57, 165, 167, 169, 171, 185, 191, 192, 193, 194, 195, 198, 201, 205, 223–24, 227, 234–35, 256–57
Knopf-Mencken enterprises, 40

Labatt's brewery, 205
La Eddy. *See* Eddy, Mary Baker
Lancashire, 42. *See also* Merseyside
Landmines, 144–45

Landon, Alfred M., 47, 52
Lang, The Most Reverend Father in God Cosmo Gordon, (Archbishop of Canterbury), 57
Laski, Joseph, 47
Last Men and First Men (O. Stapledon), 62–63
League of Nations, 171–73
"Le Roi". *See* Roosevelt, F. D.
"Letters and Documents Relating to the *Baltimore Sunpapers*, 1892–1941" (H. L. Mencken), 257
Lewis, Sinclair, 196; *Babbitt*, 195–96
Lincke, Paul, 115–16; *Beautiful Spring*, 115–16
Lincoln, Abraham, 51, 214
Lindemann, F., 29
Literary Guide, The, 123, 215–16
Little Book in C Major, A (H. L. Mencken), 82
Litz, Professor Francis, 59
Liverpool, 40, 42, 46, 89, 166–67, 191; archbishop of, 45–46; bombing of, 102–3, 108, 132–33; city limits, 40, 42; *Daily Post*, 42; democracy at work in, 148; docks, 108; *Echo*, 28, 105, 168; port of, 85, 89, 166, 169, 191; street vendor, 236
Lohrfinck, Arnold W., 264–65
Lohrfinck, Mrs. John W. (Rosalind L.), 14, 70, 127–28, 158–62, 165, 214, 237–38, 241–65; "Mencken in my Life," 260–61
London, 122, 150, 171, 182, 191–93; bombing of, 191; *Daily Express*, 48, 144, 184; *Daily Mail*, 118; Dr. Louis Cheslock of, 117; Fleet Street, 122; HLM visit, 43; Knopf visit, 192; literary agents, 123; National Secular Society, 18; newspapers, 48, 118, 126, 144, 163; PEC visits, 58, 150, 170–71, 192; proposed Roosevelt visit, 82; Rationalist Society, 216; *Sunday Express*, 163; Tower of, 150
Lord God of Hosts. *See* Yahweh
Lost Languages (P. E. Cleator), 263
Louis, Joe, 203
Loyola, St. Ignatius de, 136–37
Lucifer. *See* Satan
Luftpost, 154

"Mademoiselle from Armentières" (H. Carlton and J. A. Tunbridge), 50
Making a President (H. L. Mencken), 46, 83, 189, *218*

Manchester: *Guardian*, 92; Interplanetary Society, 70
Marlowe, Christopher, 118
Marshall Field III, 195–96
Maryland, 64, 78, *153*, 162, 183, 195, 209, 257; bagpipe prohibition in, 162; Hagerstown *Almanac*, 64; Hyattesville, *153;* Madstone, 45–46, *185;* rye whiskey, 209; shores of, 183; University of, 17, 61
Massachusetts, 44; Boston, 137
Masters, Edgar Lee, 86
Mazda, 30
McGoff, Martin A., 80
McNiece, Jean R., 18
Meekins, Lynn, 196
Meiklem, Father Kenneth, 54
Meledin, H. L., 17
Mencken, Anna Abhau (HLM's mother), 37, 81
Mencken, Anna Gertrude (HLM's sister), 80–81, 120, 131–32, 255
Mencken: A Study of his Thought (C. Fetcher), 236
Mencken, August & Brother, 195–96
Mencken, August (HLM's brother), 37ff., 80f., 86, 105, 120, 140f., 145, 168, 188, 205, 222–23, 249–50, 254–55, 258–59, 261–62
Mencken, August Senior. (HLM's father), 37
Mencken, Burkhardt Ludwig (HLM's grandfather), 44
Mencken (C. Bode), 54, 83, 145
Mencken, Charles (HLM's brother), 120
Mencken Chrestomathy, A (H. L. Mencken), 76, 221–22, 223, 226–27, 234–35
Mencken-Cleator wartime relationship, 54
Mencken Estate, 17, 236
Mencken epigraphs, 83, *93, 141, 175, 190, 199, 208, 218, 225*
Mencken, Henry Louis: agnosticism of, 11, 30; alcoholic drinking, 197, 203, 242; alias Meekins, 195–96; alleged anti-Semitism, 52; ancestry, 52, 66; and abdication of King Edward VIII, 56–57; and agnosticism, 30; and Aldous Huxley, 66; and American women, 50, 56–57; and anti-Semitism, 52; and armed conflict, 63, 90–91, 93–94; and atmospheric pollution, 79; and bagpipes, 162; and Baltimore, 88, 225; and barking dogs, 183, 188; and behests

of Holy Writ, 58; and bureaucracy, 11, 55, 62, 136–37, 140, 143, 154, 156, 165, 169, 175, 188, 217, 226, 230; and burning at the stake, 54; and cannibalism, 165; and Christian Science, 210; and clothing problems, 162–64, 205–6, 211; and Communism, 80; and Congress, 79–81; and Congressmen, 58; and Father Coughlin, 49; and the Declaration of Independence, 62, 75; and democracy, 80, 147; and dentists, 43; and Thomas E. Dewey, 158–59; and diet, 137–38, 144, 156, 165, 170, 224; and ethyl alcohol, 197; and Father Divine, 67–68; and feminine wiles, 56–57; and fleas, 216; and Florida, 56; and forbidden terms, 139–40, 142–43; and the Fortean Society, 201–2; and high humidity, 131, 145, 158, 194, 215–16; and HLM salutation, 12, 70, 193, 195–96; and the Holy Writ, 58, 83; and hops, 106; and hospitals, 69; and houses and homeowners, 97–98; and Cordell Hull, 78–79; and human reasoning, 64; and illness, 197–98; and indexing, 161, 163–64, 215–16, 219–20; and Jews, 51–52, 54, 79; and journalistic jargon, 48; and Justices of the Peace, 77; and Alfred M. Landon, 47; and lawyers, 196; and lunatic asylums, 68; and lynching, 54; and Marshall Field III, 195–96; and metaphysicians, 125; and Methodist parsons, 139; and the mother tongue, 48, 55; and Munich beer, 61–63; and the New Deal, 65–66, 78, 80–81, 224; and nursing homes, 69; and officialdom, 55, 136, 140, 143, 145–46, 154, 156, 165, 188, 230; and W. P. Pitkin, 55; and politicians, 10–11, 45–48, 90, 108, 125, 158, 176, 234; and printers, 138, 168, 177–78; and Prohibition, 50, 79, 94, 103–4, 108, 130, 149, 157; and psychologists, 139; and publishers, 58, 193–94, 200; and radio broadcasting, 63; and religion, 39; and F. D. Roosevelt, 16, 48, 51, 65, 78, 82–83, 100; and the Russians, 220; and sin, 58; and Socialists, 169; and space travel, 38, 50; and a Supreme Being, 30; and suburban curates, 39; and surgery, 38, 60, 189; and taxation, 81, 114, 119, 147, 151, 156, 158, 189, 217; and Dr. Francis E. Townsend, 47; and Harry S. Truman, 232–33; and Unitarians, 46; and the University of Maryland, 61; and the universe, 30; and unwelcome intrusions, 182, 192, 195; and vaccines, 64, 97, 115, 121, 135, 171, 173; and vitamins, 119–20, 135, 137, 148–50; and Henry A. Wallace, 230, 232; and Wendell Willkie, 100–101; and witches and demons, 43; and the YMCA 39; as alphabetical mountebank, 21; as amateur pathologist, 12, 130; as applicant for baptism, 210; as attendant of national conventions, 45–47, 101, 158–59, 227, 229–30; as bearded journalist, 44; as Benedictine, 193; as bricklayer, 145; as candidate for Hell, 23, 40, 60, 78–79, 137; as Christian (and a patriot), 123, 138, 207, 210; as compulsive letter answerer, 14, 22; as confirmed hypochondriac, 12, 39; as connoisseur of man's ills, 12; as dirty liar, 21; as genuine bishop, 102; as gourmet, 67, 98–99, 107, 116, 120, 137–38, 144, 156, 165, 168, 170, 224, 242; as a homeowner, 98; as humane man, 138; as intellectual nihilist, 21; as jackal, 21; as maggot, 21; as near centenarian, 197, 213; as nudist, 162, 205; as optimist, 98; as parasite, 21; as pick and shovel man, 143; as pole-cat, 21; as political prophet, 12, 51–52, 66, 78, 80–81, 83, 89, 101, 119, 189, 227, 229–30; as potential bishop, 102; as prancing gazelle, 194; as professing Christian, 79, 138, 183; as prospective angel, 114; as radio broadcaster, 63; as rhetorician, 78; as senile ox, 194; as sceptic, 39; as supposed Jew, 52; as the Old Man, 220; as torch for all eternity, 40; as turkey buzzard, 21; as would-be debtor, 235–36; association with G. J. Nathan, 40, *53,* 118, *120;* buffoonery, *41,* 44, 50, 54–55, 60–62, 76, 114, 118–20, 157, *184;* change of address, 38; Christian works, 37; cruising, 68–69, 108; daily devotions, 55; death of, 17, 21, 119, 221, 252, 256–57; diaries of, 257; entertaining royalty, 86, 88; epigraphs, 83, *93, 141, 175, 190, 199, 208, 218, 225;* excursions abroad, 22–23, 38, 42–43, 45, 68–69, 73, 75–76, 78, 108;

family references, 37–38, 50, 58, 60–61, 80–81, 140; garmenture exchange, 209–15; generosity of, 14, 109, 111–12, 115, 189, 191, 207, 209–15; holidays, 14, 55, 58, 158, 223; imaginary relatives, 50, 60–61, 119–20, 195; last days, 14, 241–56; marriage, 98; music making, 115–17; notepaper, 38, 70, 166, 177–78, 184, *186*, 197, 206; partnership with Nathan, 40; private correspondence, 14–15, 17–18, 21, 222, 257; pro-German sympathies, 52, 111; proposed contribution to the *BIS Journal*, 44–45, 47; proposed literary undertakings, 39, 59, 67, 70, 75, 91, 106–7, 138–39, 150, 164–65, 174, *208*, 223, 226–27; proposed meeting with PEC, 14, 22–23, 54, 60, 73, 77, 84–85, 87, 98–99, 102, 105, 114, 161, 166, 168, 171, 183, 191, 219, 242–46, 250–53, 256; reading, 55, 62, 73, 77; scientific interests, 11, 135; spiritual advisors, 55, 98, 105, 123, 135, 149, 161, 168, 172, 174–75, 181–82, 215; under arrest, 136–37; vilification of 21; weather reports, 48, 62, 64, 76, 80, 84–88, 112, 114, 131, 142, 145, 156–59, 169, 205, 213, 215–16, 223; working procedure, 67, 260. Maladies and afflictions: apoplexy, 14, 23, 89, 158, 165; asthma, 115, 162–63; bursitis, 183, 198, 201; celebral paralysis, 11, 14, 237–57; double vision, 165; eye strain, 63, 241; gastralgia, 73–74, 112; gout, 183–84; hay fever, 39, 64, 103–4, 114–15, 135, 146–50; 160, 171, 173, 249; heart trouble, 158; hospitalization, 56, 82, 127 passim, 170–71, 237–38, 244–56; nasal infection, 131; overwork, 69, 73–74, 108–9, 237; prostatitis, 168; sinusitis, 130–31, 141, 184, 187; surgical experiences, 56, 59–61; 130–31, 167, 198, throat infection, 56, 127–31; tonsilitis, 130; tracheitis, 229; unspecified ailments, 67, 73, 80, 82, 89, 118–19, 142, 148, 154, 158. Unpublished manuscripts: "Additions and Corrections" (to *Days Books*), 251; "Letters and Documents Relating to the *Baltimore Sunpapers*, 1892–1941, 257; "My Life as Author and Editor," 114–15, 139–40, 257; "Thirty-five Years of Newspaper Work," 114–15, 121, 257. Works: *American Language, The,* 12, 37, 50–52, 59, 76, 99, 106, 111, 115, 132, 136, 139, 142–43, 146–48, 150–54, 161, 171–72, 181–82, 213–14, 224; *American Language, The, Supplement I,* 51, 59, 99, 106, 111, 115, 132, 136, 139, 142–43, 146–48, 150–52, 156, 159–61, 163, 167, 169–70, 171–73, 182, 205, *225; American Language, The, Supplement II,* 12, 154, 159, 164, 167, 174, 177, 181–82, 184, 192–93, 195–97, 201, 203, 205–6, 211–13, 215–16, 219–21, 224, *225*, 226–27; *American Language, The, Supplement III,* 227; *Americana 1925,* 77, 92, 113, 187; *Americana 1926,* 41, 77, 92, *199; Book of Burlesques, A,* 82, 189; "Bulletin on 'Hon,'" *141; Christmas Story, 176; Damn—A Book of Calumny,* 68; *Happy Days,* 85, 89–90, *93,* 97–98, 136, 189, 191; *Heathen Days, 93,* 128, 131–32, 136–39, 158; *Heliogabalus* (with G. J. Nathan), 113, 118, 185; *In Defense of Women,* 70, 189, 197–98, 201–2; *Little Book in C Major, A,* 82; *Making a President,* 46, 83, 189, *218; Mencken Chrestomathy, A,* 76, 221–22, 226–27, 234–35; *Menckeniana,* 21, 52, *208; Minority Report,* 256–57; *New Dictionary of Quotations, A,* 67–68, 106, 109, 113, 121, 123–24, 126; *Newspaper Days, 93,* 109, 113–14, 136; *Prejudices* (series I–VI), 30, 37, 39, 68–69, 187, 189, *190,* 202; *Treatise on the Gods,* 11, 30, 175, *176,* 195–96, 216; "War Slang," *141;* "War Words in England," 106–7, *140,* 141.

Menckeniana (H. L. Mencken, ed.), 21, 52, *208*
Mencken in my Life (R. L. Lohrfinck), 260–61
Mencken, Johann Burkhardt, 58–59; *The Charlatanry of the Learned,* 58–59, 66
Mencken, Mary (HLM's sister-in-law), 120
Mencken, Sara Haardt (HLM's wife), 38, 44, 120, 173
Mencken, Virginia (HLM's niece), 120
Mendeleef, D. I., 135
Mercantile-Safe Deposit and Trust

275

Co., 17, 259
Mersey River, 42, 108, 166, 183
Merseyside, 13, 26, 29, 42, 130, 166; bombing of, 13, 21, 102–11, 130, 132–33, *134;* Liverpool, 40, 42, 46, 89, 166–67, 191; Wallasey, 36, 40, 42, 98–99
"Messages in Morse from Mars" (P. E. Cleator), 221
Mexico, 93
Middle West, the U.S., 47–48, 105
Milan, archbishop of, 137
Minority Report (H. L. Mencken), 256–57
Missing correspondence, 21–22, 89–90, 94, 97, 99–100, 106–8, 111, 132–33
Moffett, E. Edwin, 117
Montgomery, General Bernard L., 142
"Moon and Mr. Farnsworth, The" (P. E. Cleator), 205
Moon, reaching the, 38, 50, 151, 181, 205, 221
"Moonshine" (P. E. Cleator), 67
Morrison, Mrs. David S. (Virginia Mencken), 120
Mussolini, Benito, 65
"My Life as Author and Editor" (H. L. Mencken) 114–15, 139–40, 257
"My Kingdom for a Hearse" (P. E. Cleator), 118, 120, 122–23, 125–26, 128, 131, 217, 219, 221–22, 224–26, 229, 258–59
"My Old Kentucky Home" (S. Foster), 50

Nathan, George Jean, 40, 52, *53,* 113, 120, *121; Heliogabalus* (with H. L. Mencken), 113, 118, 185
National Recovery Act, 65
Nazis, the, 52, 70, 73, 103, 113, 151, 220
"Nearer My God to Thee" (J. B. Dykes), 143
Netzer, Ewald, 52
New Deal, 65–66, 78, 80–81, 224
New Dictionary of Quotations, A (H. L. Mencken, ed.), 67–68, 106, 109, 113, 121, 123–24, 126
New Horizons (F. E. Townsend), 48
New Lands (C. Fort), 202
New Mencken Letters, The (C. Bode, ed.), 22, 30, 47–48, 52, 54, 57, 67, 86, 165, 168
Newnes, George, 70

Newspaper Days (H. L. Mencken), *93,* 109, 113–14, 136; "Additions and Corrections," 257
News Review, 60, 92
New Statesman and Nation, The, 77; "This England," 77
New York: Broadway, 118; Fifth Avenue, 200; Public Library, 18, 21–22, 37, 89, 97, 100, 107, 115, 144, 154, 222, 252, 257–58; Stork Club; *121;* Wall Street, 100
Noah, son of Lamech, 122
No More Peace (E. Toller), 113, 212
Norwich, 173
NRA. *See* National Recovery Act

Occupational profanity, 140
Odhams Press, 60
Ogden, Charles Kay, 147–48; Basic English, 147–48
Oklahoma, 114
"Old Age Pension Man," *See* Townsend, Dr. F. E.
Old Moore's *Almanack,* 64
"On Giving up Shaving" (P. E. Cleator), 42, 44, 65
"Onward Christian Soldiers" (A. Sullivan), 166
"Operation" (P. E. Cleator), 62, 68
O'Regan, Dick, 90–91, 93–94, 97, 120, 122
Ostend, Belgium, 62

Past in Pieces, The (P. E. Cleator), 253
Paul (Saul of Tarsus), 55, 65
Peacop, Dianne, 18
Pearl, Dr. Raymond, 116–17
Penicillin, 161
Pennsylvania: Lancaster, 120; Philadelphia, 46, 93–94, 100, 122, 229, 232
"Periodic Problem, The" (P. E. Cleator), 135, 139, 245
Perleman, Dr. Jakow I., 43
Philadelphia: Democratic convention at (1936), 46–47; *Bulletin,* 93–94, 122; proposed HLM visit, 97; Republican convention at (1940), 100–101
Philological exchanges, 14, 50–51, 54, 57, 59–60, 61, 65–66, 69–70, 76, 78, 80, 84, 87, 101, 105–6, 111–12, 113, 115, 118–19, 125–26, 136, 139–40, 143, 145, 147–48, 150–52, 154, 156, 158–62, 164, 166–67, 174, 177, 181–82, 184, 189, 197, 201, 213, 220,

276

223, 227, 231, 234, 236–37, 247; "accident tout," 51; "ambulance chaser," 51; "car clinic," 61; "casualty," 181; "dilutees," 118; "latrineograms," 181; "mobile police," 51; "side-walk," 50; "speed cop," 51; "to script," 177; "umber-bloody-ella," 50–51
Pi, 29
Pitkin, Walter P., 55; *A Short Introduction to the History of Human Stupidity,* 55
Plain Words (H. M. Stationery Office). 227. 229
Pointless obscenities, 143
Poland: corridor, 88–89; German attack upon, 89, 94; Dantzig, 88–89; Vistula River, 89
Politics, 12, 48, 78, 125, 158, 193
Polonius, 132
Population Bulletin, 224
"Possibilities of Interplanetary Travel, The" (P. E. Cleator), 28
Postal: censorship, 100, 102–3, 106, *110,* 116, 118, 143–44, 146–47, 150–51, 170, 173, 175; losses and delays, 21–22, 106–8, 111, 115, 125–26, 128, 154–55, 172, 216–17, 219
Pratt, Enoch, 82; Library, 37, 82, 115, 221–22, 227, 260
Predestination, 84
Presbyterianism, 143, 175
Presidential candidates, U.S. *See* United States presidential candidates
Presidents, U.S. *See* United States presidents
Prejudices (series I—VI (H. L. Mencken). 30, 37, 39, 68–69, 187, 189, *190,* 202
Prohibition: failure of, 149; literature, 127–28; renewed activity, 127, 130, 157–58
Provost, Heinz, 119–20, 123; "Intermezzo," 119–20, 123
Publishers: Alfred A. Knopf Inc., 17, *41,* 100–101, 117, 126, 152, 156–57, 165, 167, 169, 171, 185, 191, 192, 193, 194, 195, 198, 201, 205, 223–24, 227, 234–35, 256–57; Allen & Unwin, 37, 152, 154, 169, 182, 185–86, 189, 191, 193–94, 200, 224, 227, 229; Associated University Presses, 17; Chambers, W. & R., 18; George Newnes, 70; Harper & Row, 263; John Day Company, 263; Jonathan Cape, 101, 183; Odhams Press, 60; Reader's Digest Association, 18;

Simon & Schuster, 37, 195–96; Thomas Y. Crowell, 200, 250, 263; W. Heffer & Sons, 70; William Sloane Associates, 219, 221, 223–24, 225–26, 227, 229
Punch, 61, 87
Pygmalion (G. B. Shaw), 142
Purdom, Frank C., 117

Quack Quack (L. S. Woolf), 67

RAF. *See* Royal Air Force
Rascoe, Burton, 202
Rationalist Society, the British, 216
Rationing, 126–31, 136, 138, 144, 154
Reader's Digest Association, The, 18
Reader's Digest, The, 99–100
Reade, Winwood, 29
Reaver School of Chiropractic, The, 204
Reith, Sir John, 142–43
Religion, objection to, 30
Republican National Convention: (1936), 45–47; (1940), 100–101; (1948), 229–30
Republican Party, 52, 159, 224
Resurrection Morn, 21
"Riddle of the Earth-Moon Double Planet, The" (J. Weisberger), 151
Rinin, Professor Nikolas, 43
Robertson, John M., 29
Robot Era, The (P. E. Cleator), 249, 253–54, 259
Rocket research, 50–51, 80–82, 84, 230–31
Rockets Through Space (P. E. Cleator), 11, 37–38, 181–82
Roget, Peter Mark, 212; *Thesaurus,* 212
Rome's Gift (A. T. Sheppard), 63–64
Rommel, Field Marshal Erwin, 142
Roosevelt, Franklin Delano, 12, 46–47, 51–52, 65–66, 79–83, 90–91, 99–101, 105, 107, 111–12, 148, 158–59, 162, 167, 169–70, 231–32; as a member of the Trinity, 78; death of, 167, 169–70
Rotarians, 197
Royal Air Force, 56–57, 154; *Magazine,* 56–57
Russell, Bertrand, 29
Russia: and American diplomacy, 79; as Asiatic barbarians, 220; Berlin blockade, 232; collapse, 124; coming war with, 210, 231–32; godless hordes of, 90, 232; Hitler-Stalin alliance, 93–94; in Siberia, 235; in Westminster, 235; Leningrad, 43;

277

victories, 166
Salvation Army, 76
San Quentin, 200
Satan, 44, 122, 198
"Satanic Soliloquy" (series, P. E. Cleator), 67, 75
Saturday Night Club, 18, 86, 116
Schickelgruber, Adolf. *See* Hitler, Adolf
Schleyer, Johann, 120; Volapuk, 120
Schuyler, George S., 54
Science and Health (M. B. Eddy), 210
Scientific Book Club, 200
Scott, Elizabeth, 18
Seaman, Herbert W., 51–52, 173, 249–50
Shaw, George Bernard, 142; *Pygmalion*, 142
Sheppard, A. T., 63–64; *Rome's Gift*, 63–64
Short Introduction to the History of Human Stupidity, A, (W. P. Pitkin), 55
"Sidelights on the Slaughter" (P. E. Cleator), 90–91, 97, 150, 154, 169–71, 223–24, 226
Sidgwick, Dr. N. V., 212; *The Electronic Theory of Valency*, 212
Simon & Schuster, 37, 195–96
Simon, Sir John, 50–51
Simpson, Mrs. Wallis Warfield, 49, 57; as a prospective queen of England, 49
Sloane, William, 223, 226
Smart Set, The, 40
Smith, Dr. Howard, 168
Smith, Ralph A., 154
Socialism, 25, 169, 172
Society for Space Travel, the German, 28
Son of Yahweh, 45, 65, 193, 196
Soddy, Dr. Frederick, 135
Sonneck, O. G. T., "The Star Spangled Banner," 50
South Africa: as a prospective intellectual desert, 233; Capetown, 243; *Die Transvaler,* 247; Johannesburg, 247
Space Research and Exploration (D. R. Bates, ed.), 229
Space travel, 37–38, 42, 45, 50–51, 78, 151, 196, 221, 229; theological implications of, 45
Spencer, Herbert, 29
Staffe, W., "John Brown's Body," 166
Stalin, Josef V., 93–94

Stapledon, Olaf, 62–63; *Last Men and First Men,* 62–63
"Star Spangled Banner, The" (O. G. T. Sonneck), 50
Star, the Washington, 204
Strauss, Johann, 90
Sturmer, the, 52
Sullivan, Arthur, "Onward Christian Soldiers," 166
Sumer: organised warfare among Sumerians, 94; Sumero-Babylonian folklore, 30
Sunday Express, the London, 163
Sunpapers, Baltimore, 257
Sun, the Baltimore, 44, 62, 73, 122, 137, 196, 231–32; history of, 44
Sun, the Chicago, 196
Supreme Being, belief in a, 30
Switzerland: Basle, 62; Geneva, 122; Lucerne, 62; Zurich, 62

Tasker, Robert, 200–201; *Grimhaven,* 200–201
Taxation, 25, 61, 114, 119, 127, 147, 151, 156–57, 209, 215, 217
Taylor, S. C., 202
Thatcher, Margaret, 25
Thayer, Tiffany Ellsworth, 201–202
Thesaurus (P. M. Roget), 212
"Thirty-five Years of Newspaper Work" (H. L. Mencken), 114–15, 121, 257
"This England" *(New Statesman and Nation),* 77
Thor, 30
Time Magazine, 48
Toller, Ernst, 113, 212; *No More Peace,* 113, 212
Tomorrow, 81
Torovsky, Adolf, 117
Townsend, Dr. Francis E., 47–48; *New Horizons,* 48
Treatise on the Gods (H. L. Mencken), 30, 175, *176,* 195–96, 216
Trinity, the Christian, 29
Truman, Harry S., 14, 169–70, 206, 217, 223–24, 227, 229–30
Tully, Jim, 200
Tunbridge, J. A. (with H. Carlton), "Mademoiselle From Armentières", 50
Twelve Apostles, the, 64–65
Tydings, Millard, 78

U-Boats, the German, *93,* 100, 131
Uncle Lionel. *See* Gamlin, L.

Unexploded bombs, 133, 183
Unitarians, 46
United States: Allegheny Mountains, 46; Army, 155, 181, 231; as God's chosen playground, 207; burning at the stake in, 49, 54; Cheka, 79; Congress, 79–81, 156, 158, 184, *185;* Congressmen, 58; Constitution, 157, 184–85; Customs Agents, 88; Dachau, 99; Dartmouth College, 115; Declaration of Independence, 75, 211; Democracy, 80, 149; Democratic National Convention (1936), 46–47 (1940), 101, 158–59 (1948), 230–31; Democratic Party, 46, 229, 233; Depression, the Great, 65, 80, 126; G. I. Bill of Rights, 204; Government, 203–4; history, 214; Hollywood, California, 63; Information Office, 91–92; Interplanetary Society, 28; Jurisprudence, 45; Justices of the Peace, 77; national anthem, 49–50; national conventions, 44–47, 100–101, 158–59, 227, 229–30; national debt, 107; national imbecilities, 55, 78, 137, 140; National Recovery Act, 65; Mount Vernon, 86; negroes, 54, 74, 184, *185,* 230; New Deal, 65, 78–79, 81, 224; officialdom, 11, 55, 136, 140, 143, 145–46, 154, 156, 165, 188, 230; politics, 12, 48, 125, 158, 193; Post Office, 55, 107, 155; Proclamation of 1863, the, 184, *185;* Prohibition, 50, 79, 94, 103–4, 108, 130, 149, 157; Pure Food Laws, 224; Republican National Conventions (1936), 45–46 (1940), 100–101 (1948), 229–30; Republican Party, 52, 159, 224; San Quentin, 200; Senators, 78–79, 230, 236; State Department, 140; the greatest show on earth, 66; weather reports, 48, 56, 64; women, 50, 56–57; Washington, George, 86–87. *See also* Cleveland, Florida, Idaho, Illinois, Kansas, Maryland, New York, Oklahoma, Pennsylvania, U.S. presidential candidates, U.S. presidents, Washington D.C.
United States presidential candidates: Rev. Charles Coughlin, 49; T. E. Dewey, 158–59, 162, 224, 230, 233–34; H. C. Hoover, 79; A. M. Landon, 47, 52; F. D. Roosevelt, 46–47, 51, 65, 83, 91, 158–59, 231; F. E. Townsend, 47–48; H. S. Truman, 169–70, 227, 229–30; H. A. Wallace, 230–32; W. L. Willkie, 100–101
United States presidents: W. G. Harding, 56; H. C. Hoover, 65, 79–80; A. Jackson, 214; A. Johnson, 214; A. Lincoln, 51, 214; F. D. Roosevelt, 12, 46, 51–52, 65–66, 79–83, 90–91, 99–101, 105, 107, 111–12, 148, 158–59, 162, 167, 169–70, 231; H. S. Truman, 14, 169–70, 206, 217, 223–24, 227, 229–30, 232
Untermeyer, Louis, 52
USSR, *see* Russia

Veblen, Professor T. B., 202
Veritype machine, 224
Verein für Raumschiffahrt (VfR), 28
Verne, Jules, 28; *De la terre à la lune,* 28
Versailles, Treaty of, 89
Virgin Birth, the, 29
Volapuk (J. Schleyer), 120
Voltaire (F. M. Arouet), 29

Wagner, Richard, 90–91
Wallace, Henry A., 230–32
Wallasey, 26, 40, 42, 98–99, 141, 166, 175–76, 220; as an erstwhile Cheshire town, 26; bombing of, 13, 21, 102–11, *110,* 127, 132–33, *134,* 144, 149, 183; Fireguard Association, 163–64, 166; Grammar School, 27; maniac on the loose in, 175–76; supposed Liverpool suburb, 40–41; proposed HLM visit to, 98–99, 102, 105, 161, 166, 168, 171, 183, 191, 219; repairs to raid damage, 141–42
Walsh, Richard J., 263–64
War and post war shortages: alcoholic beverages, 106, 122–23, 149, 157, 160, 204; automobile tires, 126, 128; building materials, 13, 188; cooking fat, 13, 129; clothing, 14, 126, 162–63, 164, 205–6, 220; foodstuffs, 12, 92, 126, 128–29, 157, 164–65, 170, 205–6, 220, 222, 225, 232; fuel, 126, 128–29, 131; hops, 106; leather, 126; paper, 12, 92, 123, 125–26, 154, 161, 167, 169–70, 182, 189, 191, 194, 216
"War Slang" (H. L. Mencken), 99–100
War Damage Bill, 92
Wartime: blackout, 124, 162; neologisms, 159; 161; rationing, 126–31, 136, 138, 144, 154; taxation, 160

"War Words in England" (H. L. Mencken), 106–7, 140–41
Washington D.C.; as an abode of Marxian jobholders, 169; bureaucratic outpourings, 137; diplomatic activities in, 78; infestation of by chiropractors, 203–4; National Museum, 213; transport difficulties, 136; *Star,* 204; summer climate of, 80, 85–86, 88; volcanic threat to, 77
Washington, George, 86–87
"Water" (P. E. Cleator), 27
Weapons of War (P. E. Cleator), 94
"We Call it Air" (P. E. Cleator), 27
Weisberger, Edouard, 152
Weisberger, Emil A., 152, *153*
Weisberger, Josef, 150–52; "The Riddle of the Earth-Moon Double Planet," 151
"Weisberger Moon" (P. E. Cleator).151
Wells, H. G., 28; *The First Men in the Moon,* 28
West Indies, 68–69
Whiskey, 106, 122–23, 125, 136, 160, 204, 209
Whitaker, F., 70; *Good and Bad English* (with W. Whitten), 70
Whitaker, Joseph, 212; *Almanack,* 212
White, Andrew D., 29
White, Walter, 54
Whitten, W., 70; *Good and Bad English* (with F. Whitaker), 70
William Sloane Associates, 219, 221, 223–24, 227, 229
Willkie, Wendell, 100–101

Winchell, Walter, 115–16
Witches and demons, 43–44
Woolf, Leonard Sidney, 67; *Quack Quack,* 67
Woolton, Lord and Lady, 215
World War I, 52, 54, 89, 111, 176
World War II, 11–12, 21, 26, 83, 89–91, 98, 143, 186, 258; as a Crusade, 105, 109, 155, 215; predictions as to the duration of, 12, 92, 98, 100, 103–5, 107, 111, 114, 131, 145, 149, 151, 154–56, 158, 161–62, 166
World War III, 210, 231–32
Wotan, 30

Yahweh, 12, 26, 30, 39, 44–45, 51, 56–57, 60, 62, 67–68, 73, 75, 77, 83–85, 93, 103, 105–6, 115, 118, 123–24, 129, 132–33, 137–38, 140, 142, 145–46, 149–52, 158, 161–162, 163, 164, 165, 168, 170, 174–175, 176, 181, 183, 193, 197–98, 200, 203, 206–7, 209, 215–16, 220, 222, 224–25, 232, 235–36; son of, 45, 65, 193, 196; triadic associates, 67, 73, 97, 103, 115, 161, 200
Yale Review, 42
Yelton, Donald C., 18
YMCA. *See* Young Men's Christian Association
Yorkshire, 51
Yoseloff, Thomas, 17
Young Men's Christian Association, 39

Zamenhof, Dr. L. L., 120
Zeus, 30